The Middle Ages
in the
North-West

The Middle Ages in the North-West

Papers presented at an International Conference sponsored jointly by the Centres of Medieval Studies of the Universities of Liverpool and Toronto

EDITED BY

Tom Scott *and* Pat Starkey

LEOPARD'S HEAD PRESS

In conjunction with the
LIVERPOOL CENTRE FOR MEDIEVAL STUDIES

Published in 1995 by
LEOPARD'S HEAD PRESS
1–5 Broad Street, Oxford OX1 3AW

© T. Scott and P. Starkey 1995

ISBN 0 904920 31 3

Typeset by Denham House, Yapton, West Sussex
and printed in Great Britain by
Progressive Printing (UK) Limited, Leigh-on-Sea, Essex

Contents

Page

List of Maps and Figures   vii

Acknowledgements   ix

Notes on Contributors   xi

Abbreviations   xv

Introduction — *Tom Scott and Pat Starkey*   xvii

1 — Territorial organization in pre-Conquest Cheshire
    Nick Higham   1

2 — Open fields and rural settlement in medieval
    west Cheshire
    Graeme White   15

3 — Scandinavian ornamental influence in the Irish Sea
    region in the Viking Age
    David M. Wilson   37

4 — The Irish Sea vikings: raiders and settlers
    James Graham-Campbell   59

5 — Aspects of time in the battle poetry of
    early Britain
    David N. Klausner   85

6 — Discretion and deceit: a re-examination of a
    military stratagem in *Egils saga*
    Ian McDougall   109

7 — From Throndheim to Waltham to Chester:
    Viking- and post-Viking-Age attitudes in the
    survival legends of Óláfr Tryggvason and
    Harold Godwinson
    Marc Cohen   143

                                                        page

8 — The cult of king Harold at Chester
        Alan Thacker   155

9 — Recognition of worth in *Pearl* and *Gawain and
        the Green Knight*
        Nick Davis   177

10 — Constructing bliss: Heaven in the *Pearl*
        E. Ruth Harvey   203

11 — The Chester Mystery Plays and the limits
        of realism
        David Mills   221

12 — Marian devotion in post-Reformation Chester:
        implications of the smiths' 'Purification' play
        Sally-Beth MacLean   237

13 — 'Selling the Bible to pay for the bear': the value
        placed on entertainment in Congleton 1584–1637
        Elizabeth Baldwin   257

Index   269

List of Maps and Figures

Page

Graeme J. White

Map 1 — The thirty-two townships in the study
area   16

Map 2 — Reconstruction of possible open arable field
in Tilson   18

Map 3 — Reconstruction of possible open arable fields
in Aldersey Green   19

Map 4 — Tilson, from OS 25 ins. to mile, 1911   20

Map 5 — Barton, from OS 25 ins. to mile, 1898   24

Map 6 — Aldersey Green, from OS 25 ins. to mile,
1874   24

Map 7 — Clotton, from OS 25 ins. to mile, 1898   26

Map 8 — Burton, from OS 25 ins. to mile, 1910   26

Map 9 — Duddon, from OS 25 ins. to mile, 1898   28

David M. Wilson   *between pages* 52–53

Figure 1 — Strap-end from Sandvor, Rogaland, Norway

Figure 2 — Ornament of the cup from the North
Mound at Jelling, Jutland, Denmark

Figure 3 — Cross-slab from Kirk Bradden, Isle of Man

Figure 4 — Bossed penannular brooch from Orton Scar,
Cumbria

Figure 5 — Sword-guard from a burial at
Hesket-in-the-Forest, Cumbria

Figure 6 — The Gosforth Cross, Cumbria

Figure 7 — Cross from Dearham, Cumbria

Figure 8 — Gautr's cross, Kirk Michael, Isle of Man

between pages 52–53 (continued)

Figure 9 — Fragment of a cross-slab from Inchmarnock, Bute

Figure 10 — Cross-slab from Malew, Isle of Man

James Graham-Campbell   *page*

Figure 1 — The kingdom of Man and the Isles at its greatest extent   60

between pages 68–69

Figure 2 — Berdal-type oval brooch from Oronsay

Figure 3 — Hiberno-viking arm-ring hoard from Anglesey

Figure 4 — Iron weapons found in 1789 at Aspatria, Cumberland

Figure 5 — Viking grave-goods found in 1822 at Hesket-in-the-Forest, Cumberland

Figure 6 — Some important Norse sites on the Isle of Man

Figure 7 — Remains of the conical iron shield-boss from the Balladoole boat-burial, Isle of Man

Figure 8 — Plan of the 'Pagan Lady's' grave on St Patrick's Isle, Isle of Man

Sally-Beth MacLean   *between pages 244–45*

Figure 1 — East window of East Harling church

Figure 2 — Painted glass windows of Malvern Priory

Figure 3 — The Circumcision, depicted on part of an alabaster table

Figure 4 — Alabaster table in the Germanic Museum at Nuremberg

Figure 5 — The Circumcision, depicted in an English woodcut

Figure 6 — The angel chorus, from the west front of Chester Cathedral

Figure 7 — The Purification, east window, East Harling church

Acknowledgements

THE EDITORS WISH to express their gratitude for the generous subventions towards the costs of this volume received from the Marc Fitch Fund; the Friends of the University of Liverpool; the Historic Society of Lancashire and Cheshire; Ocean Trading plc (P. H. Holt Trust); the Eleanor Rathbone Charitable Trust; the Isobel Thornley Bequest Fund; the Irene Scouloudi Foundation; and the Liverpool Centre for Medieval Studies. Assistance in editing the volume was given by Andrew Hamer, Victoria Mirfin and Lorna Stevenson, and the map on p.16 was drawn by Sandra Mather, to all of whom the editors are most grateful. Permission to reproduce the maps on pp.20, 24, 26 and 28 has been given by Cheshire Record Office; the photograph of the Hesket sword guard between pp.52-53 is reproduced by permission of the Tullie House, City Museum and Art Gallery, Carlisle. The woodcut of The Circumcision, between pp.244-45, from *Edward Hodnett's English Woodcuts 1480-1535*, revised edition, (Oxford, 1973) is reproduced by permission of Oxford University Press. Above all, the editors wish to record their sincere thanks to the Director and Secretary of the Marc Fitch Fund, Roy Stephens, who provided advice and encouragement at an early stage, and who agreed to publish the volume under the imprint of the Leopard's Head Press.

Notes on Contributors

Elizabeth Baldwin, was Leverhulme Research Associate in the Department of English at the University of Liverpool, and is now at University College, Dublin. She is editing, with David Mills, the Cheshire volume for *Records of Early English Drama*.

Marc Cohen is a postgraduate student at the University of Toronto, who has just published a major study on the ethnographic dimensions of conversion. His other interests include post-Conquest English cultural history and the sociological background to Jewish conversions in the High Middle Ages.

Nick Davis is a lecturer in the Department of English Language and Literature at the University of Liverpool. He works on literature written in English between the fourteenth and seventeenth centuries and is currently engaged in a study of Spenser's *The Faerie Queene*.

James Graham-Campbell is Professor of Medieval Archaeology in the Institute of Archaeology, the University of London. He is a specialist on the archaeology of the vikings and of the late Celtic period in Britain and Ireland.

E. Ruth Harvey is a professor in the English Department at the University of Toronto. She is currently working on the medieval literature of tribulations and the connections between human and animal in medieval thought.

Nick Higham is Senior Lecturer in the Department of History, the University of Manchester. His primary interests are the early Middle Ages, local and regional history in north and north-west England in the Middle Ages and landscape and settlement history.

David Klausner is Professor of English and Medieval Studies at the University of Toronto. His research interests include relations between Old English and early Welsh poetry, and medieval and early Tudor drama in English and Welsh.

Sally-Beth MacLean is Executive Editor of the *Records of Early English Drama* series. She has written on Chester art as well as articles on travelling players, patronage and folk drama.

Ian McDougall is an Assistant Editor at the Dictionary of Old English Project at the University of Toronto. His research has focused on medieval Iceland and included a study of foreigners and foreign languages and accounts of surgery.

David Mills holds a Personal Chair in the Department of English Language and Literature at the University of Liverpool. His major field of research is early English drama. He is a member of the Editorial Advisory Board of *Records of Early English Drama* and Director of the Leverhulme-funded research project into the Cheshire records for that series.

Tom Scott is Reader in History at the University of Liverpool. His principal research has focused on problems of regionalism and town-country relations in late medieval south-west Germany.

Pat Starkey is a Research Fellow in the Department of History at the University of Liverpool with interests in women's history and the history of pacifism. She was formerly Administrator of the University of Liverpool Centre for Medieval Studies.

Alan Thacker was formerly Editor of the *Victoria County History of Cheshire* and Research Fellow in the Department of History at the University of Liverpool. He is now Deputy Editor of the *Victoria County History of England*. His research interests include the cult of saints' lives and the ecclesiastical history of Anglo-Saxon England.

Graeme White is Head of History at Chester College. His research interests include the reign of king Stephen and medieval landscape history.

David Wilson was Director of the British Museum from 1977–92. He is an honorary professor at University College, London and a Fellow of the British Academy.

Abbreviations

CCRO	Chester City Record Office
CRO	Cheshire Record Office
EETS	*Early English Text Society*
EPNS	*English Place-Name Society*
MGH	*Monumenta Germaniae Historica*
MLR	*Modern Language Review*
MPG	J. P. Migne, ed., *Patrologiae cursus completus. Series graeca*, Paris, 1857–1934
MPL	J. P. Migne, ed., *Patrologiae cursus completus. Series latina*, Paris, 1843–1890
PMLA	*Proceedings of the Modern Language Association*
PRO	Public Record Office
REED	*Records of Early English Drama: Chester*

Introduction

TOM SCOTT and PAT STARKEY

THIS VOLUME BRINGS together papers delivered at an international conference on the Middle Ages in the North-West, held at the University of Liverpool in July 1993. Its occasion was also marked by the mounting of an exhibition of medieval manuscripts from Merseyside collections, treasures brought to the area in the eighteenth and nineteenth centuries by Liverpool patrons and collectors and shown in Liverpool and London in the summer and autumn of that year. The conference organizers wished to highlight the rich medieval legacy enjoyed by north-west England: from the recently discovered viking hoard at Cuerdale, through the allegorical poetic tradition embodied in the *Pearl* and *Sir Gawain and the Green Knight*, to the pageantry and symbolism of the Chester mystery plays, the North-West can boast a distinctive artistic and intellectual history created by foreigners and natives alike. The conference was sponsored jointly by the Centres for Medieval Studies at the Universities of Liverpool and Toronto. Its purpose was to range widely through the fields of archaeology, art history, literature and drama, as well as local history and geography, in order to convey both the vigour of contemporary studies of the medieval North-West and the fruits of interdisciplinary scholarship in casting new light upon topics often regarded in isolation. Not all the papers presented at the conference have found their way into the present volume — the editors regret the absence of two contributions on the territorial and administrative history of Lancashire — but further essays from

James Graham-Campbell and Alan Thacker have been
included, which complement the contributions of David
Wilson and Marc Cohen. The contributors would not wish to claim that they were
consciously writing regional history in the manner of
geschichtliche Landeskunde, the tradition of regional historical
studies amongst German scholars which deliberately integrates
history, topography, cultural and artistic life. Nevertheless, a
sense of regional identity (or continuity) has been a feature of
much recent research, both medieval and early modern, on the
history of north-west England, which is reflected in the present
volume. This identity, as Nick Higham argues, is evident in the
territorial organization of Cheshire, where the man-made
demarcations of parish and hundred, already firmly in place in
Anglo-Saxon times, were able to withstand the administrative
upheaval of the Norman Conquest and can still in many cases
be observed today. Similarly, Graeme White suggests that a
distinctive pattern of open fields was peculiar to parts of
Cheshire from remote times through the Middle Ages, and left
its mark on the tithe returns of the nineteenth century. Such
continuities do not preclude periodic dislocation, even if the
nature and extent of the disruption remain matters of controversy.
As both David Wilson and James Graham-Campbell show, the
assessment of the viking impact in the North-West is a precarious
endeavour. Both remain sceptical in the face of efforts by Scandinavian
scholars to urge an earlier and more profound influence than
commonly assumed. The artifactual evidence — spectacular in
the case of the Cuerdale hoard — obviously implies a penetrating
impact; but what were authentically viking imports and what
manufactures by viking settlers or native imitators cannot
easily be determined. Nevertheless, the artefacts, by their dispersion,
do suggest that the vikings, as sea-farers, regarded the Irish Sea
and its littoral as a maritime region, rather than the mainland:
the North-West was as much linked to Man, or Ireland, or
Galloway in the viking period as to the rest of England.

   Viking influence seen through the prism of literary evidence
is no easier to assess. To identify Bromborough on the Wirral,

in Ian McDougall's example, as the site of the battle of Brunanburh between Norse and Anglo-Saxon described in the Norse sagas, runs the risk of confusing literary *topoi* with historical or geographical fact. This theme is pursued by David Klausner in a wide-ranging consideration of the genres of Old English battle poetry, where fact and fiction are inextricably interwoven. A yet more curious instance is the cult of the last Anglo-Saxon king discussed by Alan Thacker: the legend of Harold Godwinson's survival after the battle of Hastings displays formal stylistic parallels with those of Óláfr Tryggvason, as Marc Cohen points out. Why Harold's cult should have developed, particularly at Chester, after its beginnings in the South-East, is unknown, but may well lie in those configurations of power relations in twelfth- and thirteenth-century north-west England traced by Alan Thacker.

The remaining essays turn our attention from the high to the later Middle Ages, and in particular towards the remarkable flowering of literature and drama in the North-West. The anonymous author of *Pearl* and *Sir Gawain and the Green Knight* displays a philosophical and theological profundity and breadth of learning unrivalled in later medieval England. Nick Davis is able to show how far the values evinced by the poet were firmly grounded in a speculative tradition stretching back through the Christian fathers to Aristotle and Greek mathematicians, whilst Ruth Harvey engagingly investigates the contrast in *Pearl* between the unknowable reality and man's vain imagining of heaven. That literature of such quality was composed in the North-West goes some way to counteract the view of the medieval region as backward and provincial. At the same time, the evidence of the mystery plays, performed most notably at York and Chester, testifies to a popular religiosity of impeccably Catholic devotion. David Mills describes the degree of involvement evinced by the Chester craftsmen, with each guild investing its own human and material capital in a religious dramatization which stood witness to the citizens' sense of sacral corporatism, of civic pride and mutual obligation. No wonder, perhaps, that their religious commitment was not easily broken by the Reformation: Sally-Beth MacLean demonstrates how devotion to the Virgin continued to inform the 'Purification' play enacted by the city's smiths. Here, if anywhere, is evidence of that religious conservatism which Christopher Haigh and others have attested for the North-West throughout the sixteenth century and beyond. This sense of continuity can likewise be discerned, as Elizabeth Baldwin's paper shows, in the preference for popular entertainments over the more austere pleasures of Bible study enjoined by the Protestant Reformers.

Taken together, the essays in this volume do not seek to impose an artificial homogeneity upon the history and culture of the North-West, seen as a region distinct from the rest of England. Rather, they offer insights into an historical diversity which combined the broader influence of viking activity in the Irish Sea with a certain particularity – slow to change, and in some respects set slightly apart from the mainstream of English life. It was, in other words, a region both 'open' and 'closed', not intolerant of interlopers, vikings or Welsh, yet proud of its native character — a feature of the Middle Ages which still holds good today.

1

Territorial organization
in pre-Conquest Cheshire

NICK HIGHAM

THE STUDY OF CHESHIRE'S early organization summarized in
this short essay derives from the need to place excavations in
Tatton Park, primarily of a deserted medieval settlement, in an
appropriate territorial context. Excavations began in 1978,[1]
and the wider survey in 1979, with the first fruits published in
1982.[2] Research notes were made available to Dr Alan Thacker
and some of the material incorporated into the first volume of
the *Victoria County History of Cheshire*,[3] but full publication is still
pending as this goes to press.[4] This study, therefore, is one
which has had a desultory existence over almost a decade
and a half.

When it began, few of the plethora of recent studies of early
medieval territorial organization had been undertaken, let
alone published,[5] and several of the approaches which are now
familiar to landscape historians and archaeologists had not then
been developed.[6] In addition, neither Lancashire nor Cheshire
had been extensively researched in this respect: only Dorothy
Sylvester had studied the territorial evolution of Cheshire and
it was a great privilege to follow in her footsteps,[7] and particularly
to use the same Index to the Tithe Ordnance Survey maps in
the Geography Department Library of the University of
Manchester, which she had previously annotated.[8]

Cheshire poses its own special problems: there are almost no
pre-Conquest charters and none with boundary clauses; indeed,

the region was little short of prehistoric before Domesday Book, apart from six stray references to local places or events in the Anglo-Saxon Chronicle.[9] For written evidence, therefore, this study rested on Domesday Book, with all the problems of interpretation which that brought with it. The region does, however, offer one major advantage: few local thegns or Norman knights in the period *c*.900–1200 participated in the then popular practice of founding manorial churches. Perhaps they were satisfied with the older, more extensive *parochiae* already in existence and a scarce and comparatively untutored clergy; perhaps few secular lords were sufficiently affluent to indulge in such conspicuous statements about status; perhaps few were interested in a practice which appears to have flourished primarily in East Anglia and the south and the east of England. For whatever reason, most of Cheshire's large parishes became ossified in the twelfth and thirteenth centuries and these extensive, multi-settlement units of parochial administration offer an important means of studying early territoriality, although just how early is rarely clear.

This examination began in the two north-central Domesday hundreds of Bucklow and Tunendune, and more specifically in Rostherne parish, because that is where Tatton lies. Attempts were made, with little success, to identify medieval settlements in this multi-township parish from field evidence. More successful was the examination of the hundred, parish and township boundaries, with the following tentative results. First, the parish has a geographical rationale, being centred on a ridge of well-drained soils conducive to cultivation, along which ran major and ancient routes (one, and possibly two, Roman roads),[10] and on which most township names had a settlement or topographical suffix. Second, the parish boundaries tended to follow either major topographical features — such as the river Bollin or Sink Moss — or minor features (streams, hedges, etc.) running through poorly drained clay land where medieval woodland had been extensive — on place-name evidence — and only cleared at a late stage. The M6 now runs up just such a corridor of cleared medieval woodland.[11] In addition, where appropriate, the Domesday hundred generally, but not invariably, shared a boundary with the parish and was arguably dependent on the parish for its boundary. But there are exceptions: for example, one of the two Tableys lay in Rostherne and one in Great Budworth parish. Secular lordship similarly looked in different directions, but both were recorded in 1086 as of Bucklow hundred, suggesting that intercommoning may have been practised in this marginal woodland and wet land by communities normally based on either side even later than the formal creation of the Domesday hundreds in the tenth century. And peripheral areas of well-drained land which were cut off from the central core of the parish by belts of woodland, or areas of woodland settlement, exhibit a tendency to fall away under influential thegns and become separate small parishes. This probably occurred at Lymm, for example, at the northern end of Rostherne parish. Other such marginal areas eventually became parochial chapelries, as did the Peovers.

Despite the geographical rationale of Rostherne parish, which was suggestive of an ancient *parochia*, there were two serious weaknesses in the case for its representing an early territorial unit. First, the church is undocumented at Rostherne before the later twelfth century, and a church and priest are recorded in Domesday Book under one of the two manors of High Legh.[12] This may be because Rostherne was then almost valueless and both estates were held by Gilbert de Venables, but doubts remain. Second, the place-name Rostherne is Anglo-Scandinavian.[13] This is most unusual for a name of parochial status in Cheshire away from the Wirral.

There may, therefore, have been a shift in the parochial centre or in its name, but neither implies major change to the boundaries of the *parochia* before the formation of its several dependent chapelries in the post-Conquest period. There are hints of a lost secular estate: the Domesday Book place-name 'Chapmonswiche'[14] — meaning 'trader's market' (perhaps even 'trader's salt-site', given the specific meaning attached to 'wich' locally) — implies a significant trading site at some date before 1066 on the borders of Rostherne and Great Budworth parishes; secondly, the place-name Millington suggests a mill. Given the close correlation between mills and extensive estates held by men of high status in 1086,[15] this may be a relic of a large estate which had already been dispersed long before king Edward died. Examination of Tunendune hundred to the west revealed a far clearer picture of territorial organization. The entire hundred consisted almost exclusively of two large medieval parishes, the churches and/or priests of which were recorded in 1086, one at Great Budworth, the other on the Halton estate, so presumably at the mother church of Runcorn.[16]

Each *parochia* consisted of a core of well-drained terrain, characterized by settlement-type township names. That of Runcorn exhibits the only complete set of directionally named townships in Cheshire — Norton, Sutton, Aston, Weston — suggesting that they had been dependent parts of a large estate.[17] They do not relate directionally to Runcorn or Halton — the late Saxon and Norman capital manor.

A consistent belt of poorly-drained townships with woodland names divides them. Curiously, the parish boundary fails to follow this line, but this is arguably due to a major reorganization of this territorial system consequent on the foundation of the Mercian defensive *burh* at Runcorn in 915. The woodland belt should probably — on numerous local analogies — be viewed as the earlier boundary between these two parochial systems.

Both have at the core of the *parochia* a secular estate of large size and high status in 1086. Halton barony was the senior of these, descending from an extensive estate held by the powerful thegn Orm in 1066.[18] Other local landholders inside the parish may have been his tenants. Great Budworth was the capital manor of a significant subinfeudation of that barony in 1086 held by one Pagen and extending into several townships.[19] It had been held by another apparently prosperous and influential local thegn in 1066, named Edward, who survived in the locality to 1086 in the service of Osbern fitz Tezzo.[20]

At neither is it certain that the Domesday church site predates the Viking Age: St. Bertelin's at Runcorn is surely a product of

Æthelflæd's reorganization in 915, perhaps being relocated from either Preston-on-the-Hill or Daresbury, in the centre of the parish: although a ridge-top site (like Bowdon), God and All Saints at Great Budworth lies at a site the name of which is unique among parish names in the shire, where -worth names are more normally attached to dependent settlements of low status in the settlement hierarchy. The manor was small in 1086, despite the presence of a hall and church,[21] and the possibility that the church has been relocated should be taken seriously, perhaps in the same tenth-century shake-up that affected Runcorn.

Several characteristics do emerge from this more extended study, which have since been confirmed by attention to other parts of the shire. In the first place, large medieval parishes do exhibit clear evidence of a 'core and periphery', with cleared land evidenced by distinctive settlement-type place-naming in the core and woodland wetlands, uplands and so on at the periphery. This is not just a description of landscape. These are very clearly resource-conscious units and can only be understood by invoking parish-wide economic systems involving integrated land-use across the whole, and the partial segregation of specific types of land-use (such as ploughland or permanent pasture) in specific parts of the territory. If such parishes were characterized by integrated economies, they were necessarily also territorial units of a secular kind, such as might very loosely be termed estates, or shires of the Northumbrian kind.[22] They were, therefore, units for the regulation of economic, social and religious activity. Additionally they were units in terms of the renders paid by the farming community to maintain a secular court and tithes to a minster church, and presumably hidated as such.

Moreover, wherever possible, they use boundaries of high status: the Mersey, Weaver and Bollin rivers, with their sometimes extensive mosses, were supplemented by belts of unenclosed woodland, probably used for a variety of extensive purposes and not just grazing, within which the actual boundary might eventually be attached to a topographical feature of far less magnitude, or even a man-made feature such as a ditch and/or hedge. To a marked extent the Anglo-Saxon hundreds shared these boundaries. And with a handful of very minor exceptions, the Domesday hundreds of Tunendune and Bucklow both consist of two large minster parishes. In each case, one was associated with a large, late-Saxon estate of some political and strategic significance along what had been the Mersey frontier of Mercia — that which became Dunham barony in Bowdon parish and that which re-emerges as Halton barony in Runcorn parish.

Hundreds consisting of two large parishes were probably the norm in pre-Conquest Cheshire, although the situation has been partially obscured by the subdivision of parishes consequent upon the foundation of some manorial churches in the tenth and eleventh centuries. The 'two parish' formula is clearly visible in Ruloe hundred, supposing only that the parish of Thornton-le-Moors (in the developing eleventh-century ploughlands of the lower Gowy) had become detached from the mother church of Frodsham.[23] If so, the parishes of Frodsham and Weaverham made up the hundred. Rushton hundred arguably derived from the combination of the bishop's minster and estate at Tarvin (from which Tarporley and Over parishes probably became detached) and earl Edwin's minster of Bunbury. 'Wa(e)rmundestrou' hundred — later Nantwich — probably derived from earl Morcar's Acton estate and minster in combination with the bishop's minster at Wybunbury. Middlewich hundred apparently derived from the fragmented *parochia* of a minster at Sandbach, probably under episcopal patronage (given its superb carvings), linked with a smaller but longer-surviving *parochia* based on Astbury. Chester's two minster churches, in episcopal and secular patronage respectively, may similarly have been the two minsters for the Wirral, or at least a large part thereof, although here the early parochial structure is more obscure than elsewhere. Scandinavian 'settlement', subsequent reorganization and the comparative affluence of its landholders all probably contributed to the obscurity of its territorial development by the eleventh century.

The pattern that emerges suggests two further possibilities.

One, that there is a comparatively regular and uniform structure of territories throughout most of Cheshire identifiable through examination of early parishes, which was incorporated into the hundreds little changed, so predating the shiring of the tenth century. And two, that minster churches in secular patronage are frequently paired with similar in episcopal patronage to constitute hundreds. This pattern is too commonplace to be accidental. Again, these pairings must necessarily predate the shire.

In some sense, therefore, the hundreds of Cheshire are of earlier origin than the shire, although they will not, of course, have been called hundreds. The antiquity of this pattern is obscure but worthy of examination. 'Dudestan' hundred (later Broxton hundred), in the south-west corner of Cheshire, is perhaps the most interesting example by which to illustrate the points summarized above, and also to unravel a little more of the history and organization of this apparently ancient pattern of territoriality.

This hundred also has well-defined geographical boundaries: to the west is the river Dee and to the south (if we ignore for the moment the presence of Maelor Saesneg inside the hundred in 1086) is the steep little valley of the Wych Brook. This is augmented by boggy and well-wooded land to the east in a trench now occupied by the Shropshire Union Canal, the southern end of the mid-Cheshire ridge to the north-east and more well-wooded wetlands to the north.

The southern half of the hundred consists of Malpas parish, whose core was an estate of earl Edwin in 1066, the caput of which became a baronial centre by 1086.[24] The entire parish was held of the barony in 1086 and may well have been held of earl Edwin thitherto. Despite the lack of documentary evidence for a church earlier than the thirteenth century, it seems very likely that St. Oswald's, Malpas was a pre-Conquest minster church, at the core of an estate then called 'Depenbech' — a toponym irrelevant to the later township but probably named after the deep valley of the Wych Brook on the southern edge of the parish. St. Oswald was a favoured saint in pre-Conquest Mercia and this probably royal Mercian estate could have had a church dedicated to St. Oswald from as early as the late-seventh century, although Ethelred and Æthelflæd may equally have been responsible since it was they who moved his relics from Bardney in the Danelaw to Gloucester.[25]

At the core of the parish is a group of township names with either settlement or topographical suffixes, with a periphery on most sides of woodland names (predominantly -leah),[26] but the township names may convey even more information concerning the integrity of the early territory than this: two contain elements which refer to bees, so honey (Bickerton, Bickley); one to bullocks, so beef (Bulkeley); one to dairying (Stockton); and one to either salt working or trade (Wychough). Collectively these names suggest economic specialization across an early territory, with renders paid in specific commodities by different sections of the community occupying various localities within it.

Similar patterns of place-names relating to renders occur elsewhere in Cheshire, but this is probably the set which exhibits least change in the later Anglo-Saxon period, when so many new manorial names were apparently being formed from personal names. The long-lived secular estate of high status should probably be given credit for this conservatism although 'personal name + suffix' type place-names (for example, Cuddington) do occur, particularly among what may have been tenancies held by the thegns of the earl and bishop in 1066.

That place-naming here was comparatively conservative is demonstrated by the survival of Macefen — from Old Welsh 'Maes y ffin' ('open land near a boundary').[27] There is no reason to concur with the view of the late, lamented Professor John Dodgson that this referred to an early boundary between Wales and England.[28] Instead, it was probably the boundary of this major land-unit to which the name refers. Macefen does lie on the edge of the core of the territory, up against the belt of woodland place-names which may have been pasture common to this and another land-unit to the east. It provides a crucial hint that this estate system pre-dates English place-naming, so perhaps pushing the system back at least to the early Anglo-Saxon period — at latest the seventh century. The Old Welsh origin of the name Tarvin, the early name of the river Gowy which also means 'boundary', supports this.[29] This boggy river separated two parochial systems and two hundreds in 1086, and the antiquity of this frontier role is once more established by its pre-English name. Again, there is no reason to interpret this as an Anglo-Welsh 'national' frontier, but it may have been the boundary of Chester's legionary *prata* or *territoria* in the Roman period, as David Mason has suggested.[30]

At Domesday, only three priests (but no churches) were noted in 'Dudestan' hundred: one was at Bettisfield, earl Edwin's large estate in Maelor Saesneg; the remaining two were the bishop's tenants of one and a half hides at St Chad's, the episcopal minster church at Farndon. By 1066 there were two large estates of this name, the bishop's and the earl's, which emerged later as Aldford parish.[31] The boundary between the two is clearly artificial, as is that between the later medieval parish of Farndon, with its detached portion, and the parishes of Tilston, Coddington and Shocklach. The early parish of Farndon probably encompassed everything inside the hundred excluding Malpas, so everything between the Dee and the mid-Cheshire Ridge.

The boundary between the parishes of Farndon and Malpas looks older, in its alignment, than those of the townships on either side, but it is the only boundary of either *parochia* which runs across terrain characterized by well-drained soils and settlement type place-names. The woodland place-name belt on the eastern edge of Malpas parish runs all the way round to the Dee at the northern end of Farndon's parish. It seems possible, therefore, that the entire hundred had an early territorial integrity which predates the primary division into the two estates and parishes, which were themselves later united once more as a hundred.

Tentative support for this hypothesis comes from several additional factors. Broxton — meaning 'burial place' — shares a border with five medieval parishes, which may indicate a desire to remain in contact with that township during the period of fission; in which case a cemetery at that site may have been one of the foci of an earlier territory approximating to the Domesday Book hundred. Such a focus might be associated with Maiden Castle, an Iron Age hillfort which could, on numerous parallels, have attracted the presence of a Romano-British shrine or a sub-Roman cemetery. That the hundred eventually took the name of Broxton may imply that the early hundredal place of assembly — 'Dudd's stone' — lay there. Otherwise it is difficult to explain why this relatively inaccessible manor of nondescript status gave its name to a hundred in which lay far more important, and more accessible, centres. And a single nucleated Romano-British site (probably 'Bovium', on Watling Street, near Tilston) lay at the core of the territory. This pattern recurs across Cheshire, with single nucleated Roman sites in the hundreds of Wirral, Nantwich and Middlewich, at least — with other hundreds grouped around scarce Roman sites, just as Ruloe, Tunendune and Bucklow were ranged around Northwich.

This brief examination of 'Dudestan' hundred does, therefore, suggest that the territory which can be identified at Domesday as a hundred is older than the shiring of Cheshire, in the tenth century. There are signs of a territory-wide system of exploitation, at least within its principal component *parochiae* and more probably within the whole. There are indications that the landscape which was characteristic of this economic system predates the English conquest. It could be a pre-Christian system, with the ancient cemetery site recalled in the place-name Broxton surviving as a place of assembly, even though displaced by Farndon — with its circular churchyard — as the spiritual centre. That a royal residence existed at Farndon seems clear from king Edward's death there,[32] and the site's subsequent use by king Edgar (or perhaps Aldford). The combination of minster and palace at or near Farndon may reflect the presence of an important secular focus of considerable antiquity. If the river crossing was active in the Roman period, then Farndon arguably ought also to be Roman in date. It may have been when that site was placed under episcopal control that secondary centres of secular lordship emerged up and down Watling Street, at Aldford and Malpas.

Much of this is necessarily very hypothetical, as much because of the poor quality of the evidence as of the need to compress ideas into a brief précis, but certain features do recur across much of Cheshire and are worth summarizing. Pre-Conquest Cheshire was characterized by large parishes which reveal a regular pattern of core and periphery in both terrain and township-names. Before the Viking Age these were arguably far more regular than was the case in the high Middle Ages — the period from which our evidence mostly derives. These parishes owed their existence to pre-existing units of secular organization, or land-units, traces of which are preserved both in the Domesday Book structure of estates and in the hierarchy of place-names. Many have parochial names which use the suffix *burh* (Wybunbury, Bunbury, etc.) or a topographical element ('Depenbech', Sandbach), which are likely to reflect early names given to high status settlements. From a very early date, some (at least) of these units were organized in pairs, of which one was normally under episcopal and the other under secular, control (Ruloe is exceptional in having two units under the control of the earl in 1066). There are hints that these paired parochial units derive from the sub-division of pre-existing territories. That the links between them remained significant is implicit in the fact that pairs re-emerged in the tenth century as ready-made hundreds. A partnership between secular and spiritual lordship seems, therefore, to have been a continuing characteristic of the system. Subdivision apparently relates in some way to the wholesale granting of approximately a half-share in most (if not all) territories to the church. This could have occurred under Rome, after Christianity first became the religion of government. It could have occurred in the sub-Roman period under British control; it could have occurred under Mercian control, perhaps in the later seventh century, when Caedwalla's grant of a quarter of the Isle of Wight to the church provides a parallel which might be relevant.[33]

That the subdivision was a pre-English phenomenon is rendered less likely by the problems implicit in the descent of the pattern virtually intact into the control of English kings who may initially have been pagan, but the possibility that some British church lands reached Anglo-Saxon bishops cannot be ruled out. The basic organization of Cheshire certainly retained the remote imprint of pre-English organization as late as the Conquest. That organization should probably be linked with major changes in the Roman period which were consequent upon the establishment of a legionary fortress at Chester, but in the countryside it may well have its origins in the tribal past of the Cornovii, then the Wrocen sæte — that early medieval tribal kingship into which the Roman and sub-Roman Cornovii eventually evolved. Whatever its exact origins (and these are unlikely ever to be known), there underlies Cheshire's basic framework a very early system of organization which was adapted and altered over a long period but which proved both durable and elastic. As a system of land-units it was largely dismembered in the manorialization of the late Anglo-Saxon and later medieval periods but its linked parishes formed the basis of the tenth-century hundreds. Those relict minster parishes proved more resilient here than in many regions of England and it was these institutions which carried the basic geographical structure of the early Middle Ages down into the early modern period.

References

1 N. J. Higham, *Tatton: the history and prehistory of one Cheshire township*, Chester, forthcoming.

2 N. J. Higham, 'Bucklow hundred: the Domesday survey and the rural community', *Cheshire Archaeological Bulletin*, 8 (1982), pp.15–21. For further comment, see also *idem*, 'The Cheshire landholdings of earl Morcar in 1066', *Transactions of the Historic Society of Lancashire and Cheshire*, 137 (1988), pp.139–47; *idem*, 'Patterns of settlement in medieval Cheshire: an insight into dispersed settlement', *Annual Report of the Medieval Settlement*

Research Group, 2 (1987), pp.9–10; *idem*, 'Forest, woodland and settlement in medieval Cheshire', *Annual Report of the Medieval Settlement Research Group*, 4 (1990), pp.24–5.

3 A. T. Thacker, 'Anglo-Saxon Cheshire', in B. E. Harris and A. T. Thacker, eds, *Victoria County History of Cheshire*, vol. I, London, 1987, p.264.

4 N. J. Higham, *The origins of Cheshire*, Manchester, 1993.

5 For example, D. Hooke, *Anglo-Saxon landscapes of the West Midlands: the charter evidence*, Oxford, 1981; J. Blair, 'Secular churches in Domesday Book', in P. H. Sawyer, ed., *Domesday Book: a reassessment*, London, 1985, pp.104–42; J. Blair, ed., *Minsters and parish churches. The local church in transition, 590–1200*, Oxford, 1988; J. Blair and R. Sharpe, eds, *Pastoral care before the parish*, Leicester, 1992.

6 As, for example, the study of the relationship between modern field systems and Roman roads, or systematic field walking for artifactual remains.

7 For example, D. Sylvester, 'The manor and the Cheshire landscape', *Transactions of the Lancashire and Cheshire Antiquarian Society*, 70 (1960), pp.1–15; *idem*, 'Parish and township in Cheshire and north-east Wales', *Journal of the Chester Archaeological Society*, 54 (1967), pp.23–36.

8 My thanks to the map curator, Mr Chris Perkins, for his generous assistance.

9 G. N. Garmonsway, ed., *The Anglo-Saxon Chronicle*, London, 1972: *Brunanburh*, versions A, E, F, for AD 937; Chester, A, 894; C, 907; E, 972; E, 1016; C, 1055; Eddisbury, C, 914; Farndon, C, D, 924; Runcorn, C, 915; Thelwall, A, 922.

10 One is Watling Street. See also E. M. Hughes, 'A Roman road between Hatton and High Legh, Cheshire', *Cheshire History*, 13 (1984), pp.13–18.

11 N. J. Higham, 'Bucklow hundred', pp.15–21.

12 *Domesday Book,* f.267.

13 J. McN. Dodgson, *The place-names of Cheshire*, parts 1–5 (*EPNS*, XLIV–XLVIII), Cambridge, 1970–81, pt 2, pp.56–7.

14 *Domesday Book*, f.267.

15 N. J. Higham, *Origins of Cheshire*, pp.196–7.

16 A. T. Thacker, 'Anglo-Saxon Cheshire', p.272.

17 N. J. Higham, 'The Cheshire *Burhs* and the Mercian frontier to 924', *Transactions of the Lancashire and Cheshire Antiquarian Society*, 3 (1988), pp.203–6; P. Greene, *Norton Priory: the archaeology of a medieval religious house*, Cambridge, 1989, pp.29–31.

18 *Domesday Book*, f.266.

19 Holding Cogshall from Richard de Vernon, and Aston (by Budworth), Great Budworth and Whitley (the last jointly with Odard), all from William fitz Nigel, baron of Halton.

20 In 1086, Edward held Dutton, Lymm and Grappenhall from Osbern fitz Tezzo.

21 *Domesday Book*, f.266.

22 J. E. A. Jolliffe, 'Northumbrian institutions', *English Historical Review*, 41 (1926), pp.1–42; G. W. S. Barrow, *The kingdom of the Scots*, London, 1973.

23 N. J. Higham, *Origins of Cheshire*, pp.151–2.

24 *Domesday Book*, f.264.

25 G. N. Garmonsway, *Anglo-Saxon Chronicle*, p.94, version C, 909.

26 N. J. Higham, *Rome, Britain and the Anglo-Saxons*, London, 1992, p.135.

27 J. McN. Dodgson, *The place-names of Cheshire*, pt. 4, p.135.

28 *Idem*, 'The English arrival in Cheshire', *Transactions of the Historic Society of Lancashire and Cheshire*, 119 (1967), pp.1–37.

29 *Idem*, *Place-names of Cheshire*, pt. 3, p.281.

30 D. Mason, 'The *prata legionis* at Chester', *Journal of the Chester Archaeological Society*, 69 (1986), pp.19–43.

31 For the bishop's manor, *Domesday Book*, f.263; for earl Edwin's descending to Bigot, f.266.

32 G. N. Garmonsway, *Anglo-Saxon Chronicle*, p.105, version C, AD 924.

33 B. Colgrave and R. A. B. Mynors, eds, *Bede's ecclesiastical history of the English people*, Oxford, 1969, IV, 16.

2

Open fields and rural settlement in medieval west Cheshire

GRAEME J. WHITE

MEDIEVAL CHESHIRE has fairly been described as 'a distinctive landscape in which patterns of settlement and patterns of [land] exploitation differed markedly from Midland England': a county of relatively low population, dispersed settlement and irregular field systems.[1] As such, it deserves far more attention than it has hitherto received from scholars engaged in medieval landscape studies. Until the 1950s, interpretations of the medieval English countryside were dominated by the concept of nucleated villages and great open fields worked in common, the origins of both usually being traced back to the early Saxon period. Over the past three decades, the combined skills of historians, geographers, archaeologists and philologists have shown that this was only one form of land use and settlement among many and that its occurrence can be attributed to a variety of factors, the centuries between the eighth and the thirteenth generally being seen as the critical formative period.[2] Current scholarship rejects the notion that the so-called 'midland system' of common fields usually associated with nucleated villages was in some sense the norm, with other patterns as aberrations. It is also inappropriate to consider one pattern as inherently superior to, or more developed than, another.[3] Where settlements were dispersed, not nucleated, and where fields took the form of closes held in severalty rather than unenclosed strips farmed in common, we have a

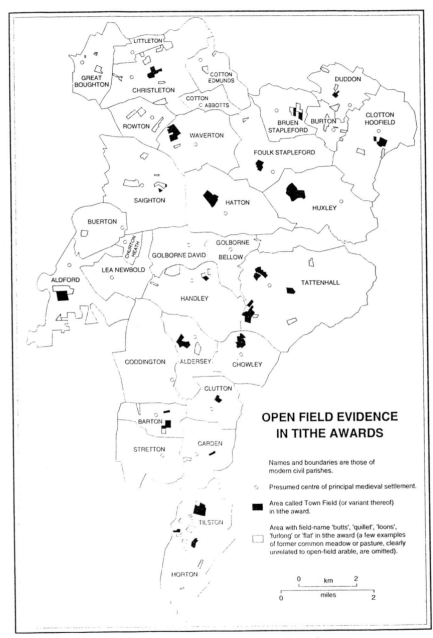

OPEN FIELD EVIDENCE
IN TITHE AWARDS

Names and boundaries are those of
modern civil parishes.

○   Presumed centre of principal medieval settlement.

■   Area called Town Field (or variant thereof)
    in tithe award.

☐   Area with field-name 'butts', 'quillet', 'loons',
    'furlong' or 'flat' in tithe award (a few examples
    of former common meadow or pasture, clearly
    unrelated to open-field arable, are omitted).

0   km   2

0   miles   2

Map 1 — The thirty-two townships in the study area.

phenomenon which deserves study in its own right, as the local or regional response to changing demographic and economic pressures and as a contribution to our knowledge of the immensely varied settlement and field patterns of the medieval English countryside as a whole. This paper, which focuses upon thirty-two vills in the Dee and Gowy valleys south and southeast of Chester, is offered as such a contribution.[4]

Although common field agriculture has come to be associated with nucleated settlement in much recent writing, the connection was by no means automatic.[5] Significantly, in the extreme south-west of Cheshire adjacent to the Welsh border, there survives to this day a forty-acre meadow divided into doles, in which five local farmers continue to have a stake: this serves not a nucleated settlement but a series of dispersed clusters of dwellings. The meadow is Gwern-y-ddavid in Shocklach Oviatt (grid reference: SJ 425484), which in the 1830s still consisted of thirteen strips and today has seven, used for the growing of hay or silage. Eighteenth-century stones (one with a decipherable date, 1765) continue to mark the boundaries between some of the strips. The doles are now worked independently; yet common grazing, under regulations whereby cattle could be 'turned in' on the Monday after the second Sunday in August and had to be taken off by Christmas, and each farmer was entitled to graze one cow or two heifers per acre, only came to an end in the 1960s.[6] No nucleated settlement is known to have existed here: the small Norman church stands isolated in Church Shocklach at the confluence of several rights of way, but no trace of a settlement has been found in its immediate vicinity. Gwern-y-ddavid remains as a precious reminder of a number of similar open meadows which appear on eighteenth-century field maps, such as those of Aldford and Farndon in the 1730s,[7] but it survives as witness to a form of communal farming in the context of dispersed, not nucleated, settlement.

Open fields, without hedges or fences between the holdings, are not necessarily the same as common fields worked as a unit,[8] and without the common grazing there is really no good

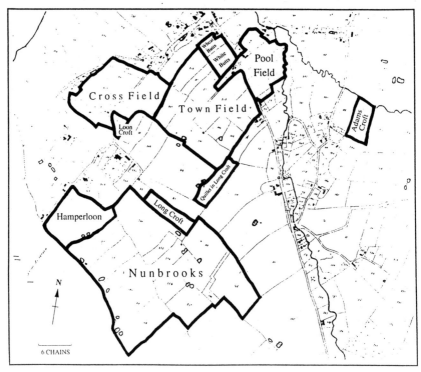

Map 2 — *Reconstruction of possible open arable fields in Tilston, based on field names in tithe award and in earlier documents.*

economic reason why the meadow at Shocklach should remain open, other than the expense of erecting barriers or of transferring and consolidating the holdings. Indeed, like the more famous open arable fields at Laxton (Notts.), its days may be numbered. Elsewhere, we know little of the regulations — common or otherwise — which governed the working of Cheshire's open arable fields, but there can be no doubt over their former widespread existence, as demonstrated by pioneer work in the 1950s,[9] and illustrated in the accompanying distribution maps. These maps are chiefly derived from the tithe awards, which furnish us with a detailed picture of field-names and of ownership/occupation patterns in the early Victorian period. In some cases, such as Aldford and Tilston, the tithe awards indicate the previous existence of open fields by identifying (as 'quillets') individual strips which still survived. Elsewhere, although any former open arable fields, or meadows, had been broken up and enclosed, some closes still bore names derived from their open-field predecessors: 'butts', 'loons', 'furlong', 'flat', or 'town field', the latter a name widely used in Cheshire for the community's principal shared field.[10] The tithe maps also record reverse-S field boundaries, normally attributed to the piecemeal enclosure of open-field strips, which themselves followed a reverse-S course. Thus, the tithe awards, although mapping what had become an almost entirely enclosed landscape, do serve as evidence of the former distribution of open arable fields, and Map 1 utilizes them as such. It is very imperfect evidence, since it relates only to that portion of former open field which left a memorial in the form of a field name, or a reverse-S boundary, by the time a tithe award was

Map 3 — Reconstruction of possible open arable fields in Aldersey Green (aka Great Aldersey), based on field names in tithe award and earlier documents and on certain areas of surviving ridge and furrow.

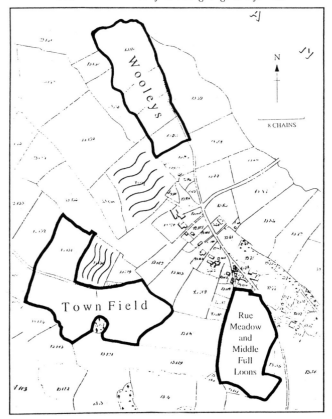

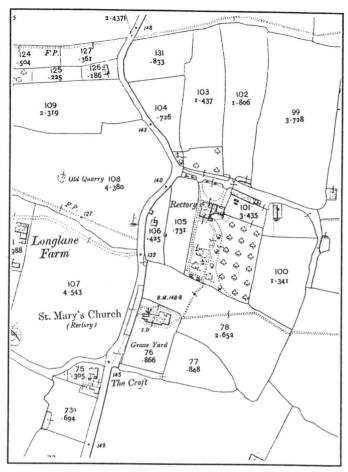

Map 4 — *Tilston, from OS 25 ins. to mile (3rd edn., 1911),*
Cheshire LX.1 (reduced).

compiled. By using earlier documentary evidence, and observing
patterns of surviving reverse-S ridge-and-furrow, it can be
argued that open-field arable once existed over a considerably
larger area than that suggested by the tithe awards: this exercise
is attempted for Aldersey Green and Tilston in Maps 2 and 3.
However, provided that it is borne in mind that tithe awards
can offer only a limited impression of the former distribution
of open fields, they are nevertheless a most useful starting-
point, and they form part of the evidence in all three discussions
which follow: of the incidence of 'town fields'; of the
occurrence of settlement planning; and of the circumstances

which led open arable fields to survive longer in some vills than in others.

First, as established in the 1950s, the tithe awards for the great majority of vills in the Dee-Gowy lowlands showed clear evidence of former open-field arable: of sixty-four townships in the region (including all those under study here), eleven still had one or more arable strips and all but ten revealed, through the names or shapes of their fields, that such strips had once existed. No less than thirty-three had one or more fields bearing the name 'town field', indicative of the open field of that name which had previously existed.[11] The acreages covered by such 'town field' names in the tithe awards were usually modest. Huxley had four adjoining closes, 'Higher town field' of fifteen acres one rood; 'Lower town field' (thirteen acres two roods); 'Near part of big town field' (sixteen acres); and 'Further part of big town field' (eight acres two roods), which suggests that the previous, open, town field had extended over at least fifty-three acres. Such an area was exceptional, however. The next largest among the thirty-two Dee-Gowy vills studied for present purposes, on the evidence of tithe awards, was that in the south-west of Tattenhall, a group of fifteen closes and quillets called some variant of 'town field' or 'Willmoor town field', comprising a total of forty-one acres. Waverton had a block of seven closes in the north of the vill, four called 'town field', the others named 'Jones town field', 'Top town field' and 'Near town field', which together made up thirty-five acres. In Tilston, ten adjacent closes variously called 'town field', 'long town field', 'part of long town field', 'townfield croft' and 'lower townfield croft' totalled twenty-eight acres. Similar groupings in Hatton (two closes); Chowley (two); Christleton (seven); and Aldersey (three) imply town fields of approximately thirty-two; twenty-nine; twenty-four and twenty-three acres respectively. At Aldford, a twenty-two-acre town field area can be reconstructed from no less than twenty-six small closes and quillets. Elsewhere, distinct town field areas can be identified within the same vill. In Tattenhall, a group of eleven fields, all called 'town field' or a variant thereof, totalling thirty acres, most of them narrow and reverse-S in shape, straddled the road leading north-west out of the vill. Another twelve-acre close called 'town field' lay to the east of the settlement, while a third group made up the forty-one-acre 'Willmoor town field' near the south-western boundary. There was a particularly interesting survival at Horton: one 'town field' group near the north-western boundary comprising nine unenclosed quillets and a close, and another of two adjacent closes less than half a mile to the east — also in the northern part of the vill — both groups consisting of some six acres. In other vills, less significant areas were covered: a single close called 'town field' at Burton, fractionally above one acre in size; three adjoining closes with the same name at Carden, two a little over an acre each, the other less than three-quarters of an acre; a single close of just under four acres at Handley; two neighbouring 'town fields' and an adjoining 'town field croft' at Duddon, where the three totalled seven acres.

The former significance of these fields as areas of open-field arable can occasionally be illustrated by the survival of broad reverse-S ridge-and-furrow in what is today permanent pasture. This is the case, for example, in 'long town field', Tilston (SJ 460510); in the north-western 'town field', Tattenhall (SJ 482590); and — to the east of the study area — in 'town field and Coney Grey Flatts', Calveley (SJ 600595); and 'Higher town field' and 'town field flatt', Wettenhall (SJ 611617): though since a community's principal open-field arable area must be expected to contain some of its best cultivable land, the disappearance elsewhere of the physical evidence of strips as a result of subsequent ploughing should occasion no surprise.[12] There is, of course, no shortage of documentary evidence for the previous open-field regimes. Three examples may be cited from the sixteenth century. In 1546, John Aldersey, gentleman, conveyed to his illegitimate son Thomas three butts of land in Great Aldersey (now Aldersey Green) town field.[13] In Tilston in 1559, four tenants of John Leche held sixteen and a half, thirty-four and a half, five, and forty-eight loondes respectively in the three town fields, which went under the names of 'infield', 'middlefield' and 'outfield'; a note in his rental says that three loondes in the town fields made an acre, and that for every loonde held therein, it was customary to put one beast into the townfields after the corn had been gathered in.[14] A survey of Sir Philip Egerton's lands, apparently dating to the reign of Elizabeth I, mentioned a headland and two butts in Horton town field and another butt in Horton higher town field.[15] It is worth stressing again that the areas dubbed 'town field' in tithe awards are no more than remnants of previous expanses of open arable field: piecemeal enclosure in west Cheshire can be traced back to the late thirteenth century, and had still not been completed when the tithe awards were produced.[16] Even so, there is some consistency in the pattern of town fields which emerges from the tithe awards and this merits further consideration here. Map 1 seeks to illustrate the pattern which is the subject of the discussion which follows.

If we measure the distance between the centre of the principal settlement within a vill, and the furthest extremity of the named 'town field' area, as mapped in the tithe awards, it is almost invariably within two-thirds of a mile. Most are between one-third of a mile (as at Barton and Chowley) and one-half (as at Aldersey and Pulford) from the centre of the principal settlement, with the portions of town field nearest the main settlement considerably closer: at Burton, for example, the field of this name lay immediately behind the back lane which bounded the crofts of the houses, while farmers at Aldersey and Clotton Hoofield would also have reached their town field from the backs of their crofts. Even where the town field's proximity to the principal settlement was not quite so striking as these, the association of the two seems clear: repeatedly, we find in the tithe awards an area of former open-field arable located a short distance from the main population centre within the vill. In its medieval heyday, the town field may in many cases have run closer to the settlement than the tithe award suggests, piecemeal enclosure of strips immediately next to the crofts having obscured the previous relationship between

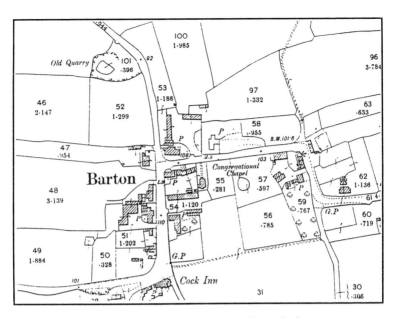

*Map 5 — Barton, from OS 25 ins. to mile (2nd edn., 1898),
Cheshire LIV.9 (reduced).*

*Map 6 — Aldersey Green, from OS 25 ins. to mile (1st edn., 1874),
Cheshire LIV.1 (reduced).*

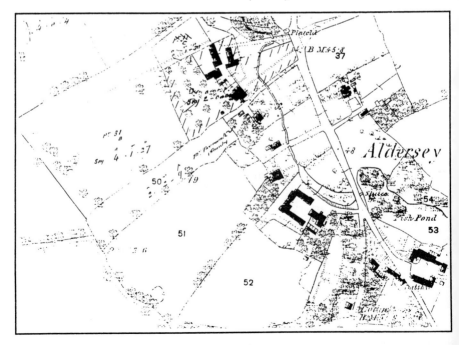

the two. Equally, early enclosure of portions of town field at an inconvenient distance from the settlement doubtless led to some changes of field-name, which have obscured the full extent of the field. What frequently survived into the early modern period, as the community's open arable 'town field', a name remembered long enough, even after final enclosure, to be preserved in the tithe award, was an area at most two-thirds of a mile from the principal settlement, rarely more than thirty acres in extent. Among the vills within the area studied, this model holds good for two of the three town fields at Tattenhall,[17] and for those at Christleton, Bruen Stapleford, Duddon, Clotton Hoofield, Burton, Foulk Stapleford, Saighton, Chowley, Clutton, Aldersey, Barton, Carden, Tilston, Horton, and (a little over thirty acres) Hatton and Waverton — although in the cases of Tilston and Waverton the centres of the principal settlements are represented by the parish churches with their late medieval towers, at Hatton the moated site at Hatton Hall and in Foulk Stapleford the hall at Hargrave in the south of the vill. The town field is also found within half a mile of the principal settlement in Handley, if this is taken to be Milton Green in the north of the vill (where nearly all the evidence of former open arable fields is to be found). Only in Aldford and Huxley does the identifiable town field area extend beyond two-thirds of a mile from the main settlement centre (taking this as the parish church in Aldford and the road junction in the present hamlet of Huxley, SJ 512615), although it is very close to Aldford and Higher Huxley Halls respectively. In Boughton, Littleton, Cotton Edmunds, Rowton and Buerton, there were no fields called 'town field' in the tithe award, but there was some other field-name evidence of former open-field arable (such as 'Six Butts', 'Long Loons' and 'Big Loons' in Littleton and 'The Flatts' in Cotton Edmunds), and this was also to be found, as a rule, within two-thirds of a mile of the main settlement nucleus; only 'Binfoot Loons', a fourteen-acre field in the western part of Buerton nearly a mile from the settlement at Bruera, was an exception. In vills which had both 'town fields' and other open-field-type names (such as Waverton, Saighton and Barton) the

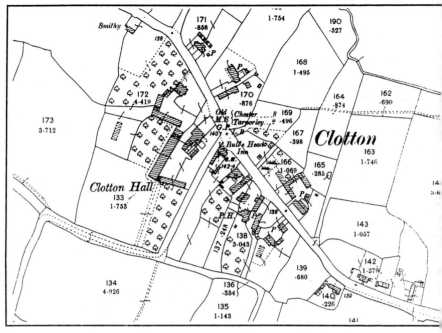

Map 7 — *Clotton, from OS 25 ins. to mile (2nd edn., 1898), Cheshire XLVII. 4 (reduced).*

Map 8 — *Burton, from OS 25 ins. to mile (3rd edn., 1910), Cheshire XLVII.3 (reduced).*

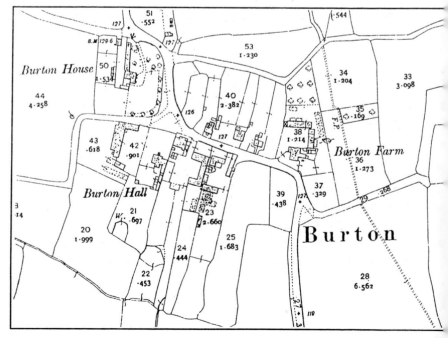

latter were also normally to be found within two-thirds of a mile of the principal settlement, although 'Big Long Loons' and 'Little Long Loons' close to the northern boundary of Christleton were nearly a mile from the village centre. Of the thirty-two vills studied, only Cotton Abbotts, Lea Newbold, Golborne David, Golborne Bellow, Coddington, Stretton, and Churton Heath yielded no evidence of former open arable fields in the form of indicative field-names in their tithe awards, although this certainly does not mean that such fields never existed, a point which will be taken up later.

The general picture in this area remains one of dispersed settlement, the minor settlements being represented today by outlying farmsteads, moated sites or the confluence of lanes and trackways, and it seems fair to picture the medieval landscape as a patchwork of arable, pasture, woodland and meadow, much of it held in severalty but with areas of open arable strips, the evidence of which was still apparent in the tithe awards. Within this pattern, most of the vills came to have a principal settlement with a recognised town field associated with it, although the indication of a quite separate field in Tattenhall possibly associated with a lost 'Willmoor'[18] and the open-field system around Milton Green distinct from the medieval ecclesiastical centre at Handley, are reminders that groups of open fields might develop around more than one settlement within a vill. As already stressed, the apparent proximity of the town field to the main settlement may be exaggerated, in the sense that more distant portions would probably have been the first to be enclosed, leaving no memory to be preserved in the field-names recorded in the tithe award. Yet the frequency with which the pattern, principal settlement-town field, recurs, is testimony to the importance of the arrangement within the west Cheshire vills.

Second, if we examine these principal settlements closely, a minority — but a significant minority — show clear signs of deliberate planning. Medieval village planning has been recognized in several northern English counties, being associated in Yorkshire with attempts to restore the economy

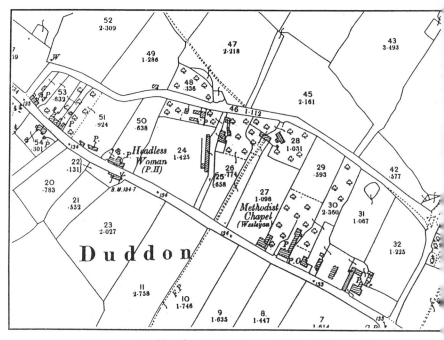

Map 9 — Duddon, from OS 25 ins. to mile (2nd edn., 1898), Cheshire XXXIX.15 (reduced).

after the 'Harrying of the North' in 1069–70 and in Cumberland with colonization following its annexation from the Scots in 1092.[19] The role of particular lords in promoting such planned settlements has also been acknowledged. Some of the elements indicative of planning can certainly be found in west Cheshire, especially rows of adjacent crofts with a common back lane which defined the crofts as a unit. This can be seen, for example, at Tilston immediately to the north of the medieval church; at Barton; at Aldersey Green; and at the neighbouring vills of Clotton Hoofield, Burton and Duddon to the east, albeit on a small scale rarely involving more than a handful of crofts. In all these cases, the former open-field area can be traced just beyond the area of the crofts (see Maps 4–9). At Clotton, five crofts with a total frontage of *c*.132 metres along the south side of the present A51 main road, are bounded to the rear by a green holloway which formerly turned at right-angles at the end of the crofts and led to the town field; there may once have been a similar number of crofts in the area immediately to the west, between the A51 and the now tarmaced continuation of this holloway, roughly where Clotton Hall Farm now stands. At Burton, seven crofts lie immediately east of a small triangular green and north of the tarmaced lane which runs through the hamlet: another green holloway forms a back lane to these crofts for *c.*125 metres at their northern end. But again this probably represents only part of the picture, for there appears to be another series of crofts, longer if less well defined, with a total frontage along the south side of the tarmaced lane of *c.*245 metres: these ran back to a stream which separated them from the former open field area. Duddon has a larger planned complex: sixteen crofts occupying *c.*480 metres along the north side of the present A51 with a back lane behind them, although the six at the western end are noticeably shorter and narrower than the remainder and probably represent an extension of *c.*92 metres to the original row. At Tilston, the total length of the row is *c.*155 metres on the northern side and *c.*177 metres on the southern, nearest the church; although only four crofts can now be identified, it is likely that the two wide ones to the east are the product of amalgamation. The crofts at Barton are not well defined, and it seems clear that there have been changes to their boundaries, but the row itself is very distinct, a rectangle marked by tarmaced lanes on the north, west and east sides and (until the present century) a footpath on the south side: the rectangle measures *c.*158 and *c.*175 metres on its long sides, *c.*100 metres in width. At Aldersey Green, the principal settlement within Aldersey, the crofts have encroached onto the village green which was still open at the time of Burdett's map in 1777.[20] But taking the building line to represent the front of the crofts and a field boundary, which in the early nineteenth century was still a trackway, as the back lane, we have here a complex of at least five crofts with a frontage of over 300 metres and a depth of nearly 250 metres.

Unfortunately, the standard explanations for planning initiatives, touched upon above, do not take us very far. The dimensions of the rows do not appear to conform to any common arithmetical formulae, even when converted to feet, so any attempt to relate them to tax assessment, as has been demonstrated for certain settlements in Yorkshire, seems doomed to failure. Three of these vills are not named in Domesday Book, the other three are entered as held by three different lords, and only one (Tilston) is recorded as having been waste. By the thirteenth century, the manorial rights in all of them had become fragmented and there had been subinfeudation to a family which took its name from the vill,[21] although this was a frequent occurrence by no means peculiar to these places. It is tempting to suggest that the planning of the principal settlement and the layout of an associated town field may have occurred as part of a manorial and tenurial reorganization at a time of rising population in the late twelfth or early thirteenth centuries. Aldersey Green, for example, is first documented (as Great Aldersey) in the thirteenth century; already by the early fourteenth century — when the settlement seems clearly to have occupied its present site — population pressure was such that the inhabitants were running out of arable and having to bring former meadow and woodland into cultivation.[22] In these circumstances, such settlement planning as occurred may have been the result of the collective decision of the community of the vill: given the fragmented manorial rights, and the relative insignificance of the seigneurial families involved, this seems a more plausible explanation than some hypothetical exercise in lordly coercion.[23] It may well be that better explanations can be offered when other planned settlements have been identified. Clutton, adjacent to both Aldersey and Barton, is one possible example. It had a town field less than half-a-mile from the main settlement and (despite an absence of well-defined crofts) an alignment of main street and back lane similar to that in Duddon. But much of this must remain speculative at present. It is sufficient to say for now that west Cheshire should not be left out of future discussions of medieval settlement planning.

Third, as noted above, a small number of vills left no trace of town fields or other open-field arable in the tithe awards. In every case, these are places which also have no modern settlement apart from isolated houses and farmsteads. This does not mean that they had never had open arable fields: Coddington's can be reconstructed from the distribution of field-names and ridge-and-furrow, and probably comprised two separate medieval open-field systems, one based at Beachin to the north where a moated site survives, the other around Coddington village itself.[24] The common characteristic of most of these vills in the early Victorian period is that they were dominated by one or two landowners: both Churton Heath and Cotton Abbotts were in single (though different) ownership, so was the whole of Lea Newbold apart from one smallholding; Coddington was shared between two major landowners, over three-quarters of Stretton was in one holding. At Golborne David and Golborne Bellow the picture was a little different, since here there were four and five landowners respectively, but nearly all held consolidated blocks of land clearly distinct from one another. By contrast, vills with clear tithe award evidence of former open fields were normally under multiple ownership, with landowning patterns which were frequently intermixed: a reflection of the previous scattered distribution of strips, which had not been entirely obliterated by enclosure. Tilston, for example, had forty-three different landowners, including four holding portions of the former town field. Christleton had fifty-seven, with two in the former town field. Clotton Hoofield had twenty-five, three in the former town field. An interesting case is Handley, where over three-quarters of the township was owned by one person, but where there were a further thirteen landowners grouped almost entirely at Milton Green in the north where the town field and other open-field evidence was to be found.

None of this should surprise us, for in a county such as Cheshire, where enclosure was largely piecemeal, we would expect open fields to survive longest where plenty of smallholders had a stake. It is worth noting that the distinction between the different townships was already apparent in the seventeenth century. The 1673–74 hearth tax returns showed Cotton Abbotts, Lea Newbold, Golborne Bellow, Coddington and Stretton with few houses but one predominant one, while Christleton (forty-four houses), Tilston (thirty-four), Clotton

Hoofield (thirty-three) and Handley (twenty-eight) were much larger communities but without prominent individual dwellings.[25] Here, certainly, there seems to be a parallel between the experience of settlements in Cheshire and in the better-documented Midlands: namely, that consolidation of ownership in the hands of one or two people increased the likelihood that open fields would be enclosed and settlements become deserted, at a time of economic and demographic downturn and slow recovery in the late medieval and early modern periods.

There are elements here from which to piece together something of the medieval landscape of west Cheshire: a landscape of dispersed settlement but frequently with a principal focus within each vill; a landscape of enclosed fields held in severalty but with areas of open-field arable and meadow, including, within each vill, at least one open arable field associated with the principal settlement; a landscape which, here as throughout the country, was obliged to respond to the pressures caused by rising and falling medieval population. Those responses still leave their mark. Coddington and Tilston both lie on boulder clay, most of their agricultural land today being classified as grade 3. There was probably no great disparity in their Domesday populations.[26] Yet in 1990, the population of Coddington was only seventy, while that of Tilston stood at 610.[27] Why? The answer lies not only in estate and local authority planning policies of the last hundred years, but also in the extent to which ownership became consolidated in the late medieval period, with a consequent impact upon settlement and field patterns. Developments and decisions which occurred over half a millennium ago continue to influence the character of the different communities to this day.

References

1 N. J. Higham, 'Patterns of settlement in medieval Cheshire: an insight into dispersed settlement', *Medieval Settlement Research Group Annual Report*, 2 (1987), pp.9–10.

2 C. C. Taylor, 'Medieval rural settlement: changing perceptions', *Landscape History*, 14 (1992), pp.5–15.

3 C. C. Dyer, 'The retreat from marginal land: the growth and decline of medieval rural settlements', in M. Aston, D. Austin and C. C. Dyer, eds, *The rural settlements of medieval England. Studies dedicated to Maurice Beresford and John Hurst*, Oxford, 1989, pp.45–57.

4 The 32 vills are as follows: (brackets indicate the reference numbers of the early-Victorian tithe awards, CRO EDT, from which much of the information in this paper is derived.) Aldersey (120), Aldford (9), Barton (40), Bruen Stapleford (73), Buerton (9), Burton near Tarvin (79), Carden (87), Chowley (120), Churton Heath (113), Clotton Hoofield (118), Clutton (119), Coddington (120), Cotton Abbotts (126), Cotton Edmunds (127), Duddon (142), Foulk Stapleford (160), Golborne Bellow (386), Golborne David (167), Great Boughton (172), Handley (185), Hatton (194), Horton (208), Huxley (216), Lea Newbold (231), Littleton (246), Rowton (344), Saighton (349), Stretton (377), Tattenhall (386), Tilston (395), Waverton (415), plus Christleton for which the tithe award reference is CRO P 28/5. I should like to record my thanks to several members of the Chester Society for Landscape History, including Malcolm and Audrey Muir, Janet and Lyn Miles, Daphne Goodwin and Margaret Lightfoot, for their painstaking work on the tithe awards, without which this paper would not have been possible.

5 For example, H. S. A. Fox, 'Approaches to the adoption of the Midland system', in T. Rowley, ed., *The origins of open field agriculture*, London, 1981, pp.64–111; V. Skipp, 'The evolution of settlement and open field topography in North Arden down to 1300', ibid., pp.162–83; T. Rowley, 'Medieval field systems', in L. Cantor, ed., *The English medieval landscape*, London, 1982, esp. p.35; C. C. Taylor, *Village and farmstead: a history of rural settlement in England*, London, 1983, esp. pp.130–1.

6 G. J. White, 'Glimpses of the open-field landscape', *Cheshire History*, 21 (Spring, 1988), esp. pp.11–12.

7 Eaton Estate MSS maps and plans no. 11 ('a map of part of the township of Aldford . . . by Thos. Badeslade, 1738'); CRO DEO 1/9 ('map of Crew and Farndon tenements, 1735'). On open meadows recorded in the tithe awards, see V. Chapman, 'Open fields in west Cheshire', *Transactions of the Historic Society of Lancashire and Cheshire*, 104 (1953), esp. pp.44–5.

8 C. C. Taylor, *Fields in the English landscape*, London, 1975, pp.71–93; J. Thirsk, 'The common fields' and 'The origin of the common fields' in R. H. Hilton, ed., *Peasants, knights and heretics: studies in medieval English social history*, Cambridge, 1976, pp.10–33; M. Aston, *Interpreting the landscape*, London, 1985, pp.120–37.

9 V. Chapman, 'Open fields', pp.35–59; D. Sylvester, 'The open fields of Cheshire', *Transactions of the Historic Society of Lancashire and Cheshire*, 108 (1957), pp.1–33; *idem*, 'A note on medieval three-course arable systems in Cheshire', ibid., 110 (1959), pp.183–6; *cf. idem*, *The rural landscape of the Welsh borderland*, London, 1969, esp. pp.267–70.

10 V. Chapman, 'Open fields', p.58; G. Elliott, 'Field systems of north-west England', in A. R. H. Baker and R. A. Butlin, eds, *Studies of field systems in the British Isles*, Cambridge, 1973, pp.42–7. The name 'town field' itself may sometimes have come into use in the early modern period, although medieval examples of its use can certainly be found: in the fourteenth century at Tushingham-cum-Grindlay and Barthomley, and in the fifteenth century at Eaton-by-Tarporley and Knutsford. See J. McN. Dodgson, ed., *The place-names of Cheshire* (*EPNS*, XLIV–XLVII), Cambridge, 1970–81, pt 2, p.75; pt 3, pp.9, 291; pt 4, p.49.

11 V. Chapman, 'Open fields', p.53.

12 *Cf.* ibid., pp.58–9: 'In the Dee and Gowy lowlands as a whole, ridge and furrow was well-marked on clay areas and absent on sandy soils, just where the strongest survivals of open fields were to be found.' On the subject generally, see G. J. White, 'Glimpses of the open-field landscape'. Field names at Calveley and Wettenhall are taken from the tithe awards, CRO EDT/84 and EDT/422 respectively.

13 Liverpool University MS 20/3 (Rental of John Leche of Nantwich), ff.8r–8v.

14 CRO DAL/177, transcribed in C. G. O. Bridgeman, *The family of Aldersey*, London, 1899, p.247.

15 PRO SC/12/1/4.

16 For example, by *c.*1280 in Poulton Lancelyn. *Cf.* J. Tait, ed. *Chartulary of the abbey of St. Werburgh, Chester* (Publications of the Chetham Society, new series, LXXIX), Manchester, 1920, no. 387; by 1491 in Tilston ('certen parcels of grownde . . . as herafor been open field') and by 1643 in Horton ('two loundes of grounds nowe inclosed and made in a crofte by itselfe'), both CRO DLE 8/1; by 1700, thirty-two in Chowley ('the town fields . . . formerly occupyd by several psons is under ye present disposition in ye tenure of one'), CRO EDD/6/7/1. Maps of Clotton (1734), Waverton (1737) and Aldford (1738) are among those which show arable strips in areas enclosed by the time of the tithe awards, CRO DDX/573/1; Eaton Estate MSS maps and plans, 14, 11.

17 Of the three town fields in Tattenhall, Willmoor Town Field was exceptional in covering 41 acres and lying up to a mile from the village nucleus, but as suggested below (p.27), it may have related to a lost outlying settlement.

18 The name 'Willmoor' was applied to four of the closes and quillets in this town field group in the tithe award. J. McN. Dodgson, *Place-names*, pt. 4, p.99, gives the meaning as 'wild marsh' but does not suggest that its origins may have been as a settlement name.

19 J. Sheppard, 'Metrological analysis of regular village plans in Yorkshire', *Agricultural History Review*, 22 (1974), pp.119–35; *idem*, 'Medieval village planning in northern England; some evidence from Yorkshire', *Journal of Historical Geography*, 2 (1976), pp.3–20; B. K. Roberts, *The making of the English village*, London, 1987, esp. pp.172–3.

20 J. B. Harley and P. Laxton, eds, *P. P. Burdett: a survey of the county palatine of Chester, 1777* (Transactions of the Historic Society of Lancashire and Cheshire, occasional series, I), Liverpool, 1974, plate vi.

21 G. Ormerod, *The history of the county palatine and city of Chester*, 2nd edn revised and enlarged, T. Helsby, ed., London, 1882, vol. II, pp.324–8; 694–5; 737–9; 748–9. The family who acquired a share in Duddon took its name from Clotton.

22 J. McN. Dodgson, *Place-names*, pt 4, p.83; CRO DBC/1720/1/3 and DBC/1720/2/1; C. G. O. Bridgeman, *Family of Aldersey*, pp.59, 73; G. J. White, 'Aldersey, Chowley and Coddington: a study of the medieval landscape', *Cheshire History*, 7 (Spring, 1981), pp.32–49.

23 C. C. Dyer, 'Power and conflict in the medieval village', in D. Hooke, ed., *Medieval villages: a review of current work*, Oxford, 1985, pp.27–32.

24 G. J. White, 'Aldersey, Chowley and Coddington', and for the moated site, *Medieval Settlement Research Group Annual Report*, 7 (1992), pp.27–32.

25 PRO E/179/86/155.

26 The recorded population of Coddington in Domesday Book was 10, that of Tilston 16, but both entries may refer to more than one vill. J. Tait, ed., *Domesday survey of Cheshire* (Publications of the Chetham Society, new series, LXXV), Manchester, 1916, pp.108–9; 120–3.

27 Cheshire County Council, *Research and intelligence: population estimates for mid-year 1990*, 1991.

3

Scandinavian ornamental influence in the Irish Sea region in the Viking Age

DAVID M. WILSON

A SYNTHETIC REAPPRAISAL of Viking-Age ornamental elements in the Irish Sea region is overdue, partly because of the considerable amount of work which has been published in the last ten years concerning the region, but also because of the great advances in the understanding of Viking-Age ornament in Scandinavia itself. This understanding has been achieved through the work of a handful of scholars who have moved the subject into the 1990s, both by a reappraisal of the ornamental evidence itself but also through the application of dendro-chronological evidence to the whole story of the Viking Age.[1]

In the last twenty years the study of the vikings has become much more professionally inter-disciplinary. No one would now dare to tackle this subject without a reasonably solid knowledge not only of ornamental history and archaeology, but also of its historical and philological background. It is also becoming increasingly plain that a thorough knowledge of Scandinavian developments in this area is a *sine qua non*. In what follows I shall not be confining myself totally to ornament — although this will be my main theme — for I shall also take into account work in other disciplines and other geographical areas which are essential to the general understanding of the Scandinavian ornamental influences in the Irish Sea region. Although the results of this survey may well be seen to be minimal, the process of achieving them may not be without interest.

Richard Bailey was the last to tackle this subject in a coherent fashion, in a stimulating and wide-ranging paper which deserves to be better known.[2] Bailey's paper, like so many, including some of my own,[3] concentrated on the sculptural evidence, which is clearly more obtrusive. Here I shall try to be more all-embracing, by considering other ornamental media as well, for when one examines other material the picture changes subtly.

Let us first, however, define what we are looking at. What is this ornament and how is it to be studied, dated and interpreted? In Scandinavia at the beginning of the ninth century — the beginning of the Viking Age in other words — a distinct art style, known (for reasons which need not concern us here) as Style III began to emerge. One element of this style is the so-called gripping-beast.[4] Style III did not affect Britain at the time when it flourished (in general terms it is dated before the viking settlement of southern Britain), but it must be mentioned, as the gripping-beast motif was an important formative influence on a somewhat similar element in the Borre style, which was the first viking art style to be introduced into Britain.

The gripping-beast of the Borre style which grows directly out of the gripping-beast ornament of Style III forms a pretzel-like loop with its head placed either above or below the body.[5] This particular animal does not appear on any of the material from around the Irish Sea — and certainly not in the sculptural corpus. The only place it really occurs in a native English source is at York, where it is possible to trace its outline on two small white metal brooches.[6] It is important, however, to notice the occurrence of this element in the British Isles on an object made here: it shows that the motif was at least known in England and, as so little late ninth- and early tenth-century non-sculptural material has been found in the Irish Sea region, we must wonder whether it was perhaps more common. This is especially so when we see the comparatively frequent occurrence of other motifs of the Borre style in the sculpture of the Isle of Man, north-west England and Wales.

The two motifs of the Borre Style which most commonly occur are, first, the so-called ring-chain ornament, seen for example on the Norwegian strap-end illustrated in Figure 1 (with its marked central element, the form of which varies — it may be triangular, rhomboid or square) and, secondly, a knot pattern which is derived from it. The Borre style is the most ubiquitous of the art styles of Scandinavia in the late ninth and in most of the tenth century. Elements of it are found frequently in the British Isles both on imported objects and on objects made here.

The next style, the Jellinge style takes its name from the ornament on a small silver cup which was buried in a royal burial mound at Jelling, Jutland in Denmark in 958–59. The main motif is an animal with a ribbon-like body, a pigtail and a lip-lappet (Figure 2). The style is more or less contemporary with the Borre style, but was possibly introduced slightly later — elements of it occur in the furnishing of the Gokstad ship from southern Norway, which was buried between 900 and 905.[7] The Jellinge style occurs reasonably frequently in a somewhat derivative manner in English art of the tenth century, but is found rather rarely in the Irish Sea region in anything like its original form, being best represented in the Isle of Man.

It is followed by the Mammen style which is found in its classic form in the Isle of Man (Figure 3), but rarely elsewhere in our region (it is fairly rare anywhere). This style takes its name from an axe deposited in a rich grave in Denmark in the winter of 970–71.[8] The chief motif is an asymmetrical semi-naturalistic animal with a substantial body often filled with billeting and caught up in open loop-like scrolls. The style is basically of late tenth-century date.

The Ringerike style, which develops out of the Mammen style, presents a foliated animal with long tightly-placed tendril ornament, an almond-shaped eye and has a tendency towards the symmetrical arrangement of foliate motifs.[9] It is succeeded by the Urnes style where the chief motifs are smooth lissom animals often in combat with a dragon.[10] Both these styles occur in the British Isles in forms very close to their Scandinavian prototypes, but occur chiefly in our region in Ireland, although there are hints of the Ringerike style in the Isle of Man. The Ringerike style may be dated to the first half of the eleventh century and the Urnes style to the late eleventh and early twelfth century.

Now to our subject, the presence of Scandinavian ornament in the Irish Sea region.

From the Isle of Man — in the middle of the Irish Sea — one may on a clear day see from the top of Snaefell (the highest mountain) five kingdoms — Man, Scotland, Ireland, Wales and England. Wales, one must admit, is rarely seen; but the other coasts are frequently clearly defined and there is no need to make the rather dreary journey to the top of the mountain to see any of them. This visual contact is and was a very important element in communication by sea between all these countries.

In the Viking Age all these lands were affected by Scandinavian incomers. On the basis of historical, place-name and archaeological evidence we may estimate the strength of the viking influence. The distribution of the Scandinavian settlements as revealed by the distribution of Viking-Age grave-finds from the Irish Sea region is in many ways remarkably reflected by the distribution of Scandinavian place-names in the same area[11]. But such comparisons must be used with caution. Some of these lands, like Man, were discrete colonies; Cumbria and Lancashire were similarly extensively settled[12] — at least from about 900 onwards — as was Dumfries; but Galloway has produced less place-name evidence of a Norse presence.

Let us for clarity outline the historical background of this region. The North-West appears to have been little affected by the Scandinavian raids or settlement until the end of the ninth century. In 893, according to the Anglo-Saxon Chronicle, the vikings occupied Chester, a Roman city which is described somewhat mysteriously as 'waste'. The English took counter-measures and the Danes had to withdraw without establishing any settlement in the area. This must have been one of a series of raids which occurred throughout the North-West. Ingemund, fleeing from Dublin after the expulsion of the vikings in 902, came — after an abortive attempt to settle in Wales — to the Wirral, where, according to Irish and Welsh sources, he and his followers were able to settle by agreement with the formidable Æthelflæd, the Lady of the Mercians. The Scandinavians then proceeded to move northwards, and it was probably in this context that the great Cuerdale silver hoard — worth some £300,000 in modern-day money, was laid down about 905. It was presumably at this period that the few viking-type graves were laid down in this region.[13]

There is, however, no direct historical record of the settlement of this area by the vikings, although the place-names clearly indicate this and certain rather oblique remarks in some contemporary sources suggest that there was trouble in this area. Although there was no formal Scandinavian political control of north-western England after *c*.930, there seems to have been a continuous settlement there of Scandinavian-speaking people throughout the tenth century. It might be possible to adumbrate further settlement of the area during the reigns of Knut and his Danish successors (1016/19–42), when some land was passed over to incoming Scandinavians, but there is no real evidence to back such a statement. We must assume that here, as in south-west Scotland, Scandinavian influence waned after the Danish dynasty in England collapsed.

Ireland was never properly settled by the Scandinavians. At some stage trading stations or towns were developed by the Scandinavians to take advantage of the mercantile opportunities of the region, but the countryside was little settled. There are major ninth-century cemeteries just outside Dublin, at Islandbridge, but the evidence from excavations elsewhere in Ireland — and particularly in the city of Dublin itself — has produced very little early tenth-century material. This may be accidental, but the foundation of a mint at Dublin in the 990s emphasizes not the beginning of the importance of Dublin in the Irish polity, but the beginning of a sophisticated economy and real mercantile power among the viking inhabitants of that city. Other towns, Limerick, Waterford, Cork and so on, were also founded by the Scandinavians who controlled them economically, but did not settle much outside them. Until 1171 the Scandinavians controlled the mercantile economic power of Ireland and with it had a very considerable say in the organization of the north-south trade along the western coasts of Europe. In 1171, however, Henry II arrived to take charge of the conquests of the Norman lords and Scandinavian power was effectively at an end.

As for Wales,[14] apart from a few hoards,[15] a couple of graves[16] and a small number of place-names, the evidence for a viking presence (and in some cases perhaps only viking taste) is apparently confined to a handful of sculptured stones, but that would be to ignore the evidence of the historical sources, such as the tenth-century *Annales Cambriae*, which, as Henry Loyn has shown,[17] provide us with tools which allow us to guess (but little more) at the nature of settlement there. The two routes from Dublin to England, the one through the Bristol Channel and the other along the North Wales coast, are marked by a few Norse place-names — names given from the sea by Scandinavian sailors — Flatholm, Lundy, Orme's Head, Priestholm and, most important of all, Anglesey.

Another area of Scandinavian influence was the Isle of Man. Controlled by a lord or king in the tenth century, it had presumably been thoroughly settled by the end of the ninth. While there are many traces of Scandinavian settlement here — place-names, graves, sites, hoards and sculpture — its history is badly documented until the end of the eleventh century. Scandinavian power collapsed in the Western Isles and the Isle of Man after the battle of Largs in 1263 and Man came into the possession of the Scottish crown. The period between the early eleventh century and the Scottish take-over is poorly represented in the archaeological record, although there are one or two major medieval buildings, like some of the remains on St Patrick's Isle at Peel.

Before the Viking Age there was a certain community of

taste in the lands round the Irish Sea. But the evidence is so diverse and the distribution of the material is so thinly spread that it is difficult to generalize about it. There was certainly a close relationship between the art of western Scotland and Ireland and this is seen in both the metalwork and in the manu-script art. It is still impossible, for example, to say where the *Book of Kells* was made. The north-west coast of England and the Isle of Man, however, are not rich in monuments of the late eighth and ninth century, but where they are found — as with the lost slab from Santon in the Isle of Man[18] and the stone from Kirkmaiden, Lancashire[19] — they can be related to each other and to the ornament of the lands to the east and the north — if only in general terms.

A glimpse of this community of taste may be seen in a few objects found in viking contexts in different parts of the region. Tinned copper alloy mounts, for example, from a Viking-Age boat-burial from Balladoole in the Isle of Man are closely paralleled in another Viking-Age grave found at Kiloran Bay on Colonsay[20] and from the tenth-century viking levels in Dublin[21] and a not dissimilar piece, a buckle from Valtos, Uig, Lewis.[22] The ornament on all these mounts is similar, the ornament and the technique are of insular origin and the objects were all certainly made in a Hiberno-Scandinavian workshop. They were clearly to the taste of the (probably late) ninth-century Scandinavian denizens of the Irish Sea region. A small amount of such material is found in Scandinavian contexts in the Irish Sea region; it not only reflects a community of taste with the original population of the region, but also demonstrates the eclectic discernment of the settlers who were not entirely bound by their own ornamental prejudices.

Particularly interesting in the context of this community of taste are the series of bossed penannular brooches (Figure 4) which are found quite commonly in the Irish Sea region. These have recently been much discussed, particularly by James Graham-Campbell.[23] They are dated to the late ninth and early tenth century by their presence in such viking coin hoards as that from Cuerdale, Lancashire, which is dated to the very beginning of the tenth century. (An interesting find of brooches of this type has recently been made at Fluskew Pike, Cumbria and adds considerably to our knowledge of the series.)[24] Influenced by English and Celtic forms and ornamental elements, and probably made in Ireland, the bossed penannular brooches were familiar to the Scandinavians who probably provided the silver and seem to have copied them, even in their homelands — as witness the example from Hatteberg, Hordaland in western Norway.[25]

It is not without significance that the first object from the North-West known to us which is decorated with a Scandinavian pattern — and one that was possibly manufactured in the British Isles — comes from the grave of a pagan Scandinavian at Hesket-in-the-Forest in Cumbria.[26] It is the guard of a sword (Figure 5) which is decorated with a version of the Borre ring-chain. While this object was presumably not made in the North-West — it was perhaps made east of the Pennines (possibly in York); equally it could have been made in Dublin — it shows the presence of this style in our region in the early tenth century, before the viking settlers had taken Christianity totally into their system.[27]

The community of taste in this region and the presence of objects decorated with Scandinavian ornament becomes an important factor when we consider the most commonly recognized decorative motif of the first settlement period (say from about 900 onwards), the Scandinavian Borre ring-chain motif which we have already encountered on the Hesket sword-guard (Figure 5). This now became a popular motif carved in stone by craftsmen who might not always have been of Scandinavian origin. The Scandinavians at this time had little or no stone sculpture at home; only in the far east of Sweden was there any really significant corpus of stone carving (on the Baltic island of Gotland, which did not influence the colonizers who came either from Denmark or Norway). When they settled in the British Isles the Scandinavians encountered stone sculpture for the first time, particularly in the form of free-standing stone crosses — as at Irton in west Cumbria, for example, which provides us today with the best preserved cross of its type in the region.[28] As they did not settle in Ireland in any meaningful fashion at this period, the Scandinavians clearly ignored the great high crosses so liberally spread around that country. These indeed did not affect their art in any significant fashion, apart possibly for the adoption of the ring-head form. They would, however, have seen such crosses in western Scotland — at Iona, for example, which they sacked at the end of the ninth century. They could relate to the interlace ornament on these sculptures and even to some of the other ornamental elements which embellished them. When they converted to Christianity in the course of the early tenth century, they also appreciated the significance of the cross in Christian liturgy and adapted the form to their own purposes as grave-markers or, in the case of the great stone cross at Gosforth (Figure 6), as a visual record of a religious message — in this case possibly the compatibility, or at least the parallelism, of the stories in the two religions.

The ornament which appears on the tenth-century stone crosses of Cumberland and Westmorland, Lancashire and Cheshire, Dumfries and Galloway and the north coast of Wales is in many ways closely related; it reflects the community of taste to which I have already referred. The ornament is in only a few cases more than competent; the standard of carving (with the exception of that on the Gosforth cross) is not very high when compared with the great stone sculptured monuments of the pre-viking period. The ornamental repertoire includes the Borre style ring-chain of the type which we have seen at Hesket, which also occurs on the Gosforth cross and in a modified form on a slab from Dearham, Cumberland (Figure 7), and which is common on the Isle of Man (Figure 8). A few stones, from Halton and Gosforth particularly, bear narrative scenes which can be related to the myth and legend of Scandinavia.[29]

The evidence of Scandinavian taste in the Isle of Man is largely to be traced in stone sculpture. It is important to consider Man in some detail as by its nature it has discrete limits and forms a nodal point in the middle of the Irish Sea. Pagan

Scandinavian graves have been found in some quantity here[30] and, although they are not altogether easy to date, we may assume that they straddle the end of the ninth century, following which period the gradual conversion of the settlers to Christianity introduced a different burial practice, one which demanded memorial stones of a form already known in the pre-viking island. Carved in the soft native slate series, a group of well-executed expressions of Scandinavian art have been found here.[31]

One stone in particular (Figure 8) from Kirk Michael should introduce the story, for here we are able for the first time to name a craftsman. It is one of two stones decorated in the Borre ring-chain which were made — according to their runic inscriptions — by a man with a Scandinavian name, Gautr, who is said to have come from a place with a Celtic name — Kuli. On the Kirk Michael stone he proudly boasts that he made both it and 'all in Man'. Later in Scandinavia such self-advertisement becomes quite common, but this is probably only the second named Scandinavian artist anywhere. The inscriptions themselves also tell us that the population of the island was still mixed in the tenth and even the eleventh century, as a number of stones memorialize people — both men and women — who have Celtic names. This fact illuminates clearly the elements of native taste — such as the ringed cross-head.

In the Isle of Man are also found a number of stones carved with narrative scenes, some few of which can be related iconographically to the heroic mythology of Scandinavia, although (as Margeson has pointed out) their interpretation must be approached with caution.[32]

Elsewhere in the British Isles few stones similar to those found in the Isle of Man exist, but two examples have survived in a relevant area, namely the Western Isles of Scotland. One, from Inchbrock on the Isle of Bute (Figure 9), bears a wheel-headed cross carved in a similar fashion to those on the Manx stones and a runic inscription of similar character to those found in the Isle of Man. Much more closely related, but clearly somewhat degenerate, is an example from Kilbar on Barra, in the Outer Hebrides.[33] A third stone, from Iona,[34] while different in form and decoration, is not unrelated epigraphically.

There are, however, common traits linking the sculpture of the Isle of Man, north-west England, North Wales and, to a lesser degree, south-west Scotland (although there is a blank area around the head waters of the Solway). This has been emphasized on a number of occasions by Richard Bailey.[35] The Borre ring-chain is one of these common traits, being found on sculpture in the north-west of England, Wales and the Isle of Man, as has been shown, for example, on the stones from Gosforth (Figure 6) and Kirk Michael (Figure 8).

When we turn to Ireland an entirely different scenario appears. This is not unexpected for, as I have pointed out, the pattern of Scandinavian settlement was very different here in the west. There was no widespread settlement, rather a peripheral (coastal) settlement, largely concentrated on newly-founded mercantile centres like Dublin. There is, therefore, little evidence of Scandinavian influence in the sculpture of the Irish countryside until well on into the eleventh century.[36] The Irish sculpture of the ninth and tenth centuries is confined to native monastic settlements and does not appear in the newly founded Scandinavian settlements; what is more, it has had no effect on the sculpture in north-west England. But the Borre style does appear in Ireland on small articles which were certainly manufactured there and show that elements of viking taste (although very much in tune with their own predilection for interlace ornament) were present even among the native craftsmen of Christian Ireland.

It has long been known that the Borre style ring-chain motif appears on a gaming board from Ballinderry Crannog[37] and that it also appears on two or three pieces of Christian Irish metalwork including a book shrine — the tenth-century Soiscél Molaise.[38] But its occurrence on one or two of the bone motif- or trial-pieces found in the High Street excavations in Dublin[39] places it firmly in a metropolitan Norse context in Ireland, suggesting (but by no means proving) that the motif was not merely a copy by an Irishman of a Scandinavian pattern, but that it was a deliberately produced ornamental motif of a Scandinavian craftsman working in the chief Irish town. These are not of course the only pieces decorated with motifs of the Borre style from Dublin; there are also wooden objects, as for example a weaving baton with a Borre ornamented handle as well as a fragment of openwork interlace which reminds us in almost every detail of the decoration on a Manx cross-head.[40] I would like to date these pieces to the middle of the tenth century, but in reality they may be a little earlier, datable, say, to the period of the refoundation of Dublin in the 920s.

The Borre style ring-chain, then, occurs on both sides of the Irish Sea, even though the media in which it appears are different. Further, nearly everyone accepts that the ring-chain is Scandinavian inspired. Its occurrence and distribution are uneven. If, for example, we relied on the non-sculptural evidence for our knowledge of Scandinavian ornament in north-west England and the Isle of Man in the tenth century, we would be reduced to one item which might have been made in the British Isles — the sword-guard from Hesket (Figure 5). Ireland alone would present us with a unique, small, but interesting group of Borre-style items which we would either relate directly to Scandinavia or to York (where the style in most of its manifestations occurs). It is always difficult to build structures on the exiguous quantity of the material which survives in the archaeological record of the Viking Age in the British Isles. It is impossible to pretend, however, that the Borre style was well established in Dublin; the evidence certainly rules that out: but have we got the whole story?

The Jellinge style is rarely found in this region. A couple of copper alloy disc brooches decorated in the classic Jellinge style — one from Chester and the other from Dublin[41] — were almost certainly made in Scandinavia. Otherwise the style only occurs on a handful of stones in the Isle of Man (as on an example from Malew, Figure 10). It does not apparently occur on the Dublin trial-pieces. If it occurs on the eastern side of the Irish Sea it is so rare (as on the stone from Cross Canonby)[42] that one can only say that it is known. It does, however, occur on the eastern side of the Pennines and, although there is no political reason why it should not appear in the North-West, it is almost completely absent. We must, therefore, ask whether this absence is accidental or significant.

The Jellinge style is traced, however, as an element in the art of the insular Mammen style, which is seen in its best form on the crosses from Kirk Braddan in the Isle of Man (Figure 3). The style is dated, by reference to the eponymous axe from Mammen referred to above (which was deposited 970–71) and a number of other Scandinavian finds, to between 950 and 1020. It is rarely found in its pure form in the sculpture of England, and this is particularly true in the North-West, although Bailey has pointed to a shaft from Workington, Cumberland, as an example of a stone with a body billeted in a manner he suggests is 'more typical of Mammen work'.[43] I am rather doubtful of such an identification which rests largely on the pelleted body, and the fact that Bailey has to stretch his evidence to this extent emphasizes that it is practically non-existent in the North-West. What is more, it is clear that there are no distinctive finds of the Mammen style in Ireland (although a wooden chair fragment possibly decorated with elements of the style was found in Dublin)[44] or Wales. The style is indeed rarely found in a pure form in England, the most typical find being the bone plaque from the River Thames in London,[45] which could have been made practically anywhere. To the east of the Pennines it does occasionally occur, but not in such a pure form to support the assertion that 'Braddan's beasts . . . are transplants from York where they belong to a menagerie with a long English ancestry'.[46]

This can hardly be true, particularly as their form is so typical of the Mammen style that the Isle of Man has even in the past been postulated by Scandinavian scholars as the original home of the style because the ornament there is so pure. The two crosses from Kirk Braddan — known because of their inscriptions as Odd's cross and Thorleif's cross — have been accepted by Signe Horn Fuglesang as clear examples of the Mammen style in the most recent study of the style.[47] The strong billeting is a typical feature of the classic form of this style as encountered, for example, on the Mammen axe referred to above. These are difficult designs to label. I am uncertain: whilst in many ways I agree with Fuglesang's identification I must admit to having labelled them as Jellinge/Mammen style. This would chime well with Graham-Campbell's description of the rather similar ornament on the brooches in the hoard from Skaill in Orkney,[48] which is dated by coins within a bracket of 950–70 (with a tendency to a slightly earlier date within that twenty-year span), a date which agrees well with the dendro-chronological date of 970–71 for the context of the Mammen axe.

The ball-type brooch of the type found in the Skaill hoard is said by Graham-Campbell to have been manufactured in the Irish Sea region. The ball-type brooch is itself indubitably of Irish origin, but the ornament of the examples found in the Skaill hoard has suggested to Graham-Campbell that they are Manx, or at least made by a man who trained in the Isle of Man, indeed the fragment of a ball-type brooch was found in the hoard from Douglas in the Isle of Man (dated by coins to about 970).[49] The argument for a Manx origin for the brooches is based on the comparison of the Skaill ornament with that of the Braddan crosses. Such an interpretation of the Skaill ornament is perhaps rather facile. Returning to the point made earlier in relation to the Borre style in this region, while it could be said that the survival of the Braddan stone crosses overemphasizes the undoubted fact that this style was strong in the Isle of Man, the distribution map does not seem to me to be significant enough to back the statement. This does not mean that Graham-Campbell is wrong: it merely means that we should treat the suggestion with caution. As a corollary, we should be cautious at least in making too definite a statement concerning the absence of the style from the lands around the Irish Sea.

The Scandinavian polity in the Irish Sea region was by this time hardly a community united by close-knit ties. The reconquest of England in the second quarter of the tenth century and the way in which the Irish, deliberately or not, managed to keep the Scandinavians confined to their towns, reduced the overall influence of the Norse, who — now fragmented — only came together in times of trouble for mutual profit or support. In Ireland they retained considerable economic power, while in the west of Scotland and in the Isle of Man they continued to have a political base. In considering the occurrence of later viking art — the Ringerike and the Urnes styles — in the region we meet an imbalance which seems to reflect the changing circumstances. The short-lived Danish empire of Knut the Great hardly seems to have affected north-west England in ornamental terms and even in the south the few finds, like the St Paul's stone (decorated in a pure Ringerike style)[50] or the brooch from Pitney in Somerset (of the English Urnes style),[51] only emphasize that English art was recovering strength with the final blooming of Anglo-Saxon art and the first flowering of the Romanesque.

In the Isle of Man a few traces of the Ringerike style may be seen in the sculpture, but such traces are only elements of ornament and hardly the full-blown art which is so liberally provided in Ireland in the manuscripts and in the motif-pieces from the Dublin excavations. Two or three Manx stones from Kirk Michael and Ramsey show, by the presence of a pear-shaped eye or a lobe-like feature, the latest elements of viking art to appear in the Isle of Man[52] — after this ornament disappears from the record. These elements were almost certainly introduced not from Scandinavia but from Ireland. They could possibly be as late as 1020. The same may well be true of one of the few examples of the Ringerike style found in western Scotland, the Dòid Mhàiri cross-slab,[53] but it is striking that despite the undoubted, historically recorded presence of Scandinavians in the region, no single object ornamented in these late viking styles is known from north-west England.

In Ireland, however, there was an almost exuberant enjoyment of the two final viking ornamental styles, which have been well chronicled by Henry. They occur on ecclesiastical metalwork, on sculpture and in manuscripts.[54] That they were popular in the viking town of Dublin, where some of the metal objects have been made, is demonstrated by the many motif pieces executed in one of the two styles;[55] they were also present on objects of everyday use, as is attested by wooden objects in some numbers from Dublin.[56]

The two later styles of the Viking Age — Ringerike and Urnes — were accepted fully into the art of the country and reworked in line with Irish principles of design. They not only appeared, as might be expected, in the large amount of material found in Dublin, but the two styles were also accepted — perhaps assimilated is a better word — into the art of the Irish church. Sculpture, but more particularly metalwork and manuscript ornament, demonstrate clearly the high esteem in which this art was held in Ireland. The fact that the newly introduced art chimed so much with the taste of the Irish themselves in its interplay of interlace and animal ornament was presumably the reason why it was so successfully taken into the full body of Irish art.

Scandinavian art, which originally was derived — so far as its animal ornament was concerned — from the same Germanic source as elements of Irish art, melded with Irish art to produce a standard which reaches heights just short of that achieved in the eighth century. To many it may, compared for example with the art of the 'Tara' brooch or the Ardagh Chalice, appear to be somewhat effete. But the quality of craftsmanship is there and, in metalwork anyway, it was never again to be equalled in the whole history of Irish art.

Probably made in Ireland is the splendid copper alloy sword-guard found on Smalls reef off Skomer Island in Dyfed.[57] The object, which was presumably lost with the wrecking of a viking ship, is decorated by means of inlaid niello and silver wire with a version of the Urnes style which has reminiscences (in the tight and regular loops of the body) of the Ringerike style.

With the coming of the Normans, Romanesque art was introduced into Ireland — a full-blown classic art with close relations to that found in England. Occasionally reflections of

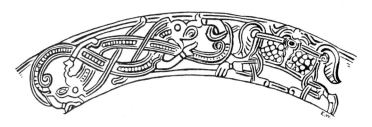

Left: *Figure 1 — Strap-end from Sandvor, Rogaland, Norway.*

Above: *Figure 2 — Ornament of the cup from the North Mound at Jelling, Jutland, Denmark.*

Below: *Figure 3 — Cross-slab from Kirk Bradden, Isle of Man.*

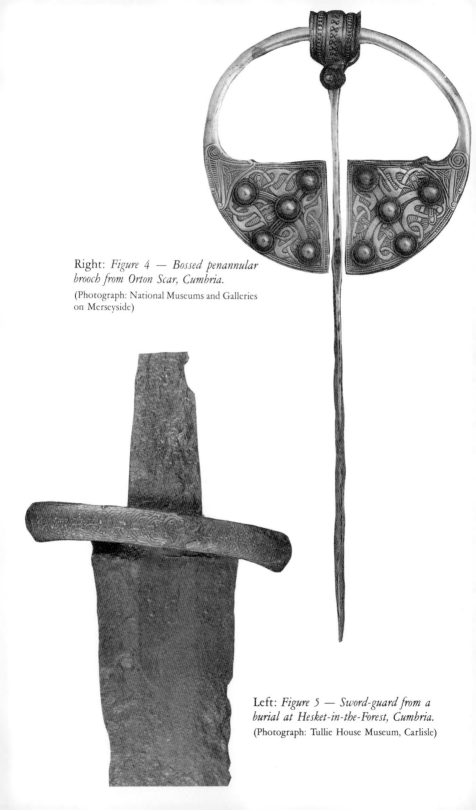

Right: *Figure 4 — Bossed penannular brooch from Orton Scar, Cumbria.*

(Photograph: National Museums and Galleries on Merseyside)

Left: *Figure 5 — Sword-guard from a burial at Hesket-in-the-Forest, Cumbria.*

(Photograph: Tullie House Museum, Carlisle)

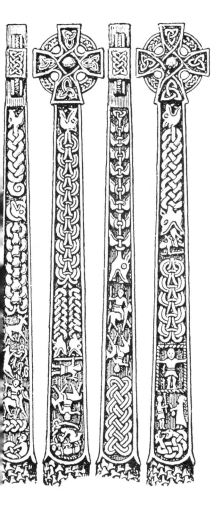

Left: *Figure 6 — The Gosforth Cross, Cumbria.*

(After W. G. Collingwood, 1927)

Right: *Figure 7 — Cross from Dearham, Cumbria.*

(Photograph: Durham University)

Left: *Figure 8 — Gautr's cross, Kirk Michael, Isle of Man.*

Below: *Figure 9 — Fragment of a cross-slab from Inchmarnock, Bute.*
(Photograph: National Museums of Scotland)

Left: *Figure 10 — Cross-slab from Malew, Isle of Man.*

the older art may be seen in the new style, but even in its most advanced and sophisticated expression it never achieved the heights of the art of the metalworker in the eleventh and early twelfth century.

What then of the rest of our region? It has been noted that slight traces of the Ringerike style are to be seen in the Isle of Man, but of the Urnes style we have nothing. By the beginning of the eleventh century the Isle of Man may be more closely related to the Western Isles, with which it seems to have formed some sort of political unity (one represented today by the title of the Manx diocese — Sodor and Man; the southern — that is the Hebridean — isles and Man). It should not be forgotten, however, that there is no major piece of metalwork, no manuscript and no piece of wood-carving surviving from the Isle of Man from the end of the tenth century until the end of the Norse period. It is conceivable that Manx patrons could have employed artists, or even commissioned work in Dublin (with which they were always in contact). But of this there is no evidence.

Lastly then to western England, Wales and south-west Scotland. Apart from a short period when a Danish king was on the throne of England — between, say, 1016 and 1042 — there was little taste for the Scandinavian style in England. It must be remembered that Knut in particular was striving to achieve acceptance by his Christian contemporaries in the Empire and was a supporter of the church and the art that went with it. The several pieces of Ringerike style which survive in England are confined to his power base in the South-East, where presumably some of his followers indulged in their home-bred taste. The strangest phenomenon is the occurrence of a few pieces of Urnes style in the period after the Danish dynasty — and even the Anglo-Saxon dynasty — had been replaced. The Pitney brooch quoted above is one such example — it may indeed have been influenced from Ireland — but it is odd in view of the undoubted presence of a submerged, but active, Scandinavian population in the North-West (as witnessed for example by the runic inscription in Carlisle Cathedral) that no traces of either the Ringerike or Urnes style is encountered there. The nearest examples geographically are a stone from Otley in Yorkshire[58] and a crozier found in an early twelfth-century bishop's grave in the chapter house of Durham Cathedral.[59] Are we again facing an imbalance of evidence, in that there is no evidence for the manufacture of fine metalwork in this period in the North-West?

In sum, then, the evidence at our disposal is varied and unbalanced. It is, however, clear that the discrete groups of material cannot be examined without reference to the whole. The mobility of jewellery more than anything else builds a community of taste — which we have seen for example in the few brooches mentioned here. Different social and religious customs and contexts and the haphazard survival of material militate against generalities. The fact that sculpture in Ireland mainly survives on monastic sites, whereas in England it is largely found in parish churches, is one example of the disparate nature of seemingly similar evidence; the absence of manuscripts illuminated in north-west England is another example. There is clearly some community of taste in the early viking period in the Irish Sea region; but as viking power collapsed in England there is a clear falling away of Scandinavian influence in the art of the North-West, although it was to survive in pockets elsewhere in the British Isles.

Acknowledgments

I am deeply grateful to James Graham-Campbell for reading the manuscript of this paper and saving me from many errors. I am also grateful to my wife for her drawings and to Durham University, the National Museums of Scotland, the National Museums and Galleries on Merseyside and the Tullie House Museum, Carlisle, for photographs.

References

1 E. Roesdahl, 'Dendrochronology and viking studies in Denmark', *Proceedings of the 12th Viking Congress*, Stockholm, 1994, pp.106–16.

2 R. Bailey, 'Irish Sea contacts in the viking period — the sculptural evidence', in G. Fellows-Jensen and N. Lund, eds, *Tredie Tværfaglige Vikingesymposium*, Højbjerg, 1984, pp.7–36.

3 D.M. Wilson, 'The art of the Manx crosses of the Viking Age', in C. Fell *et al.*, eds, *The Viking Age in the Isle of Man*, London, 1983, pp.175–87.

4 E.g., D. M. Wilson and O. Klindt-Jensen, *Viking art*, London, 1966, plate xii.

5 E.g., ibid., plate xxviii*a*.

6 A. MacGregor, 'Industry and commerce in Anglo-Scandinavian York', in R. A. Hall, ed., *Viking Age: York and the North*, London, 1978, figs 24, 25. J. Bayley does not accept my description of this object: see *idem, Anglo-Scandinavian non-ferrous metalworking from 16–22 Coppergate*, York, 1992, p.838.

7 D. M. Wilson and O. Klindt-Jensen, *Viking art*, plate xxx*d*.

8 M. Iversen, ed., *Mammen. Grav, kunst og samfund i vikingetid* (Jysk Arkælogisk Selskabs Skrifter, XXVIII), Højbjerg, 1991.

9 S. H. Fuglesang, *Some aspects of the Ringerike style*, Odense, 1980.

10 D. M. Wilson and O. Klindt-Jensen, *Viking art*, pp.147–60.

11 Compare, e.g., the maps in D. M. Wilson, 'Scandinavian settlement in the north and west of the British Isles. An archaeological point of view', *Transactions of the Royal Historical Society*, 5th series, 26 (1976), fig. 1, and A. H. Smith, *English place-name elements*, Cambridge, 1970, map 10.

12 See J. Graham-Campbell, ed., *Viking treasure from the North West. The Cuerdale hoard in its context*, Liverpool, 1992, *passim*.

13 B. J. N. Edwards, 'The vikings in north-west England: the archaeological evidence', in ibid., pp.43–8.

14 The most recent assessment of the vikings in Wales is W. Davies, *Patterns of power in early Wales*, Oxford, 1990 , pp.49–60.

15 G. C. Boon, *Welsh hoards*, Cardiff, 1986, pp.98–102.

16 N. Edwards, 'A possible viking grave from Benllech, Anglesey', *Transactions of the Anglesey Antiquarian Society and Field Club*, 1985, pp.19–24.

17 H. Loyn, *The vikings in Wales* (The Dorothea Coke Memorial Lecture in Northern Studies), London, 1976.

18 P. M. C. Kermode, *Manx crosses*, London, 1907, fig. 50.

19 W. G. Collingwood, *Northumbrian crosses of the pre-Norman Age*, London, 1927, fig. 85.

20 H. Shetelig, *Viking antiquities in Great Britain and Ireland*, pt 2, Oslo, 1940, fig. 30.

21 Unpublished. National Museum of Ireland.

22 H. Shetelig, *Viking antiquities*, pt. 2, fig. 43.

23 For references see J. Graham-Campbell, 'Bossed penannular brooches: a review of recent research', *Medieval Archaeology*, 19 (1975), pp.33–47.

24 B. J. N. Edwards, 'Vikings in north-west England', p.49.

25 J. Graham-Campbell, *Viking artefacts. A select catalogue*, London, 1980, p.54 and fig. 194.

26 J. D. Cowen, 'A catalogue of objects of the viking period in the Tullie House Museum, Carlisle', *Transactions of the Cumberland and Westmorland Antiquarian and Archaeological Society*, new series, 24 (1934), fig. 2.

27 An imported white metal Borre-style disc brooch is now in the Manchester Museum; it probably came from the Castlefield area of Manchester. J. D. Bu'lock, 'An east Scandinavian disc-brooch from Manchester', *Transactions of the Lancashire and Cheshire Antiquarian Society*, 67 (1957), pp.113–4.

28 R. N. Bailey, *Viking Age sculpture in northern England*, London, 1980, plate 1.

29 Ibid., figs 15 and 36.

30 Listed D. M. Wilson, *The Viking Age in the Isle of Man. The archaeological evidence*, Odense, 1974, pp.44ff. To which may be added the graves on St Patrick's Isle, Peel, shortly to be published in a report edited by D. Freke.

31 D. M. Wilson, 'Art of the Manx crosses'.

32 S. Margeson, 'On the iconography of the Manx crosses', in C. Fell *et al.*, *Viking Age*, pp.95–106.

33 H. Shetelig, *Viking antiquities in Great Britain and Ireland*, pt 6, Oslo, 1954, fig. 40.

34 A. Liestøl, 'An Iona stone and the world of Man and the Isles', in C. Fell *et al.*, *Viking Age*, pp.85–94.

35 R. N. Bailey, *Viking Age sculpture*, pp.216ff.

36 F. Henry, *Irish art in the Romanesque period, 1020–1170 AD*, London, 1970, plates 60, 62, 64.

37 *Idem, Irish art during the viking invasions*, London, 1967, plate 15.

38 A. Mahr, *Christian art in ancient Ireland*, Dublin, 1932, plate 57.2.

39 E.g., U. O'Meadhra, *Motif-pieces from Ireland*, Stockholm, 1979, p.39, fig. 101.

40 J. T. Lang, *Viking-Age decorated wood. A study of its ornament and style* (*National Museum of Ireland: Medieval Dublin Excavations*, series B, vol.I), Dublin, 1988, figs 13 and 14.

41 See J. Graham-Campbell in S. W. Ward, ed., *Excavations at Chester. Saxon occupation within the fortress. sites excavated 1971–81* (*Grosvenor Museum, Chester: Archaeological Excavations and Survey, Reports*, vol. VII), Chester, 1994, pp.68ff.

42 W. G. Collingwood, *Northumbrian crosses*, fig. 142.

43 R. N. Bailey and R. Cramp, *Cumberland, Westmorland and Lancashire North-of-the-Sands* (*The British Academy corpus of Anglo-Saxon stone sculpture*, vol. II), Oxford, 1988, p.155, *cf.* fig. 590.

44 J. J. Lang, *Viking-Age decorated wood*, fig. 20.

45 D. M. Wilson and O. Klindt-Jensen, *Viking art*, plate xlv*f.*

46 R. N. Bailey, 'Irish Sea contacts', p.27.

47 S. H. Fuglesang, 'Tne axehead from Mammen and the Mammen style', in Iversen, *Mammen*, p.88.

48 J. Graham-Campbell, 'Two Viking-age silver brooch fragments believed to be from the 1858 Skaill (Orkney) hoard', *Proceedings of the Society of Antiquaries of Scotland*, 114 (1984), p.297.

49 *Idem*, 'The Viking-Age silver hoards of the Isle of Man', in C. Fell *et al.*, *Viking Age*, p.3, fig. 10.

50 D. M. Wilson and O. Klindt-Jensen, *Viking art*, plate lviiia.

51 Ibid., plate lxxiiie.

52 P. M. C. Kermode, *Manx crosses*, plate xl, 89a.

53 R. B. K. Stevenson, 'The Inchyra stone and other unpublished early Christian monuments', *Proceedings of the Society of Antiquaries of Scotland*, 92 (1958–59), plate xi, 2.

54 F. Henry, *Irish art in the Romanesque period, passim*, and R. Ó. Floinn, 'Schools of metalworking in eleventh- and twelfth-century Ireland', in M. Ryan, ed., *Ireland and insular art*, Dublin, 1987, pp.179–87.

55 U. O'Meadhra, *Motif-pieces*.

56 J. J. Lang, *Viking-Age decorated wood*, figs 17, 25ff.

57 M. Redknap, 'Remarkable viking find in remote site', *Amgueddfa*, 14 (1992), p.9.

58 D. M. Wilson and O. Klindt-Jensen, *Viking art*, plate lxva.

59 Ibid., fig. 68.

4

The Irish Sea vikings:
raiders and settlers

JAMES GRAHAM-CAMPBELL

IN THE LIGHT of recent work on the origins of the viking age in Scandinavia, Professor Bjørn Myhre has recently reviewed the chronology of the early viking-period graves in Norway, as a contribution to the current archaeological debate 'about the problem of when and why the viking period actually started'.[1] It is his considered opinion that the earliest Norwegian graves containing imported objects of insular manufacture do *not* date from the period around AD 800 (as has generally been supposed), but 'could be dated to the middle and late parts, maybe even the early parts, of the eighth century'.[2] It follows for him that 'contact with Britain, and even with Ireland, may therefore have been established by that time', that is, before 'the middle part of the eighth century'.[3] This conclusion has led Professor Myhre on to the yet more controversial suggestion that some of the viking graves at Dublin 'may . . . be much earlier than 841, when, according to the written sources, Dublin was established by the vikings'.[4] The purpose of this paper is to provide a general review of the dating evidence for the beginnings of Scandinavian settlement in the Irish Sea region in the light of these claims,[5] which go far beyond such earlier observations as that by Professor Haakon Shetelig who was certain that there existed 'some intercourse between Norway and Scotland' before the end of the eighth century.[6]

The earliest reference to an attack by sea pirates on a Scottish

Figure 1 — The kingdom of Man and the Isles at its greatest extent.
(after Wilson)

monastery is that recorded in the *Annals of Ulster* in 617, 'the burning of Donnán of Eigg with 150 martyrs'. In the same year, Tory Island (off the Donegal coast) was 'devastated'; no doubt this was the work of the same fleet that had first visited the Hebridean island of Eigg (Figure 1).[7] It has been suggested that these were raiders from Norway, but it seems more probable that, in this instance, the attackers were pagan Picts who might well have had no reservations about plundering the monasteries of their Irish neighbours.[8]

It is, however, necessary to draw attention to these raids of 617 in order to emphasize the point that Shetelig himself made so clearly:

> This event stands at any rate quite alone, without any connection with the expeditions of the viking time, which did not begin till a couple of centuries after. The silence of the annals proves conclusively that calamities of this kind did not befall the monasteries and the clergy during the long intervening period — a period which came to a dramatic end in 794.[9]

In that year, according to an entry in the *Annals of Ulster*, all the islands of Britain were devastated by 'gentiles'.[10] In this case, there can be little doubt that the pagan raiders of 794 were the Scandinavian sea pirates we know as the vikings. As for their targets, in the words of Dr Alfred Smyth:

> The annalist clearly had the Scottish Isles in mind and the Northern Isles in particular, since in the following year (795) he noted the wasting and pillaging of Skye by the same gentiles who came as far south as Rathlin off the Antrim coast on that expedition. Some even ventured further south and west into the Atlantic to attack monasteries on Inismurray and . . . Inisbofin off the Connaught coast of Ireland. By 796 the Northmen were making inroads on the Irish mainland: the viking age had dawned.[11]

Dr Smyth continues: 'We have no adequate Scottish records from this period of crisis and invasion, but the fate of Iona, due to its prestige and importance, was followed carefully by Irish chroniclers.' This famous monastery, founded by Columba in the sixth century, had developed into 'the cultural and religious capital of northern Britain' and had — in consequence — much to attract the attention of viking raiders. Iona was plundered in 795, burnt in 802, and then — during a raid in 806 — sixty-eight members of the community were butchered. In consequence, the following year, the abbot felt it necessary to retreat for safety with most of his surviving monks to Kells in Ireland, although Iona was not altogether abandoned by the Church.[12]

The early records of these bloody events reveal that the initial Norse impact on northern and western Britain, as well as on Ireland, was that of viking violence. What is more, it would appear that the vikings continued to operate as seasonal raiders for at least a generation. At any rate, this would seem to be the most obvious conclusion to draw from Professor Ó Corráin's observation concerning Ireland:

> For the first four decades, from 795 to about 836, raiding follows a clear pattern. The raids themselves were hit-and-run affairs by small, sea-borne but fast-moving forces, probably independent freebooters, who appear suddenly, attack island and coastal monastic settlements, and disappear with equal rapidity.[13]

In addition, it should be noted that there are periods when there are no recorded raids on Ireland — such as the seven years from 814 to 820.

So far, two conclusions may be drawn from these records: in the first place, the Viking Age in the Celtic West began no earlier than the 790s; and, secondly, its ruthless nature makes it highly unlikely that it was preceded (as some have suggested) by a period of peaceful penetration and/or gradual settlement of the Northern Isles. Indeed, as Dr Smyth observes: 'Had there been a sizeable Norse population on Orkney, for instance, in the decades prior to the attacks of 794, Irish annalists would have taken note of such a remarkable occurrence.'[14] There is nothing in these sources to substantiate

Dr Barbara Crawford's view that the historical evidence somehow leads to the conclusion 'that pirate settlements had been
established in the Northern and Western Isles by [the last
decade of the eighth century]'.[15] On the contrary, my own
belief is that the sources indicate seasonal raiding parties direct
from Norway, at least until the 830s — and the archaeological
evidence can be seen to point in the same direction.

In the first place, there is an abundance of eighth- to early
ninth-century Celtic metalwork (both ecclesiastical and secular)
from early viking-period contexts in western Scandinavia, so
that the proceeds of the early raids were certainly reaching the
homelands,[16] even allowing for the suggestion that some of the
items may have been later merchandise or gifts.[17] Secondly,
there are no apparent archaeological traces in either the
Northern or the Western Isles of any Norse 'pirate settlements',
of the type which Dr Crawford describes as 'defensible sites on
promontories', supposed by her to have been used as viking
bases 'before farming settlements proper could be established'.[18]
Indeed, the evidence to date indicates instead the direct take-over
of native settlements.

So when *did* Norse settlement begin in Britain and Ireland?
Views vary, but one statement representative of much current
opinion is that by Dr Gillian Fellows-Jensen:

> The relatively sparse documentary and archaeological
> evidence shows that the settlement [of the Northern and
> Western Isles of Scotland] must have begun about the
> year 800, that is at about the same time as the settlement
> of the Faroe islands and the Isle of Man [and] about half a
> century before the restricted settlements in Ireland . . .[19]

It will be argued below from archaeological evidence that her
suggestions in this respect, moderate though they are, require
some modification. But Dr Fellows-Jensen is selected here for
quotation as a distinguished place-name scholar, in order to
make the point that she does *not* suggest that the Norse place-
names coined by the Scandinavian settlers have much contribution
to make to such chronological considerations — even though it

is not long since it was being proposed that the place-names themselves provided evidence for eighth-century Scandinavian settlement in the Northern Isles.[20]

As far as Ireland is concerned, it is clear that the historical evidence demonstrates that Scandinavian settlement began no earlier than the 840s, when the first viking winter-bases are recorded.[21] The fact that Professor Myhre can point to some potentially eighth-century Scandinavian material in the Dublin viking cemeteries (to be considered below) cannot be allowed to override the documentary sources. However, there is *no* contemporary documentary evidence which relates directly to the initial Norse settlement of the Northern and Western Isles of Scotland — nor any to that of the Isle of Man, or even to Cumbria. Thus it is left to archaeology to attempt to reveal the truth: only archaeology can answer the fundamental question of 'when'.

It is necessary to begin with a brief consideration of the Northern and Western Isles of Scotland, for this is the route by which many (although not all) of the Irish Sea vikings will have arrived.[22] For a recent archaeological opinion, there is Professor Christopher Morris who is 'inclined to see viking settlement in an organized sense in the Orkney Islands as coming from the late ninth century onwards, with informal contact before', although what he means by 'informal contact' is not further defined.[23] Another recent settlement excavator on Orkney, Dr John Hunter, has written: 'Whether settlement (as opposed to contact) occurred in the Orkney islands before [the later part of the ninth century] is an unresolved issue, but the evidence from Structure 16 [on the Brough of Birsay] must suggest that it did.' Hunter endeavours to use radiocarbon dates to calibrate the relative chronology of this settlement, which became the seat of the Viking-Age earls of Orkney, so establishing 'with some confidence' that the Norse take-over was 'within the later eighth or first half of the ninth century', for at least part of the site. However, Hunter is of the opinion that the first major Norse structural development on the Brough of Birsay is not likely to have taken place any earlier than the later part of the ninth century, although there is some evidence of an earlier Norse presence of unknown size and organization.[24]

Only a limited number of early viking-period artefacts can be recognized in the pagan viking graves of Scotland and their interpretation is complicated by what can be termed the 'heirloom factor'. For instance, the woman buried at Clibberswick, on the island of Unst in Shetland, wearing a pair of early viking-period oval brooches (of the so-called Berdal type which originated in the eighth century) was also dressed with a very fine middle viking-period trefoil brooch, decorated in the so-called Borre style which developed no earlier than the middle part of the ninth century.[25]

Oval brooches — those that are often known as 'tortoise' brooches — represent a unique feature of a distinctively Scandinavian form of female dress, during the eighth to tenth centuries.[26] Although in modern reconstructions all viking women are habitually portrayed as going about their daily business so attired, oval brooches will have formed part of the 'best dress' of the nobility and the well-to-do middle class, only to be worn on high-days and feast-days. As such they are prime examples of potential 'heirloom' brooches, particularly given that there is no evidence that they were manufactured anywhere in the viking settlements in the Celtic West.

There is only one other pair of Berdal-type oval brooches from Scotland (Figure 2),[27] where the majority of early viking-period oval brooches are the standard, mass-produced types which would not have been made before about 800 and so need not have been deposited before the middle of the ninth century.[28] Sigrid Kaland, the Norwegian excavator of the only viking cemetery in Scotland to have been fully explored in modern times, that at Westness on Rousay, in Orkney, found pagan Norse burials beginning only in the ninth century, although they form part of a native cemetery which had been in use from the fifth century AD (according to radiocarbon dating).[29] Her richest grave contains a fine example of an 'heirloom' ornament, in the form a grandiose eighth-century Irish pin, with gold filigree decoration, but this wealthy woman's oval brooches are of a standard early viking-period type, indicating a ninth-century date for her burial.[30] A ninth-century date is also indicated for the next most prestigious female grave known from Orkney — that found recently at Scar, on the island of Sanday. This is a triple burial placed in a boat, the elderly woman's status being marked not by oval brooches, but by a Scandinavian equal-armed brooch and a superb whalebone plaque from Norway (both of which have parallels in the Dublin cemeteries).[31]

The male graves in Scotland contain as few early viking-period artefacts as do those of the women buried in Scandinavian dress, with one possible exception. This particular grave presents us with an old problem — one that Professor Myhre is most keen to revive — as it has often been said to date from well before the beginning of the ninth century.

This was discovered in a small gravel mound in 1896 while a house was being built overlooking Lamlash Bay on the island of Arran. The rusted remains of a single-edged sword, now lost, were discovered with a poorly preserved shield-boss of conical type.[32] Shetelig convinced himself that 'if it had been found in Norway, this burial would, without hesitation, be referred to the eighth century . . . archaeologically, the conclusion appears unavoidable that at least some stray colonists were established there from the time about 750 AD'.[33] However, the single-edged sword continued to be used into the early viking period and there are several from the Dublin graves. The ninth-century (or even earlier) date which was proposed for the shield-boss in the 1920s is in urgent need of re-assessment in the light of our knowledge that conical bosses were in use on ninth-century shields in the Irish Sea area (as considered below; see Figure 7).

To turn from graves to settlement archaeology: there is one Viking-Age site in the Western Isles, the Udal in North Uist, with a radiocarbon date of significance for this chronological debate. The date, which is from a whale-bone deposited during the primary phase of the Norse settlement, is AD 859±40. On the one hand this date stands alone, but on the other it forms part of a consistent sequence, thus indicating that the vikings took over this settlement sometime during the ninth century — a date which accords well with the artefacts recovered from above, below and within this critical horizon.[34]

For Scotland, therefore, there seems no reason to reject Shetelig's confident statement: 'In summing up the list of early viking graves in Scotland we conclude with certainty that the Norse settlements in Shetland, the Orkneys, the Hebrides, and the southern isles started during the first decades after 800 AD. This conclusion is in full accordance with historical records of the first viking raids on the British Isles.'[35] For Professor Myhre this is a couple of generations too late, but his assertion that 'the argument becomes special pleading when all early objects are explained away' as heirlooms[36] is unconvincing when the evidence from Dublin and the Irish Sea region is taken into account.

It would also appear that, when the initial phase of seasonal raiding gave way to land-taking for permanent settlement, it was swift in its impact and built up rapidly. As mentioned above, no archaeological evidence has been recognized to support those who have suggested a preceding period of 'pirate settlements', in a phase of so-called 'ness-taking'. In consequence, Myhre has been forced to suggest that the Norse presence during the eighth century is, to all intents and purposes, archaeologically invisible — on the grounds that 'there was no need for the Norse population to demonstrate or express their ethnic identity through material culture. It is possible, for instance, that the first Scandinavian settlers and traders assimilated peacefully to the local population and their material culture'.[37] On the other hand, there remains the evidence of the annals for, as Smyth observed, 'these records of the earliest attacks strongly suggest that the Norwegians did not gradually infiltrate the Northern Isles as farmers and fishermen and then suddenly turn nasty against their neighbours'.[38]

According to this scenario, Scandinavian land-taking in Scotland coincided, in part at any rate, with the historically documented establishment of the first viking winter-bases in Ireland during the 840s. From these bases, which included Dublin, raiding and trading ventures were launched across the Irish Sea and to the south — ventures in which these vikings were joined by their Norse neighbours newly-established in Scotland, by such men as the wealthy viking who was buried at Kiloran Bay on the Hebridean island of Colonsay.[39]

This viking warrior was buried in a boat, some nine metres long, together with his horse; he was armed with sword, axe, spear and shield. The shield-boss is of small conical type, most closely paralleled in the Balladoole viking boat-burial on the Isle of Man (Figure 7), which also contained an equivalent set of harness mounts (possibly even from the same insular workshop in the Irish Sea region).[40] On the other hand, his silver cloak-pin is unique in the viking West, an import from Scandinavia of the so-called Vestfold type, more usually found in bronze.

In front of his body had been placed a set of scales and weights; the obvious weights number seven in all, but to them should perhaps be added the three Northumbrian copper coins (or stycas) which were recovered from the grave 'some time after the exploration was completed'. One was illegible and no longer survives, but the others are of king Eanred I (who reigned from 808 to 841) and of Wigmund (who was archbishop of York from 831 to 854); both are perforated so that they could not have been in circulation as current coin when they were buried. They demonstrate clearly that this grave can be no earlier than the mid-ninth century — and it is most probably of somewhat later date. As a set, the scale-weights are most closely paralleled by those from the Kilmainham/Islandbridge cemeteries of viking Dublin,[41] in use during the second half of the ninth century, whereas equivalent harness mounts have been excavated from the occupation levels of the tenth-century town.[42]

This grave-group is formed from a remarkable miscellany of

Figure 2 — Berdal-type oval brooch from Oronsay.
(*Proceedings of the Society of Antiquaries of Scotland*, 48, 1913–14)

Figure 3 — Hiberno-viking arm-ring hoard from Anglesey.
(Photograph: National Museum of Wales)

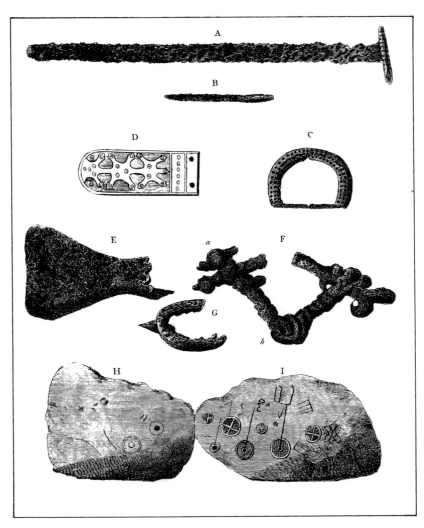

Figure 4 — Iron weapons (A, B and E), horse-bit (F) and spur (G), with a gold buckle and strap-end (C and D), stones from a viking grave in a prehistoric mound (H and I), found in 1789 at Aspatria, Cumberland.

(*Archaeologia*, 10, 1792)

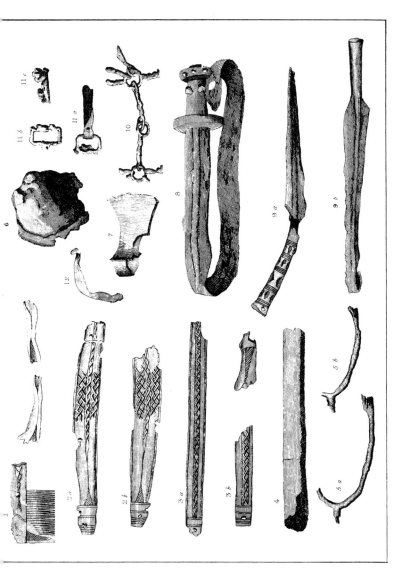

Figure 5 — Viking grave-goods, including iron weapons (nos. 6–9), horse-bit (10) and spurs (5), with a bone comb and case (1–3), a whetstone (4) and iron sickle-blade (12), found in 1822 at Hesket-in-the-Forest, Cumberland.

(*Archaeologia Aeliana*, 2, 1832)

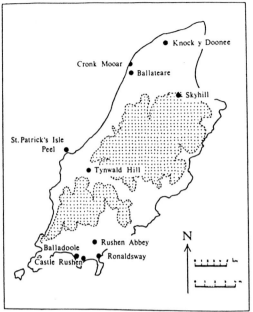

Figure 6 — Some important Norse sites
on the Isle of Man.
(after Cubbon)

Figure 7 — Remains of the conical
iron shield-boss from the Balladoole
boat-burial, Isle of Man.
(after Bersu and Wilson)

Figure 8 — Plan of the 'Pagan Lady's' grave on St Patrick's Isle (Peel Castle), Isle of Man.
(after Freke and Crawford)

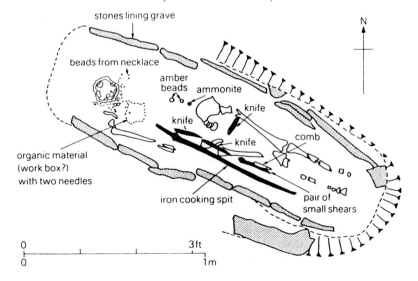

artefacts, redolent of the cross-currents of the Irish Sea in the second half of the ninth century, currents created and exploited by the viking raiders and traders of Dublin and their kinsmen — one of whom is encountered here in his Colonsay grave, with sword in one hand and scales in the other.

There seems little doubt that the power-house behind this activity was the development of viking Dublin, beginning in the mid-ninth century. The true 'viking' Dublin was that first settlement, the *longphort*, established in 841, amongst the very earliest of the winter-bases in Ireland of which it was the one best placed to become a permanent centre for both piracy and trade: until 902, that is, when the Irish defeated and expelled the foreigners of Dublin, who are said to have 'left a great number of their ships and escaped half-dead after having been wounded and broken'.[43] Where the Dublin vikings went is a matter which will be considered below, but first it is worth recalling something of the wealth that they had by then created in Ireland.

In the first place, there is the evidence of the Dublin vikings' own burials — in cemeteries situated two miles upstream from the mouth of the river Liffey in the modern suburbs of Islandbridge and Kilmainham, where a vanished early Christian monastery was sited.[44] Much of the importance of these burials has sadly been lost, for they were dug up by labourers in the mid-nineteenth century during the construction of the railway line and its terminus. From the grave-goods discovered then, and in some limited excavations in the 1930s, it is evident that a minimum of some fifty male and female viking graves is known, but what proportion this might represent of the original total is completely uncertain. The quality of the grave-goods is clearly evident from the finely embellished hilts of several of the swords, which include both Scandinavian and continental weapons. On the other hand, of the twenty-four shield-bosses listed in 1910, eighteen are conical in form and so, seemingly, of Irish Sea origin.[45] Half a dozen of the swords are single-edged — and thus of early viking-period type — while three have been deliberately bent by heating and hammering so as to render them useless as weapons, in a funerary ritual which is normally associated with the rite of cremation in Scandinavia.[46]

The majority of the surviving grave-goods are indeed weapons, with spears, axes and possibly arrows, found alongside the swords and shields already mentioned, but tools and scales were also included. Textile-working equipment accompanied some of the female burials, which are otherwise most obviously represented by Scandinavian brooches and beads. Amongst the oval brooches is a pair of a Berdal type which is known to have been in production from the eighth century, on the basis of mould debris excavated at Ribe in Denmark,[47] but that is no reason to throw out the annals by redating the origins of viking Dublin. As Shetelig himself noted:

> The greater part of swords and ornaments from Kilmainham exhibit the types that were commonly used about that eventful year [841], a date not contradicted by the fact that some of the antiquities are distinctly earlier, appertaining to the preceding generation. Some old-fashioned weapons and ornaments may still have been in use at a time when their types were generally superseded by new creations.[48]

There are no artefacts from the Kilmainham/Islandbridge cemeteries that have to be as late as the tenth century in date. Thus arguments from both the presence and the absence of diagnostic Scandinavian material amongst the grave-goods combine to date these burials to a period fully in accord with the documented existence of a viking *longphort* at Dublin from 841 to 902. Its precise location remains unknown, but the work of Elizabeth O'Brien on the local topography and the actual locations of the graves (in so far as this information can now be recovered) points in the direction of Kilmainham monastery itself.[49]

The Dublin grave-goods indicate a permanent and prosperous settlement with Scandinavian, Irish Sea and continental connections — its wealth based on both raiding and trading, the latter indicated by finds of balances and scale-weights. There seems little doubt that the commodity most coveted was silver and that the main product of the Dublin silversmiths of the period was a type of penannular arm-ring, consisting of a broad band of silver with characteristic stamped decoration, now known as the 'Hiberno-viking type' arm-ring (Figure 3).[50]

The Dublin vikings and their kin were also able to make large quantities of silver available to Irish metalworkers for the first time. These metalworkers produced splendid penannular brooches in plain silver during the second half of the ninth century and in some quantity at that, judging by the variety of surviving examples.[51] Then there is the remarkable evidence offered by three silver hoards consisting solely of massive ingots of non-Scandinavian type — hoards from the vicinity of Lough Ennell in County Westmeath.[52] The most extraordinary of these finds was that in the townland of Carrick, comprising sixty such ingots, with a total weight of almost thirty-two kilograms of silver. Samples of charcoal from the Carrick ingots have produced radiocarbon dates that place their manufacture between AD 625 and 925 (at two standard deviations). The lower end of this range lies well within the early viking period, while analysis strongly suggested, on comparative grounds, that the silver came from a viking source.

When the Irish expelled the vikings from Dublin in 902, some of this wealth got away in viking hands, as is demonstrated by silver hoards found on the opposite side of the Irish Sea, such as that consisting of an Irish bossed penannular brooch and a Scandinavian neck-ring from Orton Scar in Westmorland,[53] and the small ingot and hack-silver hoard from Gordon, Berwickshire, which also contains a gold finger-ring.[54]

The question therefore arises, what became of the Dublin vikings during the early years of the tenth century, before their return (in part, at any rate) some fifteen years later, when Dublin was re-established, but on a different site from that of the original *longphort?*

There is general acceptance that it was this crisis in Ireland that precipitated the Scandinavian settlement of north-west England, of Cumbria and the coasts of Lancashire and Cheshire, although it has been suggested that those who moved eastwards from Ireland did so to join earlier settlers. The main problem is that English historical documents are silent about these events, for knowledge of which one is largely dependent on place-name studies and archaeological, including art-historical, evidence.

There is, however, a late Irish saga, preserved in *The Three Fragments of Irish Annals*, which concerns a viking leader, Ingimund, who was expelled from Dublin in 902.[55] It tells how he headed for Anglesey, but was driven on to England where he and his followers were allowed land near Chester by the Lady of the Mercians. The historicity of this is, in part at any rate, supported by the *Annales Cambriae*, which document Ingimund's arrival in Anglesey. It is always dangerous to attempt to correlate coin-dated hoards, let alone coinless ones, with historical events, but Ingimund's intervention on Anglesey, direct from Dublin, is exactly the sort of occasion to account for the deposition and non-recovery there of a hoard of five superb Hiberno-viking rings (Figure 3).[56]

The place-name evidence on the Wirral peninsula and of south Lancashire is vivid testimony to Scandinavian settlement near Chester, and the growing strength of the Norse to the north-west of Mercia necessitated frontier fortification. If we ask the question 'Where would the main fleet of the Irish Norse in exile most likely have found its haven?', an obvious answer, as advanced by Nick Higham, is 'the Ribble estuary as the most likely harbourage, and the immediate vicinity of Preston as the most probable site for a base', having a direct trans-Pennine link to the heart of the viking kingdom of York, a link formed by the Roman road that cut through the Aire Gap.[57]

Here then is a context for the deposition of the greatest known viking treasure in both Western Europe and the Scan-dinavian homelands — the hoard weighing around forty kilograms of silver found at Cuerdale, in the south bank of the Ribble, upstream from Preston.⁵⁸ It comprised some 7,500 coins, together with about 1,100 ingots, rings and hack-silver pieces. The coins determine that the date of deposition was within a year or two of 905, many of them being fresh from the York mint.⁵⁹ On the other hand, a substantial proportion of the bullion material was of Hiberno-viking origin in the form of ring and brooch fragments. All in all, it is tempting to see the Cuerdale hoard as part of the capital of the Irish Norse in exile, newly topped up with silver from their supporters in the kingdom of York. But however that may be, its precise early tenth-century date and its Hiberno-viking elements help to fill in our outline of Norse settlement in north-west England.

No pagan viking grave from north-west England dates to the early viking period.⁶⁰ For instance, the only burial with Scandinavian oval brooches, that from Claughton Hall, between Preston and Lancaster, contains the double-shelled variety most characteristic of the middle viking period. This grave also contains a silver-gilt Carolingian mount, demonstrating again the wide-ranging connections of Irish Sea vikings.

However, Bjørn and Shetelig dated two male burials (from Rampside churchyard in Lancashire, and from Ormside churchyard in Westmorland) to the second half of the ninth century, on the basis of their 'M-type' swords.⁶¹ However, this is one of the simplest and commonest types of early to middle viking-period sword and these graves are thus as likely to date to the early tenth century as they are to the late ninth.

Amongst the viking warriors buried in Cumberland are two of undoubtedly high status — one often discussed (from Hesket-in-the-Forest) and one (from Aspatria) more generally forgotten because the grave-goods are now lost. However, the publication of the latter in 1792 shows a group of typical viking weapons, although of superior quality, given that the sword has a silver-encrusted hilt and the spear-head a silver decorated socket; equestrian equipment is also illustrated, in the form of a horse-bit and a spur (Figure 4). In addition, there is an ordinary axe and 'pieces of a shield' are referred to in the description of the find which was made in a prehistoric barrow. What is most notable, however, is the presence of a gold buckle and strap-end of Carolingian type, unique in an insular grave context.

Equestrian gear is also prominent in the Hesket warrior burial which was discovered during the clearance of a cairn in 1822; in this instance, the sword is bent back on itself twice, in the manner suggested earlier as being characteristic of cremation burials, while some of the objects show apparent signs of burning (Figure 5). The sword-hilt is encrusted in silver with the Borre-style ring-chain motif, while the two spear-heads both have distinctive bronze-rivetted sockets; all are features which indicate that this, too, is a burial of the middle viking period. There are a shield-boss and an axe, as well as the remains of a fine unburnt comb with its comb-case. The addition to the grave-goods of an ordinary sickle and whetstone might well be taken to suggest the land-owning status of this otherwise well-armed equestrian warrior.

There need be no doubt that both these burials date to the early tenth century and that both bear witness to an initial forced land-taking by pagan vikings, as in the Scottish islands and in Ireland. They would appear to represent the first generation of settlers who died pagans, but whose heirs converted to Christianity and were commemorated not by mounds, but with hogbacked tombstones or free-standing crosses, of which there is none finer than that in the churchyard at Gosforth.[62] The archaeological evidence thus accords well with the little that can be gleaned from documentary sources concerning the Norse settlement of north-west England; it agrees also with the evidence of their place-names, as well as with the artistic connections revealed by their earliest Christian sculpture.

However, both place-name and art-historical studies reveal that the Scandinavian settlement of the North-West (as also of the Isle of Man) was not confined to those of Norwegian origin who had spent time in the Scottish islands or who came from across the Irish Sea, for amongst them were some of Danish origin, settlers who had pressed westward from the Danelaw territories of eastern England. Moreover, Gillian Fellows-Jensen has argued that 'the demonstrable links between Manx names and those around the Mersey' indicate 'an anti-clockwise progression of Scandinavian settlement names from the Danelaw across the Pennines to Morecambe Bay and Man, where a Scoto-Norwegian influence made itself felt, and then back again across the Irish Sea to England'.[63] At the same time, Richard Bailey has suggested that the origins of some of the finest ornament on the Manx Viking-Age sculpture are to be found in the Anglo-Scandinavian art styles of the kingdom of York.[64]

Thus, we come finally to the Isle of Man. There is much archaeological and linguistic evidence for Scandinavian settlement on Man, including a remarkable group of tenth-century memorial crosses, many with runic inscriptions.[65] On the other hand, there is historical evidence only for the late Norse kingdom (and bishopric) of Man and the Isles (Figure 1). So once again it is left to archaeology to attempt to provide the date of its original viking settlement.

There are twenty-four possible grave sites on the Isle of Man with pagan, or at least semi-pagan, Norse burials — a remarkable total for this small area. In 1974, David Wilson proposed that the first generation of these Manx graves belonged to 'the first half, or the middle, of the ninth century'.[66] In so doing, he was revising his earlier opinion that the graves as a whole could not be dated more precisely than to 'within the century 850 to 950'.[67] It will be proposed below that it is Wilson's latter bracket that has proved to be the correct one, with the main burials most probably belonging to its middle part.

Four major Manx burials of pagan warriors, in prominent sites beneath prominent mounds, have been excavated, but there is space here only to mention two (Figure 6).[68] At Ballateare, the man was buried in a coffin but, before his mound had been capped, funerary sacrifices had taken place, for near the top it contained a layer of burnt animal bones (cattle, horse, sheep and dog), together with the skeleton of a young woman, the back of whose skull had been sliced off — a seemingly clear example of a human sacrifice. There is also a second body (also female and without grave-goods) in the Balladoole boat-burial, the most splendid of the Manx examples; it contains the set of harness mounts that could well be from the same workshop as that in the Colonsay boat-burial, while both their shield-bosses are of conical types (Figure 7). The Balladoole burial contains an insular ringed pin of a type also present in the Ballateare grave, a version of the plain-ringed, polyhedral-headed form that was particularly popular in tenth-century Dublin, but absent from the earlier Kilmainham-Islandbridge cemeteries.[69]

The pins point therefore to a date for these burials later rather than earlier within Wilson's 850–950 bracket. To this evidence may be added the fact that the Balladoole warrior was buried with spurs, such as were noted in early tenth-century burials in north-west England, but which likewise do not feature amongst the Kilmainham-Islandbridge grave-goods. There can be no doubt that the Ballateare and Balladoole burials, considered to be those of primary settlers, are close to each other in date and are most probably to be attributed to the beginning of the tenth century. Thus we return again to the importance of the events following the Norse expulsion from Dublin in 902, and the beginnings of Scandinavian settlement in north-west England.

It is most striking that, despite the number of known sites, no burial of a woman with Scandinavian brooches has yet been found on Man. This has given rise to the hypothesis that the initial land-taking involved the intermarriage of the Norse with native Christian women, so explaining also the presence of a number of Celtic names in the Norse memorial inscriptions on the mid-tenth-century cross-slabs. Intermarriage, it has been supposed, leads to conversion. But this scenario only becomes convincing if the hypothesis presented here is accepted — that the pagan burial horizon dates only from the beginning of the tenth century, with the next generation being commemorated by Christian stones, dating from the 930s onwards. Although this proposal involves a somewhat drastic curtailment of the current chronology for the viking settlement of

Man, it receives some support from the evidence of a yet unpublished group of graves which form part of a large early Christian and medieval cemetary on St Patrick's Isle, more often known as Peel Castle, also the site of the cathedral for the late Norse diocese of Sodor and Man.[70]

Seven of the excavated graves contain Viking-Age artefacts of which four are simply clothed or shrouded burials, rather than being accompanied by additional, deliberately deposited, grave-goods. However, the fill of one contained a coin of the Anglo-Saxon king Edmund (939-46), while a halfpenny of Eadred (946-55) had been placed in the grave of a child, most probably in its mouth; thus both these graves can date no earlier than the 940s or 950s. The most interesting of these graves is that of a high-status woman who had been buried fully clothed, in an elaborate lintel-grave, together with a selection of her belongings; the artefacts are of middle viking-period date (Figure 8). The 'Pagan Lady', as she has become known on Man, was wearing a necklace of exceptional quality, consisting of seventy-one glass, amber and jet beads, of Scandinavian, eastern or Mediterranean and English origin. She had no brooches, but a tablet-woven belt was ornamented with a couple of amber beads and an ammonite fossil. Her head was resting on a down-filled pillow, beside which was a bag or pouch containing a couple of needles. Beneath her was a fine Anglo-Scandinavian knife with silver ornamented hilt and beside her had been placed a cooking spit, with the wing of a goose and a bunch of herbs; a pair of shears and a comb might have hung from her belt. Near the knee had been placed a cup-shaped, bored stone with a pestle-like flint — an enigmatic and perhaps symbolic offering.

This 'Pagan Lady' is unique on Man, given that all the other known high-status burials are those of males. Her artefacts are all of Irish Sea origin or from the Danelaw (as are those in the other six graves), except for some of her exotic beads which might, however, have been obtained in viking York. There is thus no reason to suppose that this group of people was of immediate Scandinavian origin, even if of Scandinavian descent. These burials form a small group within the cemetery, dating to the mid-tenth century; they are transitional in nature and contemporary with the earliest viking-style Christian sculpture. Bearing in mind the Danelaw connections displayed by the burials and the suggestion by Fellows-Jensen of tenth-century immigration from northern England, it seems reasonable to suggest that this Peel Castle group is representative of just such a movement. The occasion for such an immigration westwards to the Isle of Man might have been some such reversal in the Danelaw as when Aethelstan captured York from the vikings in 927 — or the battle of Brunanburh in 937.

With that this review of the earliest viking settlement in the Irish Sea area is completed, leaving aside the matter of south-west Scotland, pending the publication of the Whithorn excavations. Far from following Professor Myhre's bold attempt to convince us that this process took place much earlier than supposed, it has been argued here that it should be seen as having taken place in Scotland only after 800 and in Ireland after 840 — and not before 900 in either the Isle of Man or north-west England.

References

1 B. Myhre, 'The beginning of the viking age — some current archaeological problems', in A. Faulkes and R. Perkins, eds, *Viking revaluations: Viking Society Centenary Symposium 1992*, London, 1993, pp.182–216.

2 Ibid., p.187.

3 Ibid., p.191.

4 Ibid., p.191.

5 This paper consists of the partially revised text of the Fifth Jeanette Gilbertson Lecture delivered in Chester on 11 March 1994, an earlier version of which was first given as a Munro Lecture at the University of Edinburgh in October 1989. I am most grateful to Sir David Wilson for commenting on a draft.

6 H. Shetelig, 'An introduction to the viking history of Western Europe', in H. Shetelig, ed., *Viking antiquities in Great Britain and Ireland*, pt 1, Oslo, 1940, p.8; see now P. Foote, 'Pre-viking contacts between Orkney

and Scandinavia', in R. J. Berry and H. N. Firth, eds, *The people of Orkney* (Aspects of Orkney, IV), Kirkwall, 1986, pp.175–86; C. D. Morris, 'Native and Norse in Orkney and Shetland', in C. Karkov and R. Farrell, eds, *Studies in insular art and archaeology* (American Early Medieval Studies, I), Oxford, OH, 1991, pp.61–80; G. F. Bigelow. 'Issues and prospects in Shetland Norse archaeology', in C. D. Morris and D. J. Rackham, eds, *Norse and later settlement and subsistence in the North Atlantic* (University of Glasgow, Department of Archaeology, Occasional Paper Series, I), Glasgow, 1992, pp.9–32; and J. R. Hunter, J. M. Bond and A. N. Smith, 'Some aspects of early viking settlement in Orkney', in C. E. Batey, J. Jesch and C. D. Morris, eds, *The viking age in Caithness, Orkney and the North Atlantic*, Edinburgh, 1993, pp.272–84

7 A. O. Anderson, *Early sources of Scottish history AD 500 to 1286*, vol. I, Edinburgh, 1922, pp.142–4.

8 A. P. Smyth, *Warlords and holy men: Scotland AD 80–1000*, London, 1984, p.108.

9 H. Shetelig, 'Introduction', pp.8–9.

10 A. O. Anderson, *Early sources*, p.255.

11 A. P. Smyth, *Warlords and holy men*, p.145.

12 Ibid., pp.146–77.

13 D. Ó Corráin, *Ireland before the Normans*, Dublin, 1972, p.82.

14 A. P. Smyth, *Warlords and holy men*, pp.145–66.

15 B. E. Crawford, *Scandinavian Scotland*, Leicester, 1987, p.118.

16 E. Wamers, *Insularer Metallschmuck in wikingerzeitlichen Gräbern Nordeuropas. Untersuchungen zur skandinavischen Westexpansion* (Offa-Bücher, LVI), Neumünster, 1985.

17 C. Blindheim, 'A collection of Celtic (?) bronze objects found at Kaupang (Skiringssal), Vestfold, Norway', in B. Almqvist and D. Greene, eds, *Proceedings of the Seventh Viking Congress, Dublin, 15–21 August 1973*, Dublin, 1976, pp.9–27.

18 B. E. Crawford, *Scandinavian Scotland*, p.138.

19 G. Fellows-Jensen, 'Viking settlement in the Northern and Western Isles — the place-name evidence as seen from Denmark and the Danelaw', in A. Fenton and H. Pálsson, eds, *The Northern and Western Isles in the viking world*, Edinburgh, 1984, pp.148–68.

20 Cf. the review of the evidence by F. T. Wainwright, 'The Scandinavian settlement', in *idem*, ed., *The Northern Isles*, Edinburgh, 1962, pp.117–62.

21 D. Ó. Corráin, *Ireland before the Normans*, p.90.

22 For the Danes in Ireland, see A. P. Smyth, 'The *black* foreigners of York and the *white* foreigners of Dublin', *Saga-Book of the Viking Society for Northern Research*, 19, pts 2–3 (1975–76), pp.101–17; for the vikings in the Irish sea during this period, see also his books, *Scandinavian York and Dublin*, vols. I–II, Dublin, 1975–79, and *Scandinavian kings in the British Isles, 850–80*, Oxford, 1977.

23 C. D. Morris, *The Birsay Bay project*, vol. I, *Brough Road excavations 1976–82*, Durham, 1989, p.287.

24 J. R. Hunter, *Rescue excavations on the Brough of Birsay, 1974–82* (Society of Antiquaries of Scotland Monograph Series, IV), Edinburgh, 1986, pp.172–3.

25 S. Grieg, 'Viking antiquities in Scotland', in H. Shetelig, *Viking antiquities*, pt 2, pp.103–5, figure 57, a–b.

26 I. Jansson, *Ovala spännbucklor. En studie av vikingatida standardsmycken med utgångspunkt från Björkö-fynden* (Aun, VII), Uppsala, 1985.

27 S. Grieg, 'Viking antiquities', p.42, figure 23.

28 I. Jansson, *Ovala spännbucklor*; cf. B. Myhre, 'Beginning of the viking age', pp.190–1.

29 This important cemetery has yet to be published in detail, but for a brief summary see A. Ritchie, *Viking Scotland*, London, 1993, p.50, based on S. H. H. Kaland, 'Westnessutgravningene på Rousay, Orknøyene', *Viking*, 37 (1973), pp.77–102; and *The Norse connection: Orkney-Norway, 800–1500* (Exhibition catalogue, Tankerness House Museum), Kirkwall, 1987, now part reprinted as 'The settlement of Westness, Rousay', in C. E. Batey, J. Jesch and C. D. Morris, eds, *Viking age*, pp.308–17.

30 R. B. K. Stevenson, 'The Celtic brooch from Westness, Orkney, and hinged-pins', *Proceedings of the Society of Antiquaries of Scotland*, 119, pp.239–69.

31 M. Dalland, 'Scar: a viking boat burial', *Current Archaeology*, 131 (1992), pp.475-7.

32 S. Grieg, 'Viking antiquities', pp.27–8, figure 11; B. Mhyre, 'Beginning of the viking age', p.190.

33 H. Shetelig, 'The viking graves', in *idem*, ed., *Viking antiquities in Great Britain and Ireland*, pt 6, Oslo, 1954, p.102.

34 I. A. Crawford, 'Sandscaping and C14: the Udal, N. Uist', *Antiquity*, 51 (1977), pp.124–36.

35 H. Shetelig, *Viking antiquities*, pt 6, p.103.

36 B. Myhre, 'Beginning of the viking age', p.190.

37 Ibid., p.196.

38 A. P. Smyth, *Warlords and holy men*, p.145.

39 S. Grieg, 'Viking antiquities', pp.48–61; this grave is in process of republication by myself and Trevor Cowie (National Museums of Scotland).

40 G. Bersu and D. M. Wilson, *Three viking graves in the Isle of Man* (Society of Medieval Archaeology Monograph Series, I), London, 1966, pp.20–6.

41 J. Graham-Campbell, *Viking artefacts: a select catalogue*, London, 1980, no. 308.

42 E.g. that illustrated on plate 17 of B. Ó Ríordáin, 'The High Street excavations', in B. Almqvist and D. Greene, *Proceedings of the Seventh Viking Congress*, pp.135–40.

43 D. Ó. Corráin, *Ireland before the Normans*, pp.90–5; for the expulsion from Dublin, see also N. J. Higham, 'Northumbria, Mercia and the Irish Sea Norse, 893–926', in J. Graham-Campbell, ed., *Viking treasure from the North-West: the Cuerdale hoard in its context*, Liverpool, 1992 p.24.

44 G. Coffey and E. C. R. Armstrong, 'Scandinavian objects found at Island-bridge and Kilmainham', *Proceedings of the Royal Irish Academy*, 27, section C (1910), pp.107–22; J. Bøe, 'Norse antiquities in Ireland', in H. Shetelig, ed., *Viking antiquities in Great Britain and Ireland*, pt 3, Oslo, 1940, pp.11–65; C. S. Briggs, 'A neglected viking burial with beads from Kilmainham, Dublin, discovered in 1847', *Medieval Archaeology*, 29 (1985), pp.94–108.

45 Insular shield-bosses are in need of a detailed study; there is a brief discussion by David Wilson in G. Bersu and D. M. Wilson, *Three viking graves*, pp.16–7, 60–1.

46 H. Shetelig, *Viking antiquities*, pt 6, p.83.

47 B. Myhre, 'Beginning of the viking age', pp.186–7, 190, figure 11.

48 H. Shetelig, *Viking antiquities*, pt 6, p.105.

49 Elizabeth O'Brien's research has demonstrated the existence of more than one group of burials at Kilmainham/Islandbridge and so it is obviously incorrect to continue to refer to this material as if it all derived from a single cemetery; I am most grateful to Mrs O'Brien for having shown me a draft of her article and for allowing me to refer to it here.

50 J. Graham-Campbell, 'The Viking-Age silver hoards of Ireland', in B. Almqvist and D. Greene, *Proceedings of the Seventh Viking Congress*, pp.51–2; the type has now been studied in detail by John Sheehan as part of his unpublished M.A. thesis, *Viking Age silver arm-rings from Ireland*, University College Galway, 1984.

51 O. S. Johansen, 'Bossed penannular brooches', *Acta Archaeologica*, 44 (1973), pp.63–124; J. Graham-Campbell, 'Bossed penannular brooches: a review of recent research', *Medieval Archaeology*, 17 (1975), pp.33–47, and 'Some Viking-Age penannular brooches from Scotland and the origins of the "thistle-brooch" ', in A. O'Connor and D. V. Clarke, eds, *From the stone age to the 'Forty-Five*, Edinburgh, 1983, pp.310–23.

52 M. Ryan *et al.*, 'Six silver finds of the viking period from the vicinity of Lough Ennell, Co. Westmeath', *Peritia*, 3 (1984), pp.334–81.

53 B. J. N. Edwards, 'The vikings in north-west England: the archaeological evidence', in J. Graham-Campbell, *Viking treasure*, p.50 (no.17).

54 *Idem*, 'The Viking-Age silver and gold hoards of Scandinavian character from Scotland', *Proceedings of the Society of Antiquaries of Scotland*, 107 (1975–76), pp.115, 124 and plate 14.

55 N. J. Higham, 'Northumbria, Mercia and the Irish Sea Norse', p.24 (with refs); see also W. Davies, 'Vikings', in *Patterns of Power in Early Wales*, Oxford, 1990, pp.48–60.

56 G. Boon, *Welsh hoards 1979–1981*, Cardiff, 1986, pp.98–102, figures 39–40.

57 N. J. Higham, 'Northumbria, Mercia and the Irish Sea Norse', pp.27 and 29–30.

58 J. Graham-Campbell, 'The Cuerdale hoard: a viking and victorian treasure' and 'The Cuerdale hoard: comparisons and context', in *idem*, *Viking treasure*, pp.1–20 and 107–15 (with refs).

59 M. M. Archibald, 'Dating Cuerdale: the evidence of the coins', in J. Graham-Campbell, *Viking treasure*, pp.15–20 (with refs).

60 The graves are listed in B. J. N. Edwards, 'Vikings in north-west England'.

61 A. Bjørn and H. Shetelig, 'Viking antiquitites in England', in H. Shetelig, ed., *Viking antiquities in Great Britain and Ireland*, pt 4, Oslo, 1940, pp.18–9; it is worth noting that the Ormside burial contained a further example of an insular-type shield-boss (see above, n.45).

62 R. N. Bailey, *Viking Age sculpture in northern England*, London, 1980; *idem* and R. Cramp, *Cumberland, Westmorland and Lancashire North-of-the-Sands* (*The British Academy Corpus of Anglo-Saxon Sculpture*, vol. II), Oxford, 1988.

63 G. Fellows-Jensen, 'Scandinavian settlement in the Isle of Man and northwest England', in C. Fell *et al.*, eds, *The viking age in the Isle of Man*, London, 1983, p.50; see also G. Fellows-Jensen, 'Scandinavian place-names of the Irish Sea province', in J. Graham-Campbell, *Viking treasure*, pp.31–42.

64 R. Bailey, 'Irish Sea contacts in the viking period — the sculptural evidence', in G. Fellows-Jensen and N. Lund, eds, *Tredie Tværfaglige Vikingesymposium*, Højbjerg, 1984, pp.7–36.

65 C. Fell *et al.*, *The viking age in the Isle of Man*.

66 D. M. Wilson, *The viking age in the Isle of Man: the archaeological evidence*, Odense, 1974, p.28.

67 *Idem* in G. Bersu and D. M. Wilson, *Three viking graves*, p.87.

68 The Ballateare and Balladoole burials are both published ibid., together with that at Cronk Mooar; for the important ship-burial at Knock y Doonee, see P. M. C. Kermode, 'A ship-burial in the Isle of Man', *The Antiquaries Journal*, 10 (1930), pp.126–33.

69 T. Fanning, 'The Hiberno-Norse pins from the Isle of Man', in C. Fell *et al.*, *Viking age*, pp.27–36; the ringed-pin chronology is refined in Fanning's newly published study, *Viking age ringed pins from Dublin* (1994), in the National Museum of Ireland/Royal Irish Academy series, *Medieval Dublin Excavations 1962–81*.

70 J. Graham-Campbell, 'Tenth-century graves: the Viking-Age artefacts from the Peel Castle cemetery and their significance', in D. Freke, ed., *Peel Castle excavations, 1982–87* (Liverpool, forthcoming).

5

Aspects of time in
the battle poetry of early Britain

DAVID N. KLAUSNER

THE PERCEPTION OF the passing of time is one of the most
deeply rooted processes of the brain, so deep that it is not directly
associated with any of the physical senses. And yet, however
basic it may be to our modes of thought and understanding, it is
remarkable how variable it is. It is clear to everyone that the
perception of the passage of time can vary immensely depending
on external criteria; what constitutes a long time standing in a
bus queue or waiting for the computer to save a file would in
a more pleasurable context seem a very short time.
Anthropologists, historians, and psychologists who have
considered the perception of time in a wide variety of cultures
and periods have concluded that, although there may very well
be a cultural component in the perception of time, many of
time's apparent characteristics are perceived with such
unanimity that they may well be built into our cerebral cortices.
Thus, although we have no explicit commentary on the nature
of time dating from Anglo-Saxon or Celtic Britain, it may very
well be possible to understand at least some levels of its perception
by reference to both earlier and later discussions.

On the general level, for example, it is clear that all human
beings view time to some extent as cyclical, governed by a
sequence of recurrent seasons. This perception will naturally be
stronger in temperate climates, rather than at the Arctic or near
the equator. It will be particularly strong among agricultural

communities where life revolves around the annual progression from spring rebirth to winter death. Cultural imperatives may superimpose other modes of perception; Christianity, especially in its exegetical context, tends to view time as linear, as a progression from a beginning, Creation, to an end, the Last Judgement.

On the most minute level, the level of our perception of the most basic units of time, we are fundamentally limited to two choices, depending on our answer to the question of whether time can be infinitely divided. If we answer that it can, then we will see time as a continuum. If on the other hand we understand time as consisting of a sequence of finite units which cannot be further divided, then we will see time as atomic, as a succession of instants. This division has governed man's thoughts about the fundamental nature of time since the earliest sources. It forms the basis, for example, of Aristotle's discussion of time as a continuum and his arguments countering the atomists (especially in the *Physics* 4.10, 217b29–218a30).[1] Zeno's well-known paradox about Achilles' race with the tortoise is discussed by the early philosophers as a problem in the divisibility of time as much as in the divisibility of space.[2] The distinction lies clearly behind Augustine's discussion of the nature of time in Book XI of the *Confessions*. On the other hand, Boethius' description of the human perception of time, lived 'in illo mobili transitorioque momento' in Book V, Prose 6 of the *Consolation*, would seem to echo an atomist view.

Descartes took a similar position, arguing that 'the instants at which creaturely beings exist must be discontinuous or atomic. Temporal existence must, therefore, be like a line composed of separated dots, a repeated alternation of the state of being and the state of non-being'.[3] Bergson, on the other hand, saw time as 'a continuous uninterrupted line'.[4] In more recent philosophical writing, the distinction can be seen clearly behind Heidegger's discussion of the 'mundane' perception of time as series of 'nows', a *Jetztfolge*.[5] Many scientific theories of the perception of time are based on premisses that time is perceived by the mind either as a continuum or as a succession of non-divisible instants.[6]

That this is so is important to my discussion of the way in which the passage of time is presented in the early battle poetry of the British Isles, since it allows me the possibility of referring to these modes of perception without attempting to prove that they are derived in any direct way from a reading of Aristotle, Augustine, or Boethius.[7] Similarly useful to this discussion is the scientific commonplace of the close interconnectedness of time and space, since it will allow the transference of some of my arguments concerning the presentation of the passage of time to movement in space; it is still within the recent past that 'the space-time continuum' became a cliché of the scientific journalist. From a literary point of view the two are even more inextricably linked; in countering the argument that a sense of space in literature is achieved only at the expense of a sense of time, W. J. T. Mitchell writes, 'The fact is that spatial form is the perceptual basis of our notion of time, that we literally cannot "time time" without the mediation of space. All our temporal language is contaminated with spatial imagery; we speak of "long" and "short" times, of "intervals" (literally, "spaces between"), of "before" and "after" — all implicit metaphors which depend upon a mental picture of time as a linear continuum.'[8]

The poetic description of warfare in the early Middle Ages is sufficiently common that such poems are frequently grouped together under the term 'battle poetry'. This generic classification has produced some decidedly uncomfortable bedfellows; in Old English, for example, such poems as *The battle of Brunanburh* and *The battle of Maldon* are in many ways more notable for their differences than for their similarities. More useful, perhaps, would be a generic division of the 'battle poetry' class into categories of the poetry of victory and the poetry of defeat. With such a division, the characteristics shared by poems in each group become much clearer. The sources of these poems, too, indicate such a division; the victory poem is derived principally from panegyric, while the defeat poem tends to be most closely related to elegy. This division will become important in differentiating the poet's treatment of both time and space.

The texts I wish to discuss could well be seen as a rather miscellaneous collection, perhaps covering a time period as wide as four centuries, and written in two languages whose cultures existed most often in confrontation. Of the five poems, three are from the North-West, two definitely and one probably. One comes from a bit further north and east, and one interloper concerns events in East Anglia. They include two well-known Old English poems dealing with battles of the tenth century, and a group of Welsh poems concerned with persons and events of the last half of the sixth century.

The Old English poems, *The battle of Brunanburh* and *The battle of Maldon* both describe events for which there is other supporting historical evidence, primarily in chronicle form. The Welsh poems are less well-supported. Two of them are attributed to the poet Taliesin and survive in the book named for him. Unlike much of the legendary material contained in the volume these two poems, along with ten others, deal with historical events of the sixth century and with persons referred to in the Northern History section of the *Historia Brittonum*, in the same passage that lists Taliesin as one of the foremost poets in the Welsh language. These two poems of Taliesin deal with the victories of British forces under Urien Rheged over the Anglo-Saxons of Deira and Bernicia. Urien's kingdom included the Strathclyde area as well as a good deal of northern and north-western England.

My other Welsh poem, *The Gododdin*, also has a connection, if an indirect one, with Urien. It is attributed in its manuscript epigraph to Aneirin, a poet whose career is also noted in the same passage of the *Historia Brittonum*. In contrast to Taliesin's victory poems, it deals with a disastrous defeat suffered by British troops from the area of Edinburgh, apparently in attempting to re-take territory lost to the Anglo-Saxons in the region of Catterick, Yorkshire. The 1,480 lines of *The Gododdin* comprise a series of elegies for individual warriors; later I will address the question whether it should best be seen as one poem or as a series of individual poems.

All these Welsh poems survive in manuscripts of the thirteenth century, far later than the events they purport to describe. There is considerable scholarly difference of opinion on the likelihood that they may preserve a core of poetic material dating from the sixth century, but this argument is not essential to my analysis and I intend to leave it aside.

The two poems which form my corpus of Old English poetry cause fewer problems of authenticity, although they are not entirely problem-free. In 937 King Æþelstan and his forces defeated a coalition of Constantinus, king of the Picts and Scots, and the Dublin Norse under Olaf Guthfrithsson (called Anlaf in most English sources) at Brunanburh. The location of this place-name has not been determined, though suggestions have included Bromborough, Cheshire; Burnley, Lancashire; and Burnswark, Dumfriesshire.[9] The poem on their victory is given as the annual entry in the Anglo-Saxon Chronicle. Finally, in 991 the Essex fyrd under the leadership of ealdorman Byrhtnoþ was routed by a viking raiding party at Maldon, on the river Blackwater. The manuscript of the poem commemorating their defeat was in the Cotton Library, and was destroyed in the Ashburnham House fire of 1731, but fortunately a copy of the poem had been made earlier in the century by David Casley.[10] In contrast to *The battle of Brunanburh*, *Maldon* deals with a crushing defeat, the death of ealdorman Byrhtnoþ, and the virtual obliteration of the Essex army.

Let us begin with *The battle of Brunanburh*.[11] The poem opens with a strong sense of reportage, answering in the first four and a half lines the journalistic questions expected for the Anglo-Saxon Chronicle entry: participants (Æþelstan cyning, Eadmund æþeling: Æþelstan the king, Eadmund the prince), time (her: in this year), action (geslogon æt sæcce: won in battle), manner (sweorda ecgum: with sword-blades), and place (ymbe Brunanburh: near Brunanburh). From this point, however, the poet moves from this sense of specificity to a generalized picture of the battle and its aftermath. The sense of precision in period of time and spatial dimension is subsumed in a sense of occasion enlarged by a relative vagueness of time and place. It will be useful to analyze this picture in detail.[12] The poet guides the audience's viewpoint with great care and at the same time directs much of their response to the action. Were the poet less imaginative, it would be perfectly possible for the poem to end at this point (at line 10a). If these lines did constitute the full poem, it would find an analogue both in content and in phrasing in another of the Chronicle poems, *The capture of the five boroughs*.[13]

The action begins on the battlefield with lines 10b–12. Lack of precision concerning the numbers involved (hettend, Scotta leoda, scip-flotan: the enemy, the Scots, the sailors) forces the audience to draw its own generalized picture of the tumult of the battle. This picture expands somewhat in lines 12b–13a to include the blood-stained field itself and to emphasize that the picture is still essentially earth-bound.

<blockquote>
feld dænnede

secga swate
</blockquote>

(lines 12b–13a: the field became wet with the blood of men [if that is the correct translation of the verb 'denian']).

These nine lines (5b–13a) constitute the whole narrative of the battle itself; the rest of the poem is concerned with its aftermath.

At line 13b this earth-bound viewpoint rises dramatically to follow the sun in its path from rising to setting:

<blockquote>
siðþan sunne up

on morgentid,   mære tungol,

glad ofer grundas,   godes condel beorht,

eces drihtnes,   oð sio æþele gesceaft

sah to setle.
</blockquote>

(lines 13b–17a: From when the sun, the glorious star, glided up in the morning over the land, the candle of God, the eternal Lord, until that noble creation sank to rest.)

This digression, in which the day is presented through the sun's course, is sufficiently lengthy within the context of the poem that its significance must be greater than a mere indication of the period of time occupied by the battle. The explanation lies in part, of course, in the author's reference to the sun in its cosmological sense as 'godes condel beorht', and in the ornamental appositive 'eces drihtnes'. The result of the battle upon which God's candle shines clearly reflects his will. Divine approbation is implicit in the sun's willingness to shine on the battlefield. However, just as important is the concomitant effect of this digression in moving the viewpoint of the audience from the ground to a position above from which the whole battlefield can be seen at a glance.

Again the numbers are non-specific (secg mænig: many a man) and the position of the West Saxons and the Mercians as they pursue the remnants of Anlaf's army is sufficiently unclear that the poet forces the audience to view the whole area simultaneously. The eye flashes from one part of the action to another, from the Mercians to the numbered dead of the Norse (fife . . . cyningas giunge; seofene . . . eorlas Anlafes: five young kings; seven of Anlaf's noblemen). The syntactic parallels reinforce the increase in the numbers; the specificity of this numbering is expanded to infinity with the numberless dead of the army (unrim heriges). This 'bird's eye' view, with its suggestion of omniscience is retained through the portraits of the fleeing chieftains, Anlaf and Constantinus, and the description of the departing Norse ships (lines 53–56). Temporal and spatial shifts are kept to a minimum through the avoidance of conjunctions of time and place, giving a seamless continuity to the audience's point of view.

Then, in one of the most striking shifts (or rather, non-shifts) of the poem, the eye turns to the victors. The most surprising thing about this change is its great ease; the eye, from its position above the battlefield, need hardly turn to move from defeated to victor. The smoothness of the transition is emphasized by the opening adverb 'swilce', which links syntactically the departure of the defeated with the departure of the victors:

> Gewitan him þa Norþmen   nægledcnearrum,
> dreorig daraða laf,   on Dinges mere
> ofer deop wæter   Difelin secan,
> eft Iraland,   æwiscmode.
> Swilce þa gebroþer   begen ætsamne,
> cyning and æþeling,   cyþþe sohton,
> Wesseaxena land,   wiges hremige.

(lines 53–59: The Norsemen, the bloodstained survivors, went in nailed ships on 'Dinges mere' — again the placename is not known — over deep water to seek Dublin, back to Ireland, abashed. Likewise the brothers, both together, king and prince, sought their home, the land of the West Saxons, exultant in victory.)

The parallels are, of course, even more extensive; each sentence gives the subject (Norþmen; gebroþer) and a verb of motion (gewitan; sohton) followed by their destination and an appositive (Difelin, Iraland; cyþþe, Wesseaxena land) and ending with an adjective of manner (æwiscmode; wiges hremige). The passage is also linked to the opening description of the English by the verbal parallels of 'cyning' and 'æþeling', as well as with the flight of Constantinus by the repetition of 'cyþþe' (lines 38, 58). This viewpoint is held following the departure of Æþelstan and Eadmund to give a strong picture of the desolation of the battlefield, now inhabited only by the beasts of battle (friends to the victors, enemies of the defeated) and the corpses of the slain.[14] For the epilogue which concludes the poem, this viewpoint rises further to take in not merely the field of battle and its environs, but the whole of England, as the poet places the action in its proper historical and national perspective.

The effect of this narrative, quite the opposite of the effect we will find in *The battle of Maldon*, is one of great smoothness. Because of the breadth of the poet's (and thus of the audience's) viewpoint, transitions are effected with only the slightest shift of motion or of vision. The syntax of the poem contributes to this effect, avoiding entirely the most common temporal conjunction, 'þa' (then). Instead, *Brunanburh's* hypotaxis is based on a relatively complex sequence of periods, using subordinate clauses with *swa* (7), *siðþan* (13), *oð* (16), *þæra þe* (26), *þaes* (51), and so on, in contrast to the sequential *þa* clauses we will find in *The battle of Maldon*.[15] The consistency of the metrics contributes further to the *Brunanburh's* smoothness. The caesura is never run over syntactically, and there is little evidence of the sort of minor metrical irregularities which are so common in *Maldon*.[16]

The battle of Maldon provides a contrast to *Brunanburh* from practically every point of view. It is a poem of tragedy and defeat rather than of victory, and is thus essentially elegaic in character rather than panegyric. The poet's viewpoint, his 'eye', could not differ more from the panoramic view of *Brunanburh*. In *Maldon* we are firmly rooted on the battlefield, and much of the sense of confusion and tumult is conveyed by the continual shifting of the eye back and forth, the constant use of images of 'movement apart and together', as Neil Isaacs puts it.[17] Transitions are frequent and abrupt, and the action proceeds as a series of comparatively static tableaux, which, although containing violent action in themselves, proceed in small areas of space between small numbers of individuals, in sharp contrast to the breadth, smoothness, and continuity of *Brunanburh*. Time in *Maldon* is felt very much as atomic, a series of passing moments, a slide-show perhaps rather than a video, a paratactic structure rather than a hypotactic one.[18] Although the poem is, in Wanley's phrase, 'capite et calce mutilatum',[19] and we cannot therefore know if it began with the sort of reportage we saw in *Brunanburh*, Irving's description of *Maldon* as 'a fragment of medieval journalism' seems to me fundamentally wrong.[20] The interest here is specifically non-journalistic; it is suspenseful and dramatic rather than informative, and it is more centred on the way the participants act and their motives than on the facts of their actions. This can be seen especially in the lack of interest in naming the viking participants (compare *Brunanburh*, in which the major combatants on both sides are carefully named); for the *Maldon* poet, this detail was, as R. K. Gordon noted, 'inessential to the poet of the heroic defeat', and the vikings are seen merely as 'the agent of destruction'.[21]

In contrast to *Brunanburh*, the action of *Maldon* contains very few complex subordinate clauses, but is based almost entirely on the use of the simple conjunction *þa*, which was lacking entirely in *Brunanburh*. These *þa* clauses are almost universally sequential and add to the contrast with *Brunanburh's* feeling of simultaneity. A closer look at the way the poem is constructed will clarify this difference. Allowing for some flexibility in precisely where the divisions are marked, *The battle of Maldon* is made up of about twenty-eight brief episodes ranging in length from five lines (Dunnere's speech) to thirty-six lines (the speech of the viking messenger and Byrhtnoþ's reply). A very few of these episodes involve large numbers of people: the standoff between the vikings and the Essex fyrd over the causeway, and three short episodes describing large-scale battle. Aside from these, practically all of them deal entirely or at least primarily with one person, either ealdorman Byrhtnoþ himself or one of his army. In the latter half of the poem, after Byrhtnoþ's death, practically all the episodes deal with individuals, their actions and — most important for the poet — their comments on their relationship to their dead lord.

With a very few minor exceptions, the nature of these episodes is static. This stasis may be either temporal or spatial, frequently both, but the sense of the movement of time in the poem is that it takes place largely between the episodes, not within them. Now of course a part of this sense of stasis is created by the fact that eight of the episodes are devoted almost entirely to direct speech. These speeches are very much dramatic 'set pieces'; a useful counter to the occasional suggestion that the poem is an eye-witness account because of its wealth of detail. Like Byrhtnoþ's dying prayer, spoken (apparently) quietly and calmly as the battle rages around him, they are artful expressions of the poet's theme of loyalty to death, not a reporting of what happened on the battlefield. They are static in that the battle conveniently ceases, or ceases to exist, while they speak. The movement between episodes reinforces the feeling of a slide show, so to speak, in contrast to the seamless video of *Brunanburh*.

This episodic structure is simple and sequential, with the episodes linked almost entirely by the temporal conjunction 'þa' (then, next). Allowing again for some ambiguous cases, 'þa' occurs in *Maldon* about forty times. Of the poem's twenty-eight episodes, eighteen are clearly separated from the previous narrative block by 'þa'; in almost all cases it is either the first or second word of the passage. The following lines will serve as examples of the style, and will show the extent to which the poet relies upon this simple conjunction as his major structural device:

> þa þær Byrhtnoþ ongann   beornas trymian (line 17)
> Het þa bord beran (line 62)
> þa se eorl ongann (line 89)
> þa hine heowon hæðne scealcas (line 181)

There is further evidence of the importance of 'þa' in *Maldon*: of the poem's 325 lines, only 240 lines contain actual narrative; the rest are taken up with the speeches that are such a major element of the poem's thematic concerns. 'þa' is used, then, about every six lines. It is worth remembering that the word does not appear at all in *The battle of Brunanburh*.

The metre, too, is unlike that of *Brunanburh*, where its regularity contributes to the overall effect of smoothness. In *Maldon*, the caesura is frequently ignored,[22] enjambement is common, and metrical idiosyncrasies like anacruses and shifts of alliteration are used regularly:

> þæt her stynt unforcuð   eorl mid his werode . . .

(line 51: that here stands undisgraced the nobleman with his company.)

There is a significant shift in the vocabulary, however, from line 202 as the poem becomes more formal and stylized in the 'epic diction' of the speeches of Byrhtnoþ's retainers.[23] This shift does not, however, change the poet's fundamentally atomic view of time.

Probably the largest difference between the two poems lies in the vital importance for the *Maldon* poet of the individual gesture, both in its sense of the unique reaction of a single warrior to the tragedy of defeat, and in its more universal sense as a symbolic expression of a mode of feeling common to the whole of Germanic society from Tacitus to this poem nearly a millennium later. Rosemary Woolf has suggested that the connection between these two texts may well be more poetic fiction than social fact, but this does not affect my argument.[24] It is, I would suggest, out of this sense of individuality of gesture, of unitary rather than collective experience, that the sense of unitary time grows.

Here, then, in their simplest form are the paradigms I see in these poems. The poetry of victory, as in *The battle of Brunanburh*, tends to treat time as continuous, reflected visually in the breadth of the point-of-view, verbally in the tendency to avoid conjunctions which clarify the temporal (or spatial) relationship between one action and the next, and syntactically in the use of relatively complex structures. The poetry of defeat, as in *The battle of Maldon*, tends to present the passage of time as a sequence of actions, that is atomically, reflected visually in a close and restricted point-of-view, verbally and syntactically in the relatively simple structures built up principally on the basis of a series of sequentially-linked *þa* clauses.

Now let us turn to the Welsh poems. *The Book of Taliesin* is a late thirteenth-century miscellany comprising a wide assortment of texts — religious, prophetic, elegiac, and historical or pseudo-historical. The poetry attributed to Taliesin falls in more than one of these categories, including a series of mystical obscurities sung by a legendary Taliesin who is a shape-shifter and prophet as well as a poet. The historical poems, twelve of them in the canon established by Sir Ifor Williams,[25] are heroic and bardic poems sung principally to Urien, lord of Rheged. The precise boundaries of Urien's lands cannot be established with any certainty, but the evidence from both place-name and historical sources would imply that they included a good deal of north-west England and some of south-west Scotland. The name Rheged very likely survives in the Scottish place-name Dunragit, near Stranraer. It may also survive in the name Rochdale.[26] The site of Urien's court is not known, though Carlisle has been suggested since it is mentioned as a major city of Rheged in a twelfth-century poem by Hywel ab Owein Gwynedd.[27] The information contained in the *Historia Brittonum* would lead us to date Urien's reign to a period of roughly 572–92,[28] and Taliesin's *floruit* to a similar period though perhaps including an earlier period dating from about the middle of the century.[29] Of the twelve historical poems, two are battle narratives, both victory poems celebrating Urien's triumphs against the Anglo-Saxon invaders. Place-names in the poems would suggest that the battles are probably to be located in the general area of the rivers Eden and Lyvennet in Cumbria.

The first of these poems, *The battle of Gwen Ystrat*, opens with a journalistic flavour similar to that of *Brunanburh*, if less pronounced. In the first seven lines the combatants are presented (gwyr katraeth; 'the men of Catraeth' and gwyr prydein; 'the men of Britain') and the victorious leader is named (Urien). The site (Gwen Ystrat, possibly Wensleydale)[30] and time (gan dyd; at dawn) are specified. Only the precise nature of the action and its manner are missing in comparison with *Brunanburh*. The mention in line 1 of the dawn suggests, if mildly, the description of the rising and setting sun in *Brunanburh*. We will see that a similar passage occurs in the other Taliesin victory poem as well; it may well be that the *Brunanburh* passage is an expansion of a convention of which we have a simpler version here. Since a similar reference to the rising of the sun as an indication of time occurs in the *Gododdin*, it seems possible that this is a frequent convention of the battle narrative, though the incomplete nature of *Maldon* and the uncertainty of the proper textual order of the *Gododdin* do not allow us to go further. The sense of divine guidance and approbation we saw in *Brunanburh* is given here in the lengthy description of Urien in lines 2–5. He is 'gweithuudicc gwarthegyd' (a victorious cattle-raider), 'anwawt eineuyd' (a famous chieftain). He restrains lesser monarchs (kyfedeily teyrned) and cuts them down (gofyn). Most important, he is known as 'rwyf bedyd', the leader of Christendom, against the heathen Anglo-Saxons. As defender of the faith he has the same mandate as Æþelstan, on whom 'godes condel beorht' shines.

The main body of the poem is organized about a sequence of descriptive paragraphs, each beginning with the formula 'gweleis i' (I saw). Although the viewpoint is clearly on the battlefield rather than above it, this single observer who sees all imparts a sense of simultaneity almost as strong as that of *Brunanburh*. As in the Old English poem, the actual narrative of the battle is extremely brief, and is contained in a striking phrase based on alliterative juxtaposition of a type common in early Welsh verse:

Gweleis wyr gwychyr yn lluyd.

A gwedy boregat briwgic.

(lines 11–12: I saw brave men in a host, And after morning battle, mangled flesh.)

Two descriptions of the victors are given (lines 14–16, 25–32), framing the description of the defeated English. This is presented with as much sarcasm as the portrait of the fleeing Constantinus in *Brunanburh*, and with a similar use of litotes. The understatement is especially strong in lines 19–20, where 'aethant golludyon' (they got into difficulties) seems a euphemism for 'dead' (compare 'wiges sæd: sated with battle' in *Brunanburh*, line 20). I would take the following line in a similar sense; the 'palefaces' (garanwynyon) lie rather than stand[31] in the gravel of the ford (gryt ygro) with their hands crossed in a now useless gesture of supplication (llaw yg croes). This reading is supported by line 22, in which the waves of the ford wash the tails (rawn) of their horses (kaffon), which must therefore be dead, and also perhaps by line 21 if we accept Williams' rather elaborate emendation: 'Ry fedwynt eu cynrein rywin Idon' (their chiefs have drunk too much of the plentiful wine of Eden). The defeated are 'gospeithic' and 'gospylat', a pair of words of similar meaning, probably in the range of 'dull, disheartened, haggard'. The poet quickly disposes of the bloodstained survivors (gwyar a uaglei), or possibly corpses, to return to the Welsh. Urien is 'kat gwortho', a bardic epithet of a common type linking 'kat' (battle) with another noun, here 'coverer'. The poet is amazed that he was challenged. In sharp contrast to the bloodied Anglo-Saxons, the host around Urien is 'reodic' (splendid). He is a router of enemies (galystem) and the battle is a joy (llafyn) to him. The poem ends with an invocation to Urien's men to carry their shields (aessawr), since battle is the destiny of Urien's troops. As in all but one of the poems addressed to Urien, a bardic quatrain concludes (the same in all cases), indicating Taliesin's desire to praise Urien as long as his life lasts.

The sense of continuity of vision in *The battle of Gwen Ystrat* is strikingly similar to that of *The battle of Brunanburh*. The sequence of 'gweleis i' (I saw) passages gives the same kind of tour of the battle's aftermath without physically shifting the eye, such as we found in *Brunanburh*, a tour made smoother by the same lack of temporal or spatial conjunctions. Only two or three such conjunctions are found in the *Gwen Ystrat*, *gwedy* and *gan*, both quoted earlier, and *pan* 'when' in line 29. Although *gan* is usually a preposition, 'with', here it clearly has a temporal sense, 'since' or 'after'. None of these conjunctions serves to mark a temporal change; the first two indicate a contrast between the time before and after the battle, the third simply indicates the time of the battle itself, 'I saw a splendid host around Urien when he fought with his enemy at Llech Wen'. The poem concludes very much in the manner of *Brunanburh* with a rhetorical flourish in which the victor (Urien) is praised, with an implicit comparison between his glory and the misery of his defeated enemies.

Although *The battle of Argoet Llwyfein*[32] is laid out in a somewhat different manner from *The battle of Gwen Ystrat*, it too shows many of the characteristics of *Brunanburh*. The journalistic clarity of the opening is even more striking. The Anglo-Saxon chief is specified (Flamdwyn);[33] Urien and his son Owein are not named until later in the poem, but their names would likely be implied by either the situation or the manuscript title, if it is original. The place-names 'Godeu' and 'Reget' in line 4 are probably used for the armies (as in 'England attacked'). The action (kat uawr; a great battle), the place (o argoet hyt arvynyd; from Argoet to Arvynyd), and the time (bore duw sadwrn; Saturday morning) are all given. Here the simple 'gan dyd' of the Gwen Ystrat poem is expanded to a full line: or pan dwyre heul hyt pan gynnu (line 2: from when the sun rises until it sets). It seems to me very likely that this is another example of the convention which was to find its most imaginative expression in *The battle of Brunanburh*. The place-names which define the battle-place and the participants, combined with the reference to the rising and setting of the sun, give a sense of overview similar to that of the Old English poem. This point-of-view narrows to the battlefield itself in line 7, as Flamdwyn demands hostages (gwystlon) in much the same mocking tone as that used by the viking messenger in *Maldon*. Owein's reply is delivered with the same bravado as Byrhtnoþ's and with the same use of rhetorical parallels: nyt dodynt nyt ydynt nyt ynt parawt (line 10: They have not come; they are not and will not be ready). Owein bases his reply on the honour of his ancestor, Coel Hen, just as Æþelstan and Eadmund's victory was seen as a natural result of their descent from Eadweard:

> afaran Eadweardes,   swa him geæþele wæs
> from cneomægum . . .

(lines 7–8: . . . Edward's descendants, as befit the nobility which they had from their ancestors . . .)

Urien adds his boast to that of his son: rather than talk of peace (kerennyd) they will raise their shields[34] and attack Flamdwyn. As in the Gwen Ystrat and Brunanburh poems the narrative of the battle is largely ignored; the poet simply comments that at Argoet Llwyfein there were many corpses (llawer kelein), and that the beasts of battle (here the ravens, 'brein') grew red on the blood of men: Rudei vrein rac ryfel gwyr (line 22: ravens became red from warriors). Taliesin will sing their praises for a year, and concludes with the same panegyric quatrain to Urien which closed 'The battle of Gwen Ystrat'.

The similarities between these two Welsh poems and *The battle of Brunanburh* are many, and I think they suggest that there was a common repertoire of convention which to a significant extent transcended linguistic boundaries. Many of the elements which have been noted in these poems were probably drawn from the tradition of panegyric poetry, of which little has survived in languages other than Welsh. Other poems in the Taliesin canon[35] show that the description of the victorious leader and the references to his ancestry are common in the more generalized praise poetry, while it seems likely that the exchanges of boasts and threats in *Argoet Llwyfein* and *Maldon* as well as the references to the beasts of battle come from a tradition more specific to battle poetry. References to the rising and setting of the sun may well fall into this category as well.

When we turn to the *Gododdin* of Aneirin we are on less firm ground. The poem is a non-narrative sequence of descriptive elegies on the north Welsh warriors killed in a skirmish against the English at Catraeth (Catterick, Yorkshire) in the late sixth or early seventh century; that is, in the generation after Urien Rheged. The poem survives in two texts,[36] in the same manuscript though in different hands. The language of one text is significantly more archaic than the other, although the manuscript copy of both dates from the middle of the thirteenth century.

Any consideration of time in *The Gododdin* is immediately complicated by two factors. First, the proper order of the stanzas is uncertain — if indeed there was a proper order — and has clearly become confused to some extent. Poems which are connected by some form of stanza-linking (the Welsh technique of *cymeriad*) have become separated (e.g. poems 6–14, 21, and 33), though it is not, of course, possible to prove that they were ever intended to be sequential. Second, although the poem revolves around a sequence of events which can to a certain extent be reconstructed from internal evidence, it is clearly not a continuous narrative. Even with these uncertainties, however, the *Gododdin* shows some definite similarities to the Old English poems, especially to *The battle of Maldon*.

The poem is organized largely around the idea of an exchange of service for mead, not unlike the Germanic ideal described by Tacitus. We could easily replace the mead/wine metaphor of the *Gododdin* with the traditional Anglo-Saxon metaphor of the ring (beag), and we would find the *Brunanburh* poet's description of Æþelstan as 'beorna beahgifa' (line 2: ring-giver of warriors).

In *The Gododdin*, Mynydawc Mwynvawr ('the wealthy') feasts the collected army of Manaw Gododdin[37] for a year, and in return for their mead they will fight for him. Throughout the elegies it is proclaimed of the dead warriors, 'he paid for his mead' ('med a dalhei', line 22). This idea is developed through the poem into a series of potent contrasts. The mead, though sweet, is poison to the warriors: 'glasved eu hancwyn a gwenwyn vu' (line 69: fresh mead was their drink and their poison). In exchange for the mead they give their blood:

> kyn noe argyurein e waet e lawr.
> gwerth med eg kynted gan lliwedawr.

(lines 54–55: Sooner than he should be buried his blood flowed to the ground in return for mead in the hall among the hosts.) Mead is sweet, yellow, and ensnaring: med evynt melyn melys maglawr (line 92: they drank sweet, yellow, ensnaring mead). So in *Maldon*, after the death of Byrhtnoþ, Ælfwine exhorts the men to remember the vows they have spoken over mead:

> Gemunaþ þa mæla   þe we oft æt meodo spræcon,
> þonne we on bence   beot ahofon,
> hæleþ on healle,   ymbe heard gewinn.

(lines 212–14: Let us remember the times when we often spoke over mead, when we raised a boast on the bench, warriors in the hall, about the hard battle.)

What most clearly connects *The Gododdin* with *The battle of Maldon*, however, is the poet's presentation of his material as a series of discrete moments. In *Maldon*, of course, these moments are usually taken to be sequential, though we need not necessarily see them this way, and the speeches of the various members of Byrhtnoþ's retinue could without too much difficulty be seen as simultaneous. In *The Gododdin* the moments are clearly not sequential, but the clear sense of a slide-show view of the battle, rather than of a continuous narrative, remains.[38] The sparse use of temporal conjunctions contributes to this sense of simultaneity; in the almost 1,500 lines of *The Gododdin*, 'gwedy' (after) appears ten times, always in a comparative sense, relating the time of the battle to its aftermath, or to the mead-filled time before. 'Pan' (when) occurs thirty times; twenty-six of them in descriptive clauses referring to the hero of the stanza, the others as part of a simile. The purpose of these clauses is to narrow the temporal aspect of the stanza further, increasing the sense of the battle as a series of still or scarcely moving portraits. For example, the stanza on Caradog begins:

> Pan gryssyei garadawc y gat;
> mal baed coet trychwm trychyat.
> tarw bedin en trin gomynyat;
> ef llithyei wydgwn oe anghat.

(lines 343–46: When Caradog rushed into battle like a wild boar, the slayer of three warriors, the bull of the army, a hewer in the fighting, he fed the wolves with his hand.)

The 'when' clause restricts the time of the passage to the moment of Caradog's charge, his prowess defined metaphorically in terms of feeding the beasts of battle. Temporally, this may be opened up by a reference either to the period before or after the battle. Caradog's poem ends:

> gwedy med gloew ar anghat
> ny weles vrun e dat.

(lines 351–52: After the bright mead in the hand, not one of them saw his father.)

A full analysis of *The Gododdin* along these lines would not, I think, be highly productive. It is, however, clear that the poet views the action of the battle atomically, just as the poet of *Maldon* does. The reasons for this are not far to seek, of course, and lie in the nature of the event to be memorialized. How does one celebrate a victory? Clearly as a general celebration, both of the participants and of the event. How, then, does one celebrate a defeat? Obviously not in terms of the event itself, or of the participants as a group — their failed strategy or insufficient technical competence. What remains to be celebrated, or rather memorialized, is the acts of individual heroism which give the lie to the disaster of the event. Elegy is by its very nature an individual mode.

And this is not all. I would not, of course, want to imply that these poets had necessarily thought consciously about which perception of time to adopt. I do, on the other hand, think that there is a further reason which may explain their choices, a reason which has very much to do with the subject matter of their poetry. The atomic view very much sees time in its earthly sense as a series of disparate moments of stasis, what Heidegger calls the 'mundane' concept of time. From an eschatological point of view, the writer adopting an atomic stance is very cognizant of the fact that the angel of Revelation will one day say 'Tempus amplius non erit'. For the tenth-century Anglo-Saxon poets that day would have felt very close with the possibility of the world's ending at the approaching millennium. Thus, the poet writing of defeat sees it in earthly, finite terms as an event whose importance will, quite literally, fade with time.

The poet of victory, conversely, approaches time from the obverse. Time as a continuum is very much time in its divine aspect — seamless and eternal. The events of which he writes will live forever in the most literal sense he can imagine.

References

1 See, for example, Richard Sorabji, 'Atoms and time atoms' and Fred Miller Jr, 'Aristotle against the atomists', both in Norman Kretzmann, ed., *Infinity and continuity in ancient and medieval thought*, Ithaca, NY, 1982, pp.37–86 and 87–111 respectively, and Richard Sorabji, *Time, creation and the continuum: theories in antiquity and the early Middle Ages*, Ithaca, NY, 1983, esp. pts 1 and 5.

2 R. Sorabji, *Time, creation and the continuum*, pp.321–36. For a mathematical discussion of the implications of Zeno's paradox, see G. J. Whitrow, *The natural philosophy of time*, 2nd edn, Oxford, 1980, pp.190–200.

3 Ibid., p.156.

4 Thomas Cottle, *Perceiving time: a psychological investigation using men and women*, New York, 1976, p.11.

5 Martin Heidegger, *Sein und Zeit*, 8th edn, Tübingen, 1957, p.423.

6 The latter is seen especially in the theory that 'time in the form of some minimum duration is required for consciousness' (Whitrow, *Natural*

philosophy of time, p.73 quoting J. Hughlings Jackson). Whitrow also considers mathematical theories of 'temporal atomicity' and continuity, referring specifically to Zeno's paradoxes, pp.200–5. Such ideas occur in psychological discussions of time in a variety of guises; see, e.g., Paul Fraisse, *The psychology of time*, New York, 1963, pp.99–115. Similar terminology appears in W. J. Friedman's study of memory, 'Memory for time of past events', *Psychological Bulletin*, 113,1 (1993), esp. pp.54–5.

7 Concepts of time on a larger scale in early Germanic culture and their relation to early Christian culture are discussed by Paul Bauschatz, *The well and the tree: world and time in early Germanic culture*, Amherst, MA, 1982.

8 'Spatial form in literature: toward a general theory', *Critical Inquiry*, 6, 3 (1980), p.542.

9 Alistair Campbell, ed., *The battle of Brunanburh*, London, 1938, pp.57–80. A site on the east coast of England would seem to be implied by Florence of Worcester's comment that Anlaf began his raid sailing up the Humber, but Florence is supported by no other source, and an east coast raid would seem highly unlikely for a party starting from Dublin (to which the poem clearly says the Norse party returned).

10 H. L. Rogers, '*The battle of Maldon*: David Casley's transcript', *Notes and Queries*, 32 (1985), pp.147–55.

11 E. van K. Dobbie, ed., *The Anglo-Saxon minor poems* (*The Anglo-Saxon Poetic Records*, VI), New York, 1942, pp.16–20.

12 Although this analysis resembles in its overall position that of Neil Isaacs in *Structural principles in Old English poetry*, Knoxville, TN, 1968, pp.118–26, the emphasis and many of the details are significantly different.

13 E. van K. Dobbie, ed., *Anglo-Saxon Poetic Records*, VI, pp.20–1.

14 Frances R. Lipp has discussed the 'point of view' of these last two sections of the poem, coming to conclusions rather different from mine, and emphasizing more than I would the contrast between them: 'Contrast and point of view in *The battle of Burnanburh*', *Philological Quarterly*, 48 (1969), pp.166–77.

15 The whole question of parataxis in Old English and the related question of subordination is discussed by S. O. Andrew, *Syntax and style in Old English*, Cambridge, 1940, esp. ch. XI. Useful points are also made by A. C. Bartlett, *Larger rhetorical patterns in Anglo-Saxon poetry*, New York, 1935, and by R. F. Leslie, 'Analysis of stylistic devices and effects in Anglo-Saxon literature', *Stil- und Formprobleme in der Literatur*, Heidelberg, 1959, pp.129–36.

16 D. C. Scragg points out these irregularities in his edition of the poem, but notes that they do not constitute departures from the norms as great as some earlier critics had claimed. *The battle of Maldon*, Manchester, 1981, pp.28–30.

17 N. Isaacs, *Structural principles*, p.160.

18 The classical discussion of parataxis and hypotaxis in the literary representation of time is of course Erich Auerbach's *Mimesis: the representation of reality in western literature*, Princeton, NJ, 1953, *passim*, to which I am heavily indebted.

19 E. V. Gordon, ed., *The battle of Maldon*, London, 1937, p.31, n.1.

20 E. B. Irving, Jr, 'The heroic style of *The battle of Maldon*', *Studies in Philology*, 58 (1961), p.458.

21 E. V. Gordon, *Maldon*, p.22.

22 E. V. Gordon felt this to be so strong that he printed the text without the caesura.

23 This was noted by E. B. Irving, 'Heroic style', p.460, and by Bertha Phillpotts, '*The battle of Maldon*: some Danish affinities', *MLR*, XXIV (1929), p.173.

24 Rosemary Woolf, 'The ideal of men dying with their lord in *Germania* and in *The battle of Maldon*', *Anglo-Saxon England*, 5 (1976), pp.63–81. Woolf would not deny the slight possibility that the *Maldon* poet may have known the *Germania*, though there is no concrete evidence that it was known in England. Woolf suggests *Bjarkamál* is a much more likely source of the motif for *Maldon*, but her suggestion has recently been shown to be unlikely on grounds of dating by Roberta Frank, 'The ideal of men dying with their lord in *The battle of Maldon*: anachronism or *nouvelle vague*', in Ian Wood and Niels Lund, eds, *People and places in northern Europe 500–1600: essays in honour of Peter Hayes Sawyer*, Woodbridge, 1991, pp.95–106.

25 Ifor Williams, ed., *Canu Taliesin*, Cardiff, 1960; English version by J. Caerwyn Williams, *The poems of Taliesin*, Dublin, 1968.

26 The Domesday Book entry uses the name Racedham, which in the later Middle Ages changed its suffix from -ham to -dale, assimilating the two 'd's. Its origin is uncertain, but among the possibilities are Old English reced ('house'), Welsh rac coed ('before the forest'), and Welsh Rheged.

27 I. Williams, *Poems of Taliesin*, p.xxxix; Meirion Pennar, transl., *Taliesin poems*, Lampeter, 1988, p.10.

28 Urien is said to have fought against the Northumbrians Theodric and Hussa, whose reigns the Moore Memoranda would place as 572–79 and 585–92 respectively, if we accept Bede's date for the beginning of Ida's reign as 547. *Cf.* I. Williams, *Poems of Taliesin*, pp.xi–xiii.

29 The passage which includes Taliesin's name occurs in a description of Ida's reign (see n.22) and his battles against the Welsh prince Eudeyrn. Taliesin (as well as Aneirin) is said to have flourished 'tunc . . . simul uno tempore . . .', I. Williams, *Poems of Taliesin*, p.xi.

30 J. Morris-Jones, 'Taliesin', *Y Cymmrodor*, 28 (1918), p.161.

31 As in I. Williams' note, *Poems of Taliesin*, pp.36–37, s.v. 'garanwynyon'.

32 Ibid, pp.6–7.

33 'Flame-bearer': really an epithet rather than a name. Perhaps a calque on Lucifer?

34 There is some uncertainty over the meaning of 'eidoed' (line 18), but I.Williams suggests (*Poems of Taliesin*, p.76, s.v.) that it refers to a defensive rampart, probably of raised shields, in which case it would be equivalent to the Anglo-Saxon 'bordweal' (*Brunanburh*, line 5b).

35 Especially the 'Trawsganu Cynan Garwyn', *Poems of Taliesin*, p.1. Kynan, the object of this praise poem, is identified as 'mab Brochuael' (line 15).

36 Ifor Williams, ed., *Canu Aneirin*, Cardiff, 1938. K. H. Jackson, *The Gododdin: the oldest Scottish poem*, Edinburgh, 1969, gives an English translation and annotation. All citations will be from *Canu Aneirin*.

37 The number involved is given in the A text as 300, in the B text as 363. These numbers are likely to refer only to the immediate retinue of Mynyddog, not to the supporting foot-soldiers, of which there may have been a very large number.

38 Sarah Lynn Higley has recently discussed the contrasts between continuous and discontinuous verse in Old English and Welsh, though not from the point of view of temporal perception. *Between languages: the uncooperative text in Early Welsh and Old English nature poetry*, University Park, PA, 1993, esp. pp.57–76.

6

Discretion and deceit:
a re-examination of
a military stratagem in *Egils saga*

IAN McDOUGALL

THE LAST THREE DECADES have witnessed the publication of
a great many valuable studies of the nature and extent of
Scandinavian settlement in the north-west of England during
the Viking Age. Particularly in the area of onomastics, evidence
for Scandinavian settlement both north and south of the
Solway Firth has been thoroughly investigated. W. F. H.
Nicolaisen, for example, has demonstrated the close relationship
between the distribution of Scandinavian place-name elements in
south-west Scotland and corresponding onomastic patterns south
of the border in Cumberland, Westmorland and Lancashire.[1]
W. H. Pearsall has studied the distribution of place-names in
Cumberland in relation to local geology, flora and fauna to
show that Scandinavians in these regions tended to settle areas
better suited for herding than for agriculture.[2] Detailed
evidence of Scandinavian settlement patterns and the survival
of Norse as a dominant language has been presented in, for
example, studies of place-names in the Isle of Man by Margaret
Gelling and Basil Megaw,[3] in John Dodgson's examinations of
Cheshire place-names,[4] and Melville Richards' investigation of
Scandinavian place-names in north-east Wales.[5] A complete
record of the large body of onomastic research in the field to
that date was made available in 1985 with the appearance of

Gillian Fellows-Jensen's survey, *Scandinavian settlement names in the North-West*.[6] Our knowledge of the Scandinavian presence in north-western England has been similarly advanced in recent years by R. I. Page's several studies of the runic inscriptions on the Isle of Man,[7] by the publication of new archaeological research on Man by, for instance, Marshall Cubbon,[8] James Graham-Campbell,[9] and Sir David Wilson,[10] by Steve Dickinson's report on the archaeology of Scandinavian Cumbria,[11] by Nick Higham's surveys of evidence of viking settlement in the North-West,[12] and by Richard Bailey's work on Viking Age sculpture in the North and North-West:[13] a large body of evidence distributed throughout the region, and for that reason of comparable importance to the place-name material.

When we turn to the area of written accounts of viking invasion of and settlement in the north-west of England, however, the pickings are rather slim. There is only one clear, though rather indirect, reference made to viking raids in the North-West in the Anglo-Saxon Chronicles, in the entries for 875 in all versions of the Chronicle except 'F'. There it is noted that, while wintering in Northumbria by the River Tyne, the Danish leader Healfdan and his men 'made frequent raids among the Picts and the Strathclyde Britons',[14] forays which must have taken them through parts of Cumbria and Dumfriesshire, although the chroniclers make no mention of Danes settling in that area either then or at a later date. Similarly, there is an interesting note in the eleventh-century *Historia de Sancto Cuthberto* to the effect that, some time in the early years of the tenth century, a certain Ælfred son of Brihtwulf fled east over the Pennines (presumably from Cumbria) to escape from 'pirates'.[15] Apart from scant and oblique references such as these to viking penetration of the North-West in English, Irish and Welsh annals, there are no reliable historical records of viking activity in the region. Perhaps because no wealthy monasteries with scriptoria had been established in north-west England by the tenth century, the history of the region during this period has for the most part been left unwritten. Whatever the reason, for reliable information about the Scandinavian presence in this part of Britain we must depend entirely upon non-literary sources such as the archaeological and onomastic evidence I have already mentioned.

But nature abhors a vacuum, and it is perhaps only to be expected that the less there is to say about a subject, the greater the likelihood that someone will feel compelled to say something (which goes some way toward explaining why I am writing this paper). Thus, for instance, some historians, frustrated by the lack of a detailed written account of the vikings in Lakeland, have consoled themselves by lavishing attention upon the story of the viking Hingamund recounted in the collection of Irish annals known as *The three fragments*, which mentions the expulsion of Hingamund and his troops from Ireland (apparently around the year 902), and describes their eventual settlement near Chester, where 'the Queen of the Saxons', named Edelfrida, and presumably to be identified with Æþelflæd of Mercia, is said to have granted these viking emigrés land.[16] In their zeal to illuminate a dark corner of English history, some devotees of this account are undaunted by the minor inconveniences that this event is not mentioned anywhere else[17] and that, although there may be a grain of historical truth in all this, *The three fragments* is a far from ideal historical record — a clearly modernized collection of largely legendary material based on John O'Donovan's nineteenth-century copy of a transcript made in 1643 by one Duald MacFirbis from a now lost, fragmentary manuscript, the date and provenance of which are unknown.[18]

Considerably more historians' ink has been spilt over the years in debating the historical reliability of chapters 51–54 of another late composition, the thirteenth-century Icelandic text, *Egils saga Skallagrímssonar*. This part of the saga is an account of the victory of the English king Athelstan over a combined force of Norsemen and Scots on an unidentified battlefield referred to in the saga as 'Vínheiðr'. The battle described in *Egils saga* has generally (if by sceptical historians only reluctantly) been accepted to be the same as the historical battle of Brunanburh, fought in 937 between Athelstan (accompanied by his brother Edmund), and a confederacy of Dublin Norse under Óláfr Guðfriðsson, Scots led by king Constantine II and probably Strathclyde Welsh under Eugenius (or 'Owen'). Although the account in *Egils saga* differs from what can be gleaned from English, Irish and Welsh annals, by and large it agrees with what is known of the historical battle of Brunanburh, and is striking in its narrative detail. The site of the battlefield has never been identified, although over thirty locations have been proposed.[19] I shall not rehearse the last century of speculation regarding the location of Brunanburh, and certainly have no intention of compounding the problem by proposing a favourite site of my own. However, I should like to take advantage of the fact that a good case has been made, by A. H. Smith and John Dodgson, for the identification of Brunanburh with Bromborough on the Mersey shore of the Wirral peninsula in Cheshire,[20] and use this identification as an excuse for discussing the Icelandic account of the battle in connection with the fragmentary historical record of vikings in the North-West. I wish to consider in particular various interpretations of topographic details mentioned in the description of events leading up to the battle itself, and so it will be necessary to rehearse the main points of this episode in the saga.

In the Icelandic account we are told that a Scottish king by the name of Óláfr rauði ('the red') invades England and defeats two earls whom Athelstan has set over Northumbria, Álfgeirr and Goðrekr by name. On hearing of Óláfr's success, two of Athelstan's Welsh earls, with the suspiciously Norse-looking names Hringr and Aðils,[21] desert the English king's ranks and defect to Óláfr's side with a large body of men. Faced with an overwhelming enemy force and desertion from his ranks, Athelstan asks advice of his counsellors in the field, who decide that the king himself should return south to muster reinforcements. In the meantime (however unlikely this may seem), the eponymous hero of the saga, the Icelander Egill Skallagrímsson and his brother Þórólfr are left in charge of the viking troops

they have led into service under the English king, and earl
Álfgeirr is left in command of his own troops. The English side
now devises a stratagem for stalling the enemy until the arrival
of fresh troops, although it is not clear whether this tactic has
been hit upon by the remaining English commanders or, as the
Icelandic author no doubt means to suggest, by the cunning and
resourceful Icelanders Athelstan is lucky enough to have in his
employ. At any rate, it is worth examining at least the first part
of the description of this ruse, which reads as follows:

> And when Aðalsteinn heard all this, then he held a meeting
> with his leaders and advisers, and asked what would be the
> most expedient course to take. He told the whole gathering
> in detail what he had learned of the movements of the
> Scots king and his great host ... And that plan was
> adopted, that king Aðalsteinn should return and travel
> through the south of England and bring his own levies
> north up the length of the country, because they realized
> that otherwise they would be slow in mustering as big an
> army as was needed if the king himself did not call out
> reinforcements. And the king put the chieftains Þórólfr
> and Egill in charge of the army which was already
> assembled. They were to control the company which the
> vikings had brought to the king, but Álfgeirr himself still
> had charge of his own troops ...
>
> Then they sent an envoy to king Óláfr to deliver a
> message that king Aðalsteinn wishes to 'hazel out' a
> battlefield for him, and challenge him to battle on
> Vínheiðr by Vínuskógar and that he wishes that they
> should not raid his land, and that whoever has victory in
> the battle should rule over England. He stipulated that a
> week was to elapse before they should meet in battle, but
> that whoever should arrive first should wait for his opponent
> for a week. And it was the custom then that once a field
> was 'hazelled' for a king, that he could not raid without
> dishonour before the battle was ended. King Óláfr complied
> and halted his army, did not raid, and waited for the
> appointed day. Then he moved his army to Vínheiðr. A

fort stood to the north of the heath. King Óláfr established himself there in the fort, and had the greatest part of his host there, because around it was a wide expanse of country, and to him it seemed better there for supplying provisions which the army needed to have. And he sent men of his up onto the heath where a place had been arranged for the battle. They were to select tent sites, and make ready before the rest of their army came up. But when those men came to the place where the field was hazelled, there were hazel stakes set up there over the entire area to mark off where the battle was to be. It was necessary to take care in picking out the place, so that it should be level where a great army was to assemble. Where the battle was to be it was in fact the case that there was a level heath, but on one side of it a river flowed down and on the other side of it was a great wood. But where it was the shortest distance between the wood and the river, and that was a very long space, there king Aðalsteinn's men had pitched their tents, so that they stretched the whole way between the wood and the river. They had set up their tents in such a way that there were no men in every third tent, and few in any of them at that. And when king Óláfr's men came up to them, they had a crowd of men in front of all the tents, and Óláfr's men could not go into them. Aðalsteinn's men said that all their tents were full of men, so that their troop had hardly any space there. But their tents were so high that one could not see up over them to find out whether they were many or a few rows deep. They thought that there must be a great host of men there. King Óláfr's men pitched their tents north of the hazels; and all the way to that point the land sloped downward somewhat. Aðalsteinn's men said day after day that their king was on the point of arriving or had arrived at the fort which lay to the south of the heath. Reinforcements joined them both day and night.

When the time agreed upon had elapsed, king Aðalsteinn's men send messengers to meet with king Óláfr with these words, that king Aðalsteinn is ready for battle and has an immense army, but he sends word to king Óláfr that he did not wish that they should engage in such a great slaughter as was impending. He proposed that Óláfr should rather go home to Scotland, and Aðalsteinn will give him as a pledge of friendship a silver shilling for every plough of land in his kingdom and he wishes that they would establish friendship between them. But when the messengers reach king Óláfr, he had begun to make ready his army, and intended to ride out; but when they delivered his message, the king halted his movement for that day. He sat in council, the leaders of the army with him. Men were of entirely different opinions. Some were very eager that they should accept this offer. They said that it would have turned out a most successful expedition if they returned home after receiving such a great payment from Aðalsteinn. Some held back and said that Aðalsteinn would offer much more the next time if this was not accepted; and the latter counsel was adopted. Then the messengers asked king Óláfr to grant them time to meet with king Aðalsteinn again, and find out whether he was willing to pay out more in order that there might be peace. They asked for a truce of one day for riding back, a second day for discussion, and a third for the return journey. The king granted them that.[22]

The messengers return and make Óláfr an even better offer. He demands further tribute from the English. The English envoys agree to convey this demand to Athelstan, on condition that yet another three-day truce be granted to allow time for negotiation. Óláfr agrees and sends his own messengers off to the English camp to witness a final settlement accepted by the English king, who has by now arrived with reinforcements. The story continues:

Then all the messengers ride together and meet king Aðalsteinn in the fort which was nearest the heath on the south side. King Óláfr's envoys present their message and terms for peace before king Aðalsteinn. King Aðalsteinn's men also told what offers they had made to king Óláfr and added that that had been the plan of wise men to delay the battle in this way, so long as the king had not come. And Aðalsteinn gave a quick decision in the matter, and spoke thus to the messengers: 'Take these words of mine to king Óláfr, that I will grant him permission to go home to Scotland with his army, and he may return all that property which he has seized unlawfully here in this country. Then we will establish peace between our countries, and neither shall make raids on the other. In addition, king Óláfr shall become my vassal, and hold Scotland from me and be king under me. Go back now', he says, 'and tell him that this is the way things are.'[23]

Óláfr's messengers then return to their king, who realizes too late that he has been tricked.

I am certainly not the first to note that much of this sounds more like folk-tale than fact. Sixty years ago, Lee Hollander sketched out the folk-tale structure of this episode in his article, 'The battle on the Vin-Heath and the battle of the Huns'[24] and five years later Alistair Campbell repeated Hollander's observations in the introduction to his edition of the Old English poem *The Battle of Brunanburh*.[25] They drew attention to various fictional elements in this episode of the saga, the style of which contrasts markedly with the realistic tone of much of the rest of the work. Among the stylized details in this part of the story they point to the archaic and altogether romantic motif of 'hazelling a battlefield' for an enormous army which is obliging enough to refrain from plundering and devastation for a week until terms and conditions for fighting the battle or negotiating peace have been properly settled. Equally conventional is the use made of the well-known epic device of threefold repetition — in the three requests for peace made to Óláfr and the three days' ride made by the English messengers. After the initial suggestion that Egill Skallagrímsson may be behind the stratagem employed to deceive the invaders, the Icelandic hero is nowhere mentioned in this account — as if the author has simply slotted a stock description of a battle into his narrative in order to associate the eponymous hero of the saga with a great military campaign. As Campbell points out, even when considerable chronological difficulties stand in the way, saga authors are fond of allowing celebrated Icelanders to participate in the great battles of the age — in *Njáls saga* Þorsteinn Hallsson fights at Clontarf; in *Fóstbrœðra saga* Þormóðr Bersason Kolbrúnarskáld fights at Stiklastaðir; in Snorri Sturluson's version of *Óláfs saga Tryggvasonar*, Vígfúss Vígaglúmsson fights against the Jómsvíkingar at Hjǫrungavágr.[26] It is thoroughly conventional that the sequence of events in the Vínheiðr episode is represented as a contest between a single hero, Athelstan, and a single villain, Óláfr. A similar artificial symmetry is evident in the contrast between the two faithful earls, Álfgeirr and Goðrekr, and the two treacherous Welsh defectors Hringr and Aðils. The same sort of symmetrical schematization is reflected in the conveniently placed *borg*, both north and south of the battlefield, in which the leaders of the opposing armies have their headquarters.[27] Since Hollander and Campbell drew attention to such 'unhistoric' elements in this episode, however, some historians have either ignored or dismissed their remarks in order to propose new sites for the battle; and so I should like to set some of their comments on this section of *Egils saga* against a brief re-examination of the stalling tactic described there to see whether any details in this episode can, in fact, be regarded as reliable evidence on which to base any sort of historical argument.

Typical of the most tendentious manipulation of the Icelandic account before the appearance of Hollander's article is John Henry Cockburn's commentary on the Vínheiðr episode in his book, *The battle of Brunanburh and its period elucidated by place-names*, published in 1931. It is characteristic of Cockburn's unquestioning faith in the historical reliability of the saga that he manages to deduce evidence for locating the battle-site from even the most conventional elements in the Icelandic story. He points out, for example, that since the English messengers in this episode are twice granted a three-day truce to move back and forth between the English lines and Óláfr's camp — one day to go, one to be there, and one to return — then the English camp must have been situated one day's march from Óláfr's headquarters. From little more than this simple observation Cockburn very soon locates the battlefield in West Yorkshire and reaches the abrupt conclusion that 'Olaf's head-quarters were at Castleford on the Aire. Athelstan's headquarters were at or near Aston on Riknild Street'.[28] This startling deduction is supported by a rather ingenious juggling of local names along the Roman road between Castleford and Doncaster to point up what Cockburn regards as evidence of local commemoration of the peace negotiations described in *Egils saga*, reflected, for example, in what he thinks are reminiscences of various Old English terms for the messengers mentioned in the story, preserved in surrounding place-names — terms like the rare Old English word *fricc(e)a*, 'herald, crier', which he imagines to be preserved in the name 'Frickley' (between Castleford and Doncaster), the first element of which is probably the personal name 'Frica';[29] or *boda*, 'messenger', which Cockburn sees commemorated in the West Yorkshire name 'Bodels/Bodles', a name which, according to A. H. Smith, may derive from early modern English *buddle, bothul, buddle*, 'the corn marigold'.[30] Needless to say, Cockburn's exercises in imaginative free association do little to inspire confidence. It is hardly remarkable that at one point he justifies some of his more fanciful derivations by quoting an observation made by the notorious pseudo-etymologist, Horne Tooke, to the effect that, as far as the recalcitrant spellings of certain local place-name elements are concerned, one should simply bear in mind that over time, 'letters, like soldiers in a long march', are 'very apt to desert and drop off'.[31] So much, at any rate, for the scientific value of Cockburn's methodology.

Some other commentators intent on identifying the site of Brunanburh have on the whole been undeterred by Hollander's remarks on folk-tale elements in the Vínheiðr episode of *Egils saga*. An article by O. G. S. Crawford on the site of the battle-field published in the journal *Antiquity* one year after the appearance of Hollander's article took no account whatsoever of Hollander's arguments.[32] Three years later, in the same journal, W. S. Angus likewise ignored Hollander's observations in a lengthy examination of the Vínheiðr episode entitled 'The battlefield of Brunanburh'.[33] Angus was not, at least, blithely indifferent to all previous research on this topic, however, for in his article he does pay careful attention to A. H. Smith's investigation of the onomastic evidence for modern equivalents of the Old English name *Brunanburh*.[34] As I have already mentioned, Smith demonstrated that spellings of the name of Bromborough in Wirral in charters from the early thirteenth century onwards point to an original Old English form *Brunanburh*, meaning 'Bruna's stronghold' — a connection with the form of the name in versions of the Anglo-Saxon Chronicle which has been established for no other place-name. Yet, although Smith set out convincing philological evidence that present-day Bromborough derives from Old English *Brunanburh*, the fact that the two place-names are identical does not necessarily prove that the places are the same. As John Dodgson has pointed out, although the formal identity of Bromborough and *Brunanburh* is fairly certain, 'there is a failure of place-names and field-names' at the Cheshire site 'to indicate the precise location of the battle'.[35] As far as I know, no new evidence has come forward which would support a certain identification. W. S. Angus acknowledges that the onomastic evidence in favour of Bromborough is striking; nevertheless, he ultimately rejects Bromborough as an acceptable location, preferring a Dumfriesshire site, Burnswark in Annandale near Ecclefechan[36] — a location earlier advocated by George Neilson, who based his argument on the fourteenth-century writer Fordun's description of an invading fleet landing in the Solway Firth.[37] Remarkably enough, although Angus admits that 'the philological evidence' for Burnswark, which finds a parallel only in Gaimar's name for the battlefield, *Bruneswerce*, 'is slender in comparison with that for Bromborough',[38] he rejects the Cheshire site specifically because the topography there does not agree with description of the landscape around Vínheiðr in *Egils saga* as closely as Burnswark does. In fact,

Angus goes one step further and favours a location two miles south-east of Burnswark, called Middlebie Hill (in spite of the fact that this site then loses whatever weight is to be attached to the place-name 'Burnswark'), and he does this precisely because the landscape at this location is in his opinion even closer to the topography of the battlefield in *Egils saga*. Angus argues:

> Neilson thought that Olaf and the Scots camped in the Roman earthwork immediately to the north of Burnswark hill, and Athelstan's advanced force and perhaps his whole army in that on its southern slope. If forces were so disposed, an observer on the top of the hill could count the troops camping on the lower slopes on the south side, and Egil's ruse of using more tents than his men needed would be of no avail.[39]

He continues with his description of the local topography:

> If the English wished to conceal the weakness of their advanced guard, they would seek a position visible by their enemies but not under close observation. The knoll of Middlebie hill would meet this and other tactical needs, and squares well with the story in the saga. The tents, we are told, were pitched where the heath was narrowest between wood and water, but yet a long way off from Óláf's camp. A force on Middlebie hill facing Burnswark would have on its right the gorge of the Middlebie burn, wooded perhaps then as now, and on its left the burn from Burnswark farm ... The tents of a force in this position would be on the upland, in a place which even today is not far from moorland; behind them the ground would fall away southwards to the ramparts of Birrens, a burg to which Athelstan would come if he approached by the Roman road from Carlisle. Finally, there is the ruse of the tents. The saga says that there were no men in every third tent and few in any one, and the tents stood so high, so that there was no seeing over them; and the Scots were thus misled about the strength of the English advanced force. From Burnswark hill, Birrens camp is invisible and Middlebie hill can clearly be seen. A calculation from the

contours on the map indicates that the line of vision from
Burnswark hill should skim the top of Middlebie hill and
the slopes between it and Birrens ... Burnswark hill is
conspicuous as one approaches Birrens from the
southeast, but as one drops down to the Mein Water it
sinks from view behind the trees on the rising ground
to the north of the camp, and disappears just before
one reaches the stream. Óláf's observers, therefore, if
stationed on Burnswark hill, could see tents pitched on
high ground at Middlebie hill, and could well be misled by
camouflage and propaganda about the strength of the forces
there and in Birrens camp.[40]

It is remarkable that Angus regards the Vínheiðr episode in
Egils saga as the most reliable historical source for mapping out
the battlefield at Brunanburh. Such absolute faith in the saga-
narrative as a reliable guide to the battle-site became
increasingly rare after 1938 when Alistair Campbell reiterated
Hollander's arguments against the historical reliability of the
Vínheiðr episode in the introduction to his edition of the Old
English heroic poem *The Battle of Brunanburh*. But Campbell's
denunciation of *Egils saga* as an historical source did not deter
everyone. In 1952, in the chapter on Brunanburh in his collection,
More Battlefields of England, the military historian Lt.-Colonel
Alfred Higgins Burne took issue with Campbell's dismissal of
Egils saga as a source of topographical evidence in order to use
the Vínheiðr description to support his own theory that
Brunanburh was fought on a field near the village of
Brinsworth near Rotherham in the West Riding of Yorkshire.[41]
Like others who have proposed an eastern site for the battlefield, Burne follows Florence of Worcester's statement that the
invading fleet first sailed into the Humber. But although he
rejects the historical authorities which Neilson and Angus cite
to support their identification of a west-coast battlefield, like
both of those authors Burne is quick to dismiss the philological
evidence supporting the Bromborough site as simply irrelevant,
once the local topography is tested against details in *Egils saga*.
He maintains that, 'apart from the similarity of name,

Bromborough has nothing in common either with *Egil's saga'* or with what Burne, drawing upon his experience as a military man, refers to as 'I.M.P.', or 'Inherent Military Probability'.[42] Further criticisms of the views of Campbell and Hollander were presented by Alfred P. Smyth in his book *Scandinavian York and Dublin*. Smyth draws upon details in the Vínheiðr episode to support his own thesis that Brunanburh was fought by the forest of Bromswald on the borders of Northamptonshire and Huntingdonshire.[43] Intent on tying together discrepancies in various medieval accounts of the battle, Smyth suggests that the second elements in 'Vínheiðr' and 'Vínuskógar' in the Icelandic source find identical counterparts in references to field and forest in the local names which William of Malmesbury mentions, 'Brunefeld' and 'Bruneswald'. Smyth claims to see the element *Vín*- preserved in one of the names Simeon of Durham uses for the battlefield, *Weondun*[44] (an idea proposed as long ago as 1786),[45] although, in fact, the etymology of neither name is at all certain.[46] Smyth sees a striking correspondence between William of Malmesbury's reference to 'the evenness of the green plain' which induced Athelstan to camp near Brunefeld and the emphasis in *Egils saga* on the choice of battleground at Vínheiðr, a 'level heath . . . deliberately chosen for the site of battle to accommodate large numbers of warriors'.[47] In short, Smyth rejects Campbell's representation of *Egils saga* as a completely unreliable source, and argues that the Icelandic account of Vínheiðr derives ultimately from a medieval Danelaw tradition which preserves certain accurate details.

In 1980, Campbell and Hollander were criticized once again, this time by Michael Wood in his article 'Brunanburh revisited', published in the *Saga-Book of the Viking Society*. Wood argues in favour of the Brinsworth, Yorkshire site, as Lt.-Colonel Burne had done three decades earlier, although he makes no mention of Burne's speculations. Also like Burne, Wood dismisses the onomastic evidence in favour of Bromborough in Wirral because, as he puts it, 'the geographical and political facts given by our sources do not support the identification with

Bromborough'.[48] It soon becomes apparent that 'the geographical facts' to which he refers include the topographical description of Vínheiðr in *Egils saga*. Although the main focus of Wood's argument is a presentation of his own ideas of what constituted the political background of the battle, and although he acknowledges that Hollander and Campbell have made 'forcible objections to the acceptance of traditions such as that in *Egils saga*',[49] Wood refuses to leave topographical details in the saga out of the account. Wood's comparison of landmarks at his favoured location with the description of local geography in the saga reflects much of the same faith in the reliability of topographical detail in the Icelandic source expressed by the earliest commentators on the Vínheiðr episode. He draws attention to what he describes as 'the striking correspondence between the Brinsworth site and the famous description of Vínheiðr . . . with its forts north and south of the field, its gentle slopes north and south, the steep slope to the river, and the narrow gap to the south where the river and the forest come close together'.[50]

Behind all of these studies mentioned so far, from Neilsen's at the turn of the century until Wood's in 1980 (and this is only a small sample of available commentary), lies an assumption that literary accounts such as the Vínheiðr episode can be used as reliable touchstones for the location of a place referred to in more reliable historical sources. W. S. Angus clearly regarded his use of *Egils saga* as scientific. Although he takes no account of Hollander's arguments, he does at least consider onomastic evidence, and even devotes some attention to chronological defects in the narrative of *Egils saga*, as well as other obvious difficulties such as the conflation of Constantine, king of the Scots and Óláfr Guðfriðsson into one character, Óláfr the red of Scotland.[51] However, corruptions such as this do little to shake Angus's faith in the reliability of the topographical description, which he counts as ultimately the most important evidence to consider. He argues that at any proposed site for Brunanburh, 'the battlefield should supply the features which the account in *Egils saga* requires'.[52] And it is on this basis alone that the

Cheshire site is rejected. Angus notes: 'There is an earthwork at Bromborough, but the game of fitting Egil's account to the locality does not promise success.'[53] Burne is of much the same opinion, and in fact meets Campbell and Hollander's objections head-on. He allows that *Egils saga* in general and this episode in particular may be full of errors and confusions, but seizes upon the fact that Campbell admits that 'the main outline . . . of the tradition of the battle on Vínheithr . . . may be safely assumed to refer to the battle of Brunanburh'.[54] Burne responds: 'This as a matter of fact provides us with all that we require, namely that, mingled with the myths and fantasies of the Saga, are some historical facts. The problem then is to sift the good grain from the chaff.'[55] Part of the 'good grain', he continues, are details gleaned from description of the landscape. Burne outlines his method of dealing with this material: 'Where the saga makes statements of a topographical nature for which there can be no motives for falsification I accept their essential accuracy, though allowing that slight exaggeration and errors of detail may well be present.'[56] Smyth and Wood operate under the same assumption, that since the author of *Egils saga* would have no motive for falsifying topographical details in his narrative, such details can therefore be regarded as by and large factual.

It is worth considering just what motives the saga author might have for describing the landscape as he does in this episode, and to do this it is instructive to turn once again to the passage which contains this topographical description, the story of the stratagem itself. The first thing to be noted about this *ruse de guerre* is that it involves two forms of deception — first, the presentation of a sham army and second, the use of protracted peace negotiations as a stalling tactic. The second of these stratagems is commonly referred to in military histories and military manuals. For example, the tenth-century tactical manual of Leo VI of Byzantium recommends lulling the enemy into a false sense of security through insincere peace negotiations which should give way to a sudden attack upon the other side once one is certain to catch one's opponents off guard.[57] Similarly, the Roman tactician Sextus Julius Frontinus recalls how Hannibal's brother Hasdrubal made successful use of quibbling negotiations with the Roman general Claudius Nero to distract the enemy's attention from surreptitious troop movements; and Livy recounts the same story at greater length in Book 26 of *Ab urbe condita*.[58] In her popular synthesis of ancient military manuals, *Le livre des faites d'armes et de chevalerie*, Christine de Pisan recommends that drawn-out peace talks be used precisely as they are described in *Egils saga* to deceive the enemy into allowing sufficient time for reinforcements to be mustered. William Caxton renders the relevant passage as follows:

> For yf thou canst parceyue that men holde and kepe the in talkyng as by a long trayne fyndyng alwayes som con-trouersies that nede not / But onely for to passe tyme / Knowe thou for verray certayn that al is but for a deceyte and for a delaye of the bataylle waytyng for som socours and helpe / or ellys by cause that in the meane whyle thy prouysions and stores be wasted awaye / And that thy folke be noyouse and wery of the long soiourne.[59]

Without question, for as long as battles have been fought, military commanders have commonly resorted to stalling tactics of various kinds to regroup or to avoid immediate defeat.[60] But it is not surprising to see the same sort of imaginative ruses deployed by authors of purely fictional narratives. Consider, for example, the same stratagem described in one purely literary text, the late fifteenth-century Icelandic romance *Villifers saga frœkna*. In chapter nine of the saga, Angantýr of Saxony, who has already murdered the son of king Halfdan of Holmgarðr (Novgorod), now impudently arrives with a large army to make off with Halfdan's daughter. Halfdan engages in sham peace negotiations in order to buy sufficient time to muster secretly a force of 20,000 men and launch a pre-emptive attack on his enemy:

> All of the king's sons rose from their seats and told Angantýr that that message should be sent back to

Holmgarðr, that Angantýr and his men should all be killed. Geir said that they should immediately go to war against the king. However, the king was short of troops. And when Vébjörn heard this, he submitted to the king and said that it was altogether ill-advised to fight against Angantýr with such a small force, and advised that it was better for him not to refuse their petition immediately, but rather to request a week's respite in order to take counsel with his trusted advisers, 'and in that time it will be easy to assemble sufficient troops'. The king accepted this advice, and requested a delay of one week to respond to the marriage proposal. The brothers returned to their tents and told Angantýr the king's answer, and added that the king must be utterly terrified, and that he did not dare to fight. Angantýr sent a message back to the city to inform the king that he should have his delay, and he received that news well. Now, as for the earl's plans, it can be reported that he had a war-arrow sent secretly throughout the entire country (with a summons that) the troops should be mustered into the city at nights, so that Angantýr's camp would remain unaware that the king was mustering troops. And the king sent Angantýr gifts of friendship, and said that they might very well be able to reach a settlement over the killing of Haraldr. And Angantýr believed these friendly messages from the king. Many men now flocked to the king, and in all 20,000 men assembled to support him. And when the respite which Angantýr had granted the king had expired, the king sent him a message and said that there were not going to be any settlements, but challenged him to battle the next morning. Angantýr now saw that he had been duped, and that the king's gifts of friendship had been sent to make him drop his guard.[61]

The ploy described in this passage is by no means unique as a literary device. It is, in fact, identified as a folk-tale type, number K 2369.7 ('shammed discussing of peace while getting reinforcements') in Inger Boberg's *Motif-index of early Icelandic literature*.[62]

Hollander points out an intriguing parallel in the Eddaic fragment 'The battle of the Goths and Huns' in the thirteenth-century heroic tale, *Hervarar saga ok Heiðreks*, where the Goths use both protracted negotiations and the same device described in *Egils saga* of calling a truce to mark off a battlefield with hazel branches in order to stall for time against an invading army of Huns.[63] We are told that:

> This was the law of king Heiðrekr, that if an (enemy) army was in the country, and the king of the country 'hazelled' a battlefield and designated a place for battle, then the vikings were obliged not to make raids before the battle was decided.[64]

As we have already seen, the stalling device described in *Egils saga* is dependent upon another deception which has a more direct bearing on the topographical description of Vínheiðr, the presentation of a sham army. Once again, various similar stratagems are described in both 'historical' texts and those commonly regarded as more 'purely literary'. Frontinus, for example, mentions that the Persian commander Cyrus tied wooden mannequins dressed like soldiers to masts in order to dupe his enemies into believing that a hill was occupied by his troops.[65] The same device is described in literary works, for example, in the twelfth-century chanson de geste, *Ogier le Danois*.[66] Frontinus likewise notes that Spartacus cunningly set up corpses armed with weapons to look like sentries,[67] and this latter ruse crops up again in literary contexts such as Saxo Grammaticus' *Gesta Danorum*,[68] in the Anglo-Norman *Lai de Havelock*,[69] once again, in the thirteenth-century Provençal chronicle *Philomena*,[70] and it is not surprising to see it resurface in modern works of fiction such as Alexandre Dumas' *The three musketeers*.[71] Various similar deceptions are listed as folk-tale types in Stith Thompson's *Motif-index*. Folk-tale type K 548 records escape by making attackers believe there are many defenders of a fortified place.[72] Type K 2368 covers accounts of an enemy deceived into overestimating an opponent's strength.[73] And type K 1837.6 offers the instance of women garbed as soldiers, marching repeatedly round a place in order to deceive the enemy into thinking they are watching a large army on parade[74] — a ruse described as a genuine military tactic at least as far back as the fourth century B.C., when the Greek historian Aeneas Tacticus reported it as a stratagem used successfully by the people of Sinope in their war against the Persian satrap Datames.[75]

Ancient military historians, Aeneas Tacticus, Vegetius, Frontinus, Polyaenus, Livy, Procopius, and Leo the tactician, to name but a few, describe a great variety of methods for making a small army appear numerous to the enemy — by parading patrolmen at a distance with two spears on their shoulder instead of one, so that their numbers might appear to double;[76] by ordering cavalry, pack horses and infantrymen to march in the distance in such a way as to raise as much dust as a much larger army might be expected to do;[77] or even by simply sounding as many horns as one would expect a large army to have.[78] Commentators are usually prepared to regard ancient descriptions of deceptions of this sort as historically accurate, although it is generally agreed that all the authors mentioned copy from earlier compilations and are not unwilling to include in their collections folktales about the exploits of their favourite generals, Alexander, Hannibal, or Julius Caesar. Certainly, similar ruses are found in the pages of popular military fiction, from C. S. Forester's Hornblower series to Vladimir Peniakoff's tales of Popski's Private Army. In spite of so many general analogues to choose from, however, I have to admit that I have not been able to discover a precise parallel for the tent trick described in *Egils saga* in any source ancient or modern.[79] It is, however, not terribly difficult to adduce literary analogues which parallel roughly the deception said to have been used at Vínheiðr.

One such account is available in Paul the Deacon's *History of the Lombards* in which, more or less as in *Egils saga*, the only available troops of the outnumbered Lombard army are each day paraded before Avar ambassadors in different dress and armed differently to convince the enemy envoys that new troops are constantly arriving, and that the inadequate Lombard host is immense.[80] Another, perhaps more interesting, example is available in an account by the Jewish general and historian, Josephus, of his own clever device for suppressing a revolt in the city of Tiberias during the Jewish war against Rome in 66 AD. Josephus finds himself with virtually no troops to put down this rising, for he has sent most of his soldiers out to forage for supplies. Nevertheless, he proceeds to Tiberias with all the boats he can muster, 230 in all, but each manned with a skeleton crew of no more than four sailors aboard each vessel. Having dismayed the rebel port with the sudden appearance of his sham fleet, Josephus comes forward with a fully manned launch and convinces the disheartened rebels to send out delegations to negotiate a peace. By inventing one pretext after another, Josephus conveys group after unsuspecting group out to the awaiting boats where they are promptly whisked back to Tarichaeae to be clapped in irons. In this way, 600 rebel senators and 2,000 private citizens are arrested and the entire insurgent population subdued by no more than a tiny force.[81] In his translation of this passage, William Whiston felt compelled to note: 'I cannot but think this stratagem of Josephus . . . to be one of the finest that ever was invented and executed by any warrior whatsoever.'[82] Not all historians, however, have accepted Josephus' descriptions of his own military genius as unadulterated fact. Raymond R. Newell, for example, has cautioned that 'recent studies have shown that Josephus often draws on stock historiographic phrases, motifs, and forms appropriate to the type of history he is writing at the time'.[83] Adolf Stender-Petersen has demonstrated that, particularly when describing military manoeuvres, Josephus is happy to include in his narrative anecdotes drawn from earlier sources, which he recounts as if he is describing actual historical events.[84] Like any good story-teller, however, Josephus is careful to include a detail which makes his rather fantastic stratagem of the sham fleet sound at least a little more plausible, for he points out that he kept all but one of his 230 ships 'far enough from the town to prevent the inhabitants from detecting that his ships were unmanned'.[85]

The author of *Egils saga* unfolds his account of the Vínheiðr stratagem in a manner reminiscent of this ruse-story in Josephus, but the Icelandic author is more subtle in his manipulation of incidental details. It is often noted that the cultivation of a characteristic tone of objectivity in Old Icelandic saga-narrative 'demands a highly developed sense of proportion controlling the selection of material'.[86] It is typical of the spare economy of this literary form that even apparently inconsequential details in saga-narrative tend to reveal themselves ultimately as crucial story-elements. Interestingly, the details in the Vínheiðr episode which modern historians have scrutinized for information about the battle site, while incidental to an account of the battle itself, are an integral part of the story of the ruse to buy time. If we look again at the account of the preparation for battle in *Egils saga*, we read that Athelstan's men take care to pick out a place 'where a great army' can 'be drawn up' and make sure that they have pitched their tents before Óláfr's troops arrive. Then we are told:

> Where the battle was to be it was in fact the case that there was a level heath, but on one side of it a river flowed down and on the other side of it was a great wood. But where it was the shortest distance between the wood and the river, and that was a very long space, there king Aðalsteinn's men had pitched their tents, so that they stretched the whole way between the wood and the river.[87]

In addition to the information that the English tents 'were so high that no one could see over them to find out whether they were many or a few rows deep' we are told that king Óláfr's men were forced to pitch their tents 'north of the hazels; and all the way to that point the land sloped downward somewhat'. Clearly the English tents are pitched where they are, on higher ground and between two natural boundaries, to keep the enemy from seeing round them or getting close enough to see through the deception.[88] In his deployment of these details it is the narrator who emerges as the clever strategist, for each scrap of topographical description is included not to identify the site, but in order to make the tent-ruse story work. Indeed, while it is hard to imagine how incidental topographical details of the battle-site could have survived through centuries of oral transmission when so many other details concerning the battle of Brunanburh have been completely garbled in *Egils saga*, it is quite easy to see how, as a very necessary part of the account of a stock stratagem, such details would be handed down as an integral part of the story.

It is not at all unusual for ruse-stories of this kind to attach themselves to accounts of distinguished generals in medieval historiography, whether from Iceland or elsewhere.[89] One might compare Snorri Sturluson's description of a trick supposedly used by Haraldr Harðráði Sigurðsson, of firing an impregnable fortress in Sicily by tying flaming brands to the backs of birds from the besieged citadel and sending them flying home to their nests, thereby setting fire to the rooftops of the enemy enclosure.[90] In fact, use of precisely the same fantastic stratagem is described in a wide variety of historical and not-so-historical sources and attributed to a long parade of different tacticians.[91] Saxo Grammaticus describes the same ruse used once by the Danish king Hadding Gramsson and again by Fridleif the Swift.[92] The *Russian Primary Chronicle* recounts how queen Olga captured the fortified city of Izkorostén in the same way.[93] Various British chronicles, the Welsh *Brut Tysilio*, Wace's *Roman de Brut*, Layamon's *Brut* and Giraldus Cambrensis' *Topographia Hibernica*, for example, describe how the same trick enabled the Dane Gormund to take the English city of Cirencester.[94] And if one is not too fussy about the sort of animals employed, the story can be shown to be, in fact, extremely old. Judges xv 4–5 describes Samson using flaming foxes in much the same way against the Philistines.

The main point to be borne in mind here is that before using any work, or passage in a work, for historical study it is important to ascertain the nature of the text in question and to remain alert to the different motives and focus of literary and historical sources. Some years ago, J. B. Bessinger drew attention to the difficulties inherent in using the Old English poem, *The battle of Maldon*, as a handy topographical guide for locating the site of that battlefield. He cautions:

> No map is needed to follow Byrhtnoth's last fight, or his contemporary Olaf's, or before them, Beowulf's, or after them Roland's. Indeed the attempted use of a map might trick the modern imagination into the fallacy of misplaced concreteness, since heroic poets composed without benefit of a cartographical sense that is second nature for a reader today. The bare literary topogaphy along the Pant, at Swold, on a headland near Hronesness, or at Roncesvalles is enough to serve as a setting for a traditional story . . . treating a stock theme . . . about characters shaped through tradition by bearing sometimes historical names and using traditional verse forms. [95]

In his contribution to the Maldon conference, John Dodgson quoted Bessinger's comments and responded: 'True, very nearly quite true, if one ignores the lively cartographical sense and topographical sensitivity that Anglo-Saxons often demonstrate, as in their land charters.'[96] But here it is important to bear in mind that 'charter evidence' is a very far cry from the stock formulas of Old English heroic poetry or from the narrative conventions of a literary work like *Egils saga* which, to use another phrase from Bessinger, 'deals with history without caring about history'.[97] Macaulay describes history as 'a compound of poetry and philosophy', 'a province of literature' partitioned by two hostile powers, 'imagination and reason'.[98] Furnished with a set of charter bounds, one may very well approach the business of locating an ancient site in the field with at least a reasonable hope of success; setting off to find Brunanburh equipped only with a copy of *Egils saga* offers prospects of little more than a pleasant walk and a good read. If six decades ago Alistair Campbell was too pessimistic in maintaining that, since the saga is unreliable, 'all hope of localising Brunanburh is lost',[99] he was at least correct in emphasizing that, if the battlefield is ever to be found, clues to its location will have to be provided by onomastic or, if it were possible, archaeological evidence,[100] rather than by details in a purely literary source like *Egils saga*.*

Acknowledgements

I am grateful to Roberta Frank, Richard Perkins and George Story for advice about various points in this paper.

* For reasons of space extensive quotations from primary sources in the original languages have been omitted.

References

1 See W. F. H. Nicolaisen, 'Norse place-names in south-west Scotland', *Scottish Studies*, 4 (1960), pp.49–70.

2 See W. H. Pearsall, 'Place-names as clues in the pursuit of ecological history', *Namn och Bygd*, 49 (1961), pp.72–89.

3 See M. Gelling, 'The place-names of the Isle of Man', *Journal of the Manx Museum*, 7 (1970–71), pp.130–9, 168–75; *idem*, 'Norse and Gaelic in medieval Man: the place-name evidence', in P. Davey, ed., *Man and environment in the Isle of Man* (*British Archaeological Reports, British series*, LIV,2), Oxford, 1978, pp.251–64; also printed in Th. Andersson and K. I. Sandred, eds, *The vikings*, Uppsala, 1978, pp.107–18; B. Megaw, 'Norsemen and native in the kingdom of the Isles: a reassessment of the Manx evidence', *Scottish Studies*, 20 (1976), pp.1–44; reprinted in P. Davey, *Man and environment*, pp.265–314.

4 See J. McN. Dodgson, *The place-names of Cheshire*, parts 1–5 (*EPNS*, XLIV–XLVIII), Cambridge, 1970–81; *idem*, 'The English arrival in Cheshire', *Transactions of the Historic Society of Lancashire and Cheshire*, 119 (1967), pp.1–37; *idem*, 'Place-names and street-names at Chester', *Journal of the Chester Archaeological Society*, 55 (1968), pp.29–61.

5 M. Richards, 'Norse place-names in Wales', *Proceedings of the First International Congress of Celtic Studies, held in Dublin, 6–10 July, 1959*, Dublin, 1962, pp.51–60.

6 See G. Fellows-Jensen, *Scandinavian settlement names in the North-West*, Copenhagen, 1985. See also *idem*, 'The vikings in England: a review', *Anglo-Saxon England*, 4 (1975), pp.181–206; *idem*, 'The Manx place-name debate: a view from Copenhagen', in P. Davey, *Man and environment*, pp.315–8; and G. Fellows-Jensen, 'The Scandinavian settlement in Cumbria and Dumfriesshire: the place-name evidence', in J. R. Baldwin and I. D. Whyte, eds, *The Scandinavians in Cumbria*, Edinburgh, 1985, pp.65–82.

7 See R. I. Page, 'Some thoughts on Manx runes', *Saga-Book of the Viking Society*, 20 (1978–81), pp.179–99; *idem*, 'More thoughts on Manx runes', *Michigan Germanic Studies*, 7 (1981), pp.129–36; *idem*, 'The Manx rune-stones', in C. Fell, P. G. Foote, J. Graham-Campbell and R. Thomson, eds, *The Viking Age in the Isle of Man*, London, 1983, pp.133–46.

8 See M. Cubbon, 'The archaeology of the vikings in the Isle of Man', ibid., pp.13–26.

9 See J. Graham-Campbell, 'The Viking-Age silver hoards of the Isle of Man', ibid., pp.53–80.

10 See, e.g., D. Wilson, *The Viking Age in the Isle of Man: the archaeological evidence*, Odense, 1974; G. Bersu and D. Wilson, *Three viking graves in the Isle of Man* (The Society for Medieval Archaeology Monograph Series, I), London, 1966; D. Wilson, 'Manx memorial stones of the viking period', *Saga-Book of the Viking Society*, 18 (1970–73), pp.1–18.

11 See S. Dickinson, 'Bryant's Gill, Kentmere: another "viking-period" Ribblehead?', in J. R. Baldwin and I. D. Whyte, *Scandinavians in Cumbria*, pp.83–8.

12 See, for example, N. J. Higham, 'The Scandinavians in north Cumbria', ibid., pp.37–52; *idem*, *The northern counties to AD 1000*, New York/London, 1986, esp. pp.316–35.

13 See, for example, R. N. Bailey, *Viking Age sculpture in northern England*, London, 1980; *idem*, 'Aspects of Viking-Age sculpture in Cumbria', in J. R. Baldwin and I. D. Whyte, *Scandinavians in Cumbria*, pp.53–63. *Cf.* D. Wilson, 'The art of the Manx crosses of the Viking age', in C. Fell *et al.*, *Viking Age in the Isle of Man*, pp.175–87.

14 *Anglo-Saxon Chronicle*: A [*cf.* B,C,D,E] s.a. 875, in C. Plummer and J. Earle, eds, *Two of the Saxon Chronicles parallel*, vol. I, Oxford, 1892; repr. 1965, pp.73–4: *Healfdene for mid sumum þam here on Norðan hymbre ... & se here ... oft hergade on Peohtas & on Stræcled Walas.*

15 See *Historia de Sancto Cuthberto* in T. Arnold, ed., *Symeonis Monachi Opera Omnia*, vol. I, London, 1882, p.208, § 22: *His diebus Elfred filius Birihtulfinci, fugiens piratas, venit ultra montes versus occidentem*; transl. in D. Whitelock, ed., *English historical documents c.500–1042*, vol. I, 2nd edn, London, 1979, p.287. The passage has been much discussed; see, for example, F. M. Stenton, 'Pre-Conquest Westmorland', *Westmorland (Royal Commission on Historical Monuments)*, London, 1936, p.xlix, repr. in *idem*, *Preparatory to Anglo-Saxon England*, Oxford, 1970, pp.215–6; R. N. Bailey, *Viking age sculpture*, pp.35, 80; C. D. Morris, 'Viking and native in northern England: a case-study', *Proceedings of the Eighth Viking Congress*, Odense, 1981, pp.223–4; G. Fellows-Jensen, *Scandinavian settlement names*, pp.2–3.

16 See J. O'Donovan, ed., *Annals of Ireland: three fragments copied from ancient sources by Dubhaltach Mac Firbisigh*, Dublin, 1860, pp.224–37. Compare the translation by I. L. Foster in F. T. Wainwright, *Scandinavian England*, ed. H. P. R. Finberg, Chichester, 1975, pp.79–83, and discussion by F. T. Wainwright, 'Ingimund's invasion', *English Historical Review*, 63 (1948), pp.145–69, in *idem*, *Scandinavian England*, pp.131–61, *cf.* pp.78–87. This episode in *The Three Fragments* is dated to the year 902 by comparison with the *Annals of Ulster*, which mention under this date, 'Expulsion of Gentiles from Ireland, i.e. [from] the fortress of Ath-Cliath'. See W. M. Hennessy, ed., *Annals of Ulster*, vol. I, Dublin, 1887, pp.416–7. The story has been frequently rehearsed. See, for example, J. McN. Dodgson, 'The background of Brunanburh', *Saga-Book of the Viking Society*, 14 (1953–57), pp.304–6; A. P. Smyth, *Scandinavian York and Dublin*, vol. I, Dublin, 1975, pp.61–2, 76; J. N. Radner, *Fragmentary annals of Ireland*, Dublin, 1978, pp.166–73, 206–7; R. N. Bailey, *Viking age sculpture*, pp.35–6, 216; G. Fellows-Jensen, *Scandinavian settlement names*, pp.1–2.

17 The *Annales Cambriae* record under the year 902: *Igmunt in insula món uenit. et tenuit maes osmeliavn.* See E. Phillimore, ed., 'The *Annales Cambriae* and Old-Welsh genealogies from Harleian MS. 3859', *Y Cymmrodor*, 9 (1888), p.167; *cf.* J. Williams ab Ithel, ed., *Annales Cambriae*, London, 1860, p.16. The Welsh chronicle *Brut y Tywysogyon* likewise mentions the arrival of a certain Igmund (Jgmwnd) in Anglesey and his role in a battle fought at 'Maes Rhosmeilon' (apparently an error for Osmeilon = Ostfeil[i]on, near Llanfaes in Anglesey). See T. Jones, ed., *Brut y Tywysogyon or the Chronicle of Princes: Red Book of Hergerst version*, Cardiff, 1955, pp.10–1, s.a. 900–3, and n. ad loc., 277. It is usually assumed that this figure is the same Hingamund whose adventures in Cheshire are described in such detail in *The Three fragments*. See, for example, F. T. Wainwright, *Scandinavian England*, p.140, nn.2–3.

18 To be fair, Wainwright, at least, does discuss at great length the myriad reasons for doubting the historical reliability of *The Three fragments*: see *Scandinavian England*, pp.78–9, 137–9, 146–8. He is, however, convinced that the basic facts of the story are corroborated by the appearance of the similar name Igmunt/Jgmwnd in Welsh sources.

19 See, for example, the sample list of proposed battle sites compiled by J. H. Cockburn, *The battle of Brunanburh and its period elucidated by place-names*, Sheffield/London, 1931, pp.40–8, A. Campbell, *Battle of Brunanburh*, London, 1938, pp.58–9, n.4; *cf.* K. Weimann, 'Battle of Brunanburh', in *Reallexicon der germanischen Altertumskunde*, vol. II, 2nd edn, Berlin, 1976, pp.92–3.

20 See A. H. Smith, 'The site of the battle of Brunanburh', in R. W. Chambers, F. Norman and A. H. Smith, eds, *London Mediaeval Studies*, vol. I, London,

1937, pp.56–9; J. McN. Dodgson, 'Background of Brunanburh', pp.303–16; and *idem, Place-names of Cheshire*, pt 4, pp.237–40. A. Campbell (*Battle of Brunanburh*, p.58, n.4), points out that the Bromborough site had been identified with Brunanburh as long ago as 1692, when Edmund Gibson drew attention to the similar place-name *Brunburh* in Cheshire in the index of places in his conflated edition of the Anglo-Saxon Chronicle, *Chronicon Saxonicum*. Bromborough in Cheshire was again proposed as the likely location of Brunanburh in a note published by R. F. Weymouth, *The Athenaeum* (15 August, 1885), p.207.

21 It should be noted, however, that at least the second of these names, in the form *Apisl*, appears in a Manx runic inscription, Kirk Michael III. See remarks by R. I. Page, 'A tale of two cities', *Peritia*, 1, 1982, pp.346–7; *cf. idem*, 'Manx rune stones', pp.137–8.

22 Nordal Sigurður, ed., *Egils saga Skallagrímssonar* (Íslenzk Fornrit, II), Reykjavík, 1933, ch.52, pp.130–4.

23 Ibid, pp.134–5.

24 See L. Hollander, 'The battle on the Vin-heath and the battle of the Huns', *Journal of English and Germanic Philology*, 32 (1933), pp.33–43.

25 See A. Campbell, *Battle of Brunanburh*, pp.68–80.

26 Ibid., p.73, n.1. See Einar Ól. Sveinsson, *Brennu-Njáls saga*, (Íslenzk Fornrit, XII), Reykjavík, 1954, ch.157, pp.448, 451; *Fóstbrœðra saga*, ch. 24, in Björn K. Þórólfson and Guðni Jónsson, eds, *Vestfirðinga sǫgur* (Íslenzk Fornrit, VI), Reykjavík, 1943, pp.261–76; Bjarni Aðalbjarnarson, ed., *Snorri Sturluson, Óláfs saga Tryggvasonar*, ch. 41, in *Heimskringla*, vol. I (Íslenzk Fornrit, XXVI), Reykjavík, 1941, p.283. Campbell's note that the Icelandic hero at Clontarf is Flosi Þórðarson is incorrect.

27 In connection with the artificial symmetry evident in various details in this episode of *Egils saga* it is worth noting Northrop Frye's observation that 'symmetry, in any narrative, always means that historical content is being subordinated to mythical demands of design and form, as in the Book of Judges': Frye, *The great code*, New York, 1986, p.43. *Cf.* discussion of Frye's remarks by Robert Cook, 'Russian history, Icelandic story, and Byzantine strategy in Eymundar þáttr Hringssonar', *Viator*, 17 (1986), p.71.

28 J. H. Cockburn, *Battle of Brunanburh*, p.178.

29 See ibid., p.251. A. H. Smith remarks on the name 'Frickley': 'The first el. is probably an OE pers. n. *Frica* . . .; this can hardly be from rare OE *Fricca, friccea* "herald", but it may well be formed, as Ekwall . . . has suggested, from OE *frec* "greedy, eager" which has a by-form *Fric* (*cf.* also related OE words *Frician* [*sic*, for *friclan*] "to desire", *friclo* "appetite").' See A. H. Smith, *The Place-names of the West Riding of*

Yorkshire, vol. I (*EPNS*, XXX), Cambridge, 1961, pp.89–90; *cf.* E. Ekwall, *The Concise Oxford Dictionary of English Place-names*, 4th edn, Oxford, 1960, p.187, s.v. 'Frickley'.

30 See J. H. Cockburn, *Battle of Brunanburh*, p.251, and A. H. Smith, *Place-names of the West Riding of Yorkshire*, vol. I, p.66. The etymology is uncertain. Smith's explanation of the name, based only upon late forms, is conjectural.

31 Horne Tooke, quoted in J. H. Cockburn, *Battle of Brunanburh*, p.175.

32 See O. G. S. Crawford, 'The battle of Brunanburh', *Antiquity*, 8 (1934), pp.338–9.

33 See W. S. Angus, 'The Battlefield of Brunanburh', *Antiquity*, 11 (1937), pp.283–93.

34 See A. H. Smith, 'Site of the battle of Brunanburh', pp.56–9.

35 J.McN. Dodgson, 'The site of the battle of Maldon', in D. Scragg, ed., *The battle of Maldon, AD 991*, Oxford, 1991, p.179. *Cf.* J. McN. Dodgson 'Background of Brunanburh', p.303; *idem*, *Place-names of Cheshire*, pt 4, pp.238–40; A. Campbell, *Battle of Brunanburh*, p.59n.

36 See Angus, 'Battlefield of Brunanburh', pp.284–85, 293.

37 See G. Neilson, 'Brunanburh and Burnswork', *Scottish Historical Review*, 7 (1909), pp.37–9. Burnswark was first proposed as a likely site for the battle in an article by T. Hodgkin in *Athenaeum* (22 August, 1885), p.239; noted in A. Campbell, *Battle of Brunanburh*, p.59n.

38 W. S. Angus, 'Battlefield of Brunanburh', p.289.

39 Ibid., p.291.

40 Ibid., pp.292–3.

41 See A. H. Burne, *More battlefields of England*, London, 1952, pp.44–60.

42 Ibid., p.55.

43 See A. P. Smyth, *Scandinavian York and Dublin*, vol. II, Dublin, 1979, pp.51, 72–7.

44 Ibid., pp.74, 86–7 n.49. See Simeon of Durham, *Historia Dunelmensis Ecclesiae*, II, xviii: *apud Weondune*; and *Historia Regum*, § 83: *apud Wendune*, in T. Arnold, *Symeonis Monachi*, vol. I, p.76 and vol. II, p.93.

45 See J. Johnstone, *Antiquitates Celto-Scandicae*, Copenhagen, 1786, p.56; noted in A. Campbell, *Battle of Brunanburh*, p.68, n.2.

46 On the uncertain etymology of *Weondun/Wendun*, see, for example, A. Campbell, *Battle of Brunanburh*, p.62, n.2, and p.73; E. Ekwall, *Concise Oxford Dictionary of English Place-names*, p.507, s.v. *weoh*; F. M. Stenton, Anglo-Saxon heathenism', *Transactions of the Royal Historical Society*, 4th series, 23 (1941), pp.1ff., reprinted in *idem, Preparatory to Anglo-Saxon*

England, p.291; M. Gelling, 'Further thoughts on pagan place-names', in F. Sandgren, ed., *Otium et negotium: studies in onomatology and library science presented to Olof von Feilitzen*, Stockholm, 1973, p.114; and M. Wood, 'Brunanburh revisited', *Saga-Book of the Viking Society*, 20 (1978–81), pp.212–3.

47   A. P. Smyth, *Scandinavian York and Dublin*, vol.II, p.73; *cf.* pp.75–6.

48   M. Wood, 'Brunanburh revisited', p.213, n.4.

49   Ibid., p.216, n.68.

50   Ibid.

51   See W. S. Angus, 'Battlefield of Brunanburh', pp.287–8.

52   Ibid., p.289.

53   Ibid.

54   A. Campbell, *Battle of Brunanburh*, p.70; cited in A. H. Burne, *More battlefields*, p.52.

55   Ibid., p.52.

56   Ibid.

57   See Leo VI, *Tactica*, Constitutio XVII.7, in *MPG*, CVII, Paris, 1863, 915A. *Cf.* discussion in C. Oman, *A history of the art of war*, London, 1898, pp.200–1.

58   See Frontinus, *Strategemata* I.v.19, in M. B. McElwain, ed. and C. E. Bennett, transl., *Frontinus: the stratagems and the aqueducts of Rome*, London, 1925, pp.46–7. *Cf.* Livy, *Ab urbe condita*, xxvi, 17, in F. G. Moore, ed., *Livy* (Loeb Classical Library edn), vol. VII, London, 1943, pp.64–9.

59   A. T. P. Byles, ed., *The book of fayttes of armes and of chyualrye from the French original by Christine de Pisan* (*EETS*, original series, CLXXXIX), London, 1932, I, xx, p.71. The same delaying tactic is described by Anna Comnena, *Alexiad* X.4, in E. A. S. Dawes, ed., *The Alexiad of the Princess Anna Comnena*, London, 1928, p.246. The eleventh-century Byzantine strategist Kekaumenos warns that generals must be on guard against just this sort of ruse. See Kekaumenos, *Strategikon*, ch.31 in Hans-Georg Beck, ed., *Vademecum des byzantinischen Aristokraten. Das sogenannte Strategikon des Kekaumenos*, Graz, 1956, p.37.

60   On the ancient attitude toward trickery in warfare, see E. L. Wheeler, *Stratagem and the vocabulary of military trickery* (Mnemosyne: bibliotheca classica batava, supplementa CVIII), Leiden, 1988.

61   Einar Þórðarson, ed., *Sagan af Villifer frækna*, Reykjavík, 1885, chs.9–10, pp.17–8.

62   See I. M. Boberg, *Motif-index of early Icelandic literature* (Bibliotheca Arnamagnæana, XXVII), Copenhagen, 1966, p.187.

63 See L. Hollander, 'Vin-heath and Huns', pp.38-9.

64 Guðni Jónsson and G. Turville-Petre, eds, *Hervarar saga ok Heiðreks*, London, 1956, ch.13, p.63: 'þat váru lög Heiðreks konungs, ef herr var í landi, en landskonungr haslaði völl ok lagði orrostustað, þá skyldu víkingar ekki herja, áðr orrosta væri reynd.'

65 See Frontinus, *Strategemata* III, viii, 3, in M. B. McElwain and C. E. Bennett, *Frontinus: the stratagems*, pp.230-1.

66 See *Ogier le Danois*, lines 8330-442, in Mario Eusebi, ed., *La chevalerie d'Ogier de Danemarche*, Milan/Varese, 1963, pp.341-5.

67 See Frontinus, *Strategemata* I.v.22, in M. B. McElwain and C. E. Bennett, *Frontinus: the stratagems*, pp.48-9.

68 *Cf.* J. Olrik and H. Raeder, eds, *Saxo Grammaticus, Gesta Danorum*, IV.i.20, Copenhagen, 1931-57, I, p.91; *cf.* P. Fisher and H. Ellis Davidson, eds, *Saxo Grammaticus: history of the Danes*, Cambridge, 1979-80, vol. I, p.100. *Cf.* J. Olrik and H. Raeder, *Gesta*, I.iv.11, I, p.17; P. Fisher and H. Ellis Davidson, *History*, I, p.19; and J. Olrik and H. Raeder, *Gesta*, IV.x.4, I, p.103; P. Fisher and H. Ellis Davidson, *History*, I, p.111.

69 See *Le lai d'Haveloc*, lines 1055-82 in A. Bell, *Le lai d'Haveloc and Gaimar's Haveloc episode*, Manchester, 1925, pp.218-9.

70 See H. Heyman, *Studies on the Havelock-tale*, Uppsala, 1903, p.96; L. A. Hibbard, *Mediaeval romance in England*, New York, 1924, p.113.

71 See C. Samaran, ed., *Alexandre Dumas, Les troi mousquetaires*, Paris, 1968, ch. 47, pp.563, 574-8.

72 See S. Thompson, ed., *Motif-index of folk-literature*, revised edn, 6 vols, Copenhagen, 1955-58, vol. IV, p.313.

73 Ibid., IV, p.496.

74 Ibid., IV, p.440.

75 See Aeneas Tacticus, *Fragmenta*, xl.4, in *Aeneas Tacticus, Asclepiodotus, Onasander*, Illinois Greek Club Translation, London, 1923, pp.196-7: 'Again, the people of Sinope in their war against Datamas, when they were in danger and in need of men, disguised the most able-bodied of their women and armed them as much like men as they could, giving them in place of shields and helmets their jars and similar bronze utensils, and marched them around the wall where the enemy were most likely to see them.' The author is careful to note that in this case the disguised women were not permitted to throw anything, since women cannot throw, and 'even a long way off a woman betrays her sex when she tries to throw'. Aeneas seems especially concerned about this point, for he repeats it at the end of his treatise as general advice to anyone intending to try out this particular stratagem for the first time. (See *Fragmenta*,

lvii, pp.222–23.) Comments from various (male) readers who over the years have 'nodded sage assent' to Aeneas' 'clubman's remark' are quoted in David Whitehead, *Aineias the tactitian: how to survive under siege*, Oxford, 1990, p.206. Whitehead compares Aeneas' tactic to the description of transvestite disguise in chapter 11 of Mark Twain's *Huckleberry Finn*.

76 See Aeneas Tacticus, *Fragmenta*, lviii, pp.224–25.

77 See, for example, Polyaenus, *Strategica*, VIII.xxiii.12, in R. Shepherd, transl., *Polyaenus's stratagems of war*, Chicago, 1974, p.328.

78 See, e.g., Leo VI, *Tactica*, Constitutio XIX.28, *MPG*, CVII, 919C; Anna Comnena, *Alexiad* XI.2, p.272. One might compare Bede's description of the trick employed by Germanus of Auxerre of stationing his greatly outnumbered army of Britons in a valley and having them repeat his call of 'Alleluia' in one great shout before an oncoming horde of Saxons and Picts. This battle-cry, amplified and multiplied by echoes from the hills round about, convinces the invading army that they are surrounded. See B. Colgrave and R. A. B. Mynors, eds, *Bede's ecclesiastical history of the English people*, Oxford, 1969, I.xx, pp.62–3.

79 Surprisingly, Bjarni Einarsson has nothing to say about the ruse in his otherwise very thorough commentary on the saga, *Litterære Forudsætninger for Egils saga* (Stofnun Árna Magnússonar á Íslandi, VIII), Reykjavík, 1975. On Vínheiðr see esp. pp.229–53.

80 See L. Bethmann and G. Waitz, eds, *Paulus Diaconus, Historia Langobardorum*, in *MGH, Scriptores Rerum Langobardicarum et Italicarum saec. vi–ix*, ed. G. Waitz, Hanover, 1878, V.21, p.152. I am grateful to Walter Goffart for this reference.

81 Josephus, *The Jewish war*, II.635-45, in H. St J. Thackeray, ed. and transl., *Josephus*, vol. II, London, 1956, pp.566–9. The same event is described in sections 163–9 of Josephus' autobiography; see H. St. J. Thackeray, *Josephus*, vol. I, London, 1926, pp.62–5.

82 W. Whiston, *The whole genuine works of Flavius Josephus*, vol. III, London, 1817, p.439n.

83 Raymond R. Newell, 'The forms and historical value of Josephus' suicide accounts', in Louis H. Feldman and Gohei Hata, eds, *Josephus, the Bible and history*, Leiden, 1989, p.282. On fictional elements in Josephus' writings in general, see Horst Moehring, *Novelistic elements in the writings of Flavius Josephus*, Ph.D. dissertation, University of Chicago, 1957.

84 See A. Stender-Petersen, *Varangica*, Aarhus, 1953, pp.190–1.

85 Josephus, *The Jewish war*, II.636, in H. St J. Thackeray, *Josephus*, vol. II, pp.566–7.

Discretion and deceit 141

86 Peter Foote, 'An essay on the saga of Gisli and its Icelandic background',
    in G. Johnston, transl., *The Saga of Gisli*, London, 1963; repr. 1973,
    p.105.

87 *Egils saga*, ch.52, p.132: 'En þar er skemmst var milli skógarins ok
    árinnar, ok var þat mjǫk lǫng leið. þar hǫfðu tjaldat menn Aðalsteins
    konungs; stóðu tjǫld þeira allt milli skógarins ok árinnar.'

88 The placement of tents in this passage is strikingly similar to advice
    given by the Byzantine stategist Kekaumenos, who recommends that a
    large army pitch its tents so as to make its full force clearly visible to the
    enemy. A small troop, on the other hand, should take care that its camp
    is bounded by woods or some other natural obstacle which will deprive
    the enemy of a clear view of the size of their army. See Kekaumenos,
    Strategikon, chs. 31, 35, pp.36, 39.

89 A convenient survey of Byzantine military stratagems which have been
    incorporated into Old Icelandic narratives is available in R. Cook, 'Russian
    history, Icelandic story, and Byzantine strategy', pp.75–89. See also
    A. Stender-Petersen, *Die Varägersage als Quelle der altrussischen Chronik*
    (Acta Jutlandica, VI), Copenhagen, 1934, pp.77–90.

90 L. Hollander, 'Vin-heath and Huns', p.38n., draws attention to this
    particular stratagem. See Bjarni Aðalbjarnarson, ed., *Snorri Sturluson,
    Haralds saga Sigurðarsonar*, ch. 6 in *Heimskringla*, vol. III (Íslenzk Fornrit,
    XXVIII), Reykjavík, 1951, pp.76–7.

91 See accounts of the dissemination of this particular story by Alexander
    H. Krappe, 'The sparrows of Cirencester', *Modern Philology*, 23 (1925–26),
    pp.7–16; and A. Stender-Petersen, 'Et nordisk Krigslistmotivs historie',
    Edda, 29 (1929), pp.145–64.

92 J. Olrik and H. Raeder, *Gesta*, I, p.24; *cf.* P. Fisher and H. Ellis Davidson,
    History, I, p.25; and J. Olrik and H. Raeder, *Gesta*, I, pp.102–3; *cf.*
    P. Fisher and H. Ellis Davidson, *History*, I, p.111.

93 See S. H. Cross, transl., *The Russian primary chronicle* (Harvard Studies
    and Notes in Philology, XII), Cambridge, MA, 1930,
    p.167: entry for year 6454 (AD 946).

94 See *Brut Tysilio*, in San-Marte (a.k.a. Albert Schulz), *Gottfrieds von
    Monmouth Historia Regum ... und Brut Tysylio*, Halle, 1854, p.568. *Cf.* the
    Red Book of Hergest version, cited from Jesus College Oxford MS. 61 in
    English translation by R. E. Jones, in A. Griscom, ed., *The Historia
    Regum Britanniae of Geoffrey of Monmouth*, London, 1929, p.505; Robert
    Wace, *Roman de Brut*, lines 13949–14036, in Le Roux de Lincy, ed., *Le
    Roman de Brut par Wace*, Rouen, 1836–38, vol. II, pp.242–6. G. L. Brook
    and R. F. Leslie, eds, *Layamon: Brut*, lines 14581–622 (*EETS*, original
    series, CCLXXVII), London, 1978, pp.765–6, text from BL MS. Cotton

Caligula A.IX ff. 175vb–176ra; Giraldus Cambrensis, *Topographica Hibernica*, dist.III., c.39, in J. F. Dimock, ed., *Giraldi Cambrensis Opera*, V, (Rolls Series, XXI), London, 1867, p.184.

95 J. B. Bessinger, 'Maldon and the Óláfsdrápa: an historical caveat', in S. B. Greenfield, ed., *Studies in Old English literature in honour of Arthur G. Brodeur*, Eugene, OR, 1963, p.27.

96 J. McN. Dodgson, 'Site of the battle of Maldon', p.171.

97 J. B. Bessinger, 'Maldon and the Óláfsdrápa', p.35.

98 Thomas Babington Macaulay, 'Hallam's Constitutional History', *Edinburgh Review*, September, 1828, repr. in *idem, Literary and historical essays contributed to the Edinburgh Review*, Oxford, 1923, vol. II, p.1.

99 A. Campbell, *Battle of Brunanburh*, p.80.

100 It is, of course, difficult to say what form such archaeological evidence could be expected to take. In the discussion period which followed this session in the conference, David Klausner facetiously suggested 'hazel sticks'.

7

From Throndheim to Waltham to Chester: Viking- and post-Viking-Age attitudes in the survival legends of Óláfr Tryggvason and Harold Godwinson

MARC COHEN

IN THE YEAR 1000, near the island of Svolder off the coast of Wendland, Óláfr Tryggvason fought the final battle of his life. A naval force comprised of Danes, Swedes, and inimical Norwegians surprised the Norwegian king and the small group of vessels accompanying him. Despite a heroic struggle made against overwhelming odds, the smaller fleet was soundly defeated. Óláfr Tryggvason was reported to have drowned, though his body was never recovered. As a result of this decisive sea battle, the Norwegian throne lay empty for the next seventeen years, reduced to a tributary of the Danish realm under the sway of the Jarl of Throndheim, and remained without its own independent monarch until the advent of Óláfr's successor, the future saint, Óláfr II Haraldsson.

In 1066, Harold Godwinson of England met a similar fate. He, too, fell in a decisive battle, after which his realm would be subsumed by a foreign power. And while the earliest accounts of the Norman Conquest leave little doubt about Harold's death on the battlefield at Hastings, they vary over the final resting place of the royal corpse after duke William's victory. The Anglo-Saxon Chronicles which report Harold's fall do not mention an interment of the body.[1] William of Jumièges describes how Harold was mortally wounded, but likewise discusses no burial.[2] William of Poitiers, on the other hand, notes that Harold's mother, Gytha, offered gold for her son's corpse; duke William turned down her request, however, and instead had Harold buried on the shores of Dover.[3] The *Carmen de Hastingae Proelio* also refers to his burial on these shores, adding the detail that the site was marked by a pile of stones in the manner of an old viking burial.[4] William of Malmesbury, finally, offers an altogether different version, asserting that the duke actually granted Gytha's request, and that she subsequently buried the body at Holy Cross at Waltham, the church Harold himself had richly endowed half a decade or so before the battle of Hastings.[5]

The death of a king in battle is always a dramatic event, and one which plays an important part in the development of a people's self-perceptions and national identity. However, the plights of these two kings have more in common than the obvious consequences of the fall of both king and nation with one blow; they also share a combination of lacunae and disagreement over information on the final resting place of the royal bodies.

Óláfr Tryggvason's body was never found; his final leap overboard was variously interpreted as an act of escape, suicide, or a fall in battle. Harold Godwinson's body either lay unidentified among the carnage of Hastings, or was identified and interred either near the site of battle or at Waltham. The combination of national tragedy and mystery surrounding the final days of these two figures would spawn two of the most unusual survival legends of the High Middle Ages.

Indeed, shortly after the death of Óláfr Tryggvason, rumour spread that the king had succumbed neither to his enemies' weapons nor to the Wendish littoral tide, but had been rescued by a Wendish ship and given refuge at the court of the Wendish king Boleslaw. This rumour was recorded by Óláfr's court poet, Hallfreðr Óttarsson, in a lay he composed shortly after the fatal battle.[6]

Later on, the story of Óláfr's survival received ample embellishment in the sagas of Iceland, which told of Óláfr's

pilgrimage to Byzantium, Syria, and Jerusalem after his convalescence at the Wendish king's court. Harold Godwinson
became the subject of a similar legend. In the late twelfth century,
the report that Harold may actually have survived Hastings
began to appear in numerous chronicles and other written
sources. The legend ultimately received its fullest treatment in
the *Vita Haroldi Regis*, a curious work composed shortly after
the beginning of the thirteenth century.[7] The work testifies
that Harold, too, had survived defeat, and had spent the
remainder of his days as a pilgrim and a hermit.

The parallels between these two legends suggest that they
are somehow related; indeed, as Margaret Ashdown suggests in
an article from 1959, the legend of Harold's survival of Hastings
may have been derived from its Norse counterpart.[8] The few
scholars who have examined these legends, however, have tended
to treat them as though they were static traditions, obscuring
potential processes of development and change by which such
legends might evolve. Indeed, the time in which the legends
develop spans almost three hundred years, sufficient time for
development and modification. Scholars have also failed to
recognize that the legends may have been received differently
by different audiences, and thus would have had different
meanings for people distinguished by time and by culture.

This paper will thus approach these legends as reflections of
very different societies: of viking, post-viking, Norwegian,
Icelandic, and Anglo-French cultural perspectives. It will also
attempt to discern in what regions of England and Scandinavia
the legends were most popular; how credulous or incredulous
the various chroniclers of the legends were toward the events
they were recording; and how the different audiences from
three centuries and two different kingdoms affected and
received these accounts.

Óláfr Tryggvason is perhaps best known today for his role as
the first king successfully to establish Christianity in Norway
and its north Atlantic colonies. The sagas and chronicles of
twelfth- and thirteenth-century Norway and Iceland all portray
Óláfr as the zealous and often ruthless proselytizer of the

Christian faith. Such a depiction, however, contrasts in spirit with that of his earliest 'biographies', the memorial poems composed by the Icelandic poet, Hallfreðr Óttarsson (966–1007). Hallfreðr, though baptized under Óláfr's sponsorship about a year prior to the king's death, was ambivalent towards his new faith, and had even drawn the reproach of his royal patron for showing regret toward his renunciation of the old gods. His commemorative verses, composed shortly after the king's death, thus place no emphasis on Óláfr's religious devotion, but rather on his role as a dauntless viking war-lord, fighting against immeasurable odds to the very last.

Hallfreðr's verses about Óláfr's final battle, preserved in Snorri Sturluson's *Heimskringla*, manifest the first indications that the Norwegian king was rumoured to have survived his encounter with the naval alliance. The poet, however, doubted the truth of such reports. In one verse, he says that there are conflicting reports about whether Óláfr was alive or dead. 'The news about him is uncertain',[9] he concedes. In another verse, Hallfreðr is less ambivalent about the rumours of the king's survival. 'Some men tell me', he states, 'that the king was wounded or escaped the battle east of the sea. Now it is truthfully said that he died from the great battle in the south; I give little credence to men's idle tales.'[10]

Despite the poet's scepticism, reports of Óláfr's escape persisted, and were passed down orally through the generations until recorded in the late twelfth and thirteenth centuries. One Latin chronicle and three Icelandic sagas — the sagas of Óláfr Tryggvason composed by Oddr Snorrason and Snorri Sturluson, and the anonymous *Longest Saga of Óláfr Tryggvason*, preserved in *Flateyjarbók* — all mention the legend of Óláfr's survival. They also provide additional information about events which followed the battle. The *Historia de Antiquitate Regum Norwagiensium*, written *c.*1180 by the Norwegian monk Theodoric, reports that some people say that Óláfr escaped in a skiff and later went to distant regions for his soul's salvation.[11] Snorri Sturluson, whose work dates from between 1220–40, merely mentions the report of Óláfr's rescue by Wendish ships nearby. He also mentions that some people later told stories of Óláfr's subsequent adventures, but neglects to tell anything further about these tales.[12] Oddr and the *Longest Saga* at least give the nature and locale of these adventures: Óláfr was reputed to have turned pilgrim, travelled to Jerusalem, repented his life's misdeeds, and ended his days at a monastery in Greece, Syria or Egypt, sometime during the reign of king Edward the Confessor of England.[13]

Hallfreðr does not mention Óláfr's penitence, self-exile, and pilgrimage to the Holy Land. He does mention in one verse that Óláfr was reported to have fled east, but that probably refers to eastern Europe, either to Russia, where Óláfr was said to have been raised, or to Byzantium, where vikings were beginning to take a prominent place in the Varangian guard. That the poet failed to convey accounts of Óláfr's expiation should come as no surprise. The poet, for one thing, probably composed his verses too soon after the battle for the additional legendary material to have accrued. Even had such reports been extant in Hallfreðr's time, it is unlikely he would have recorded them, given his antipathy to the Christian faith.

How early, then, did the report of Óláfr's pilgrimage to Jerusalem arise in Norway? The *Longest Saga* links Óláfr's death to the time of the English king Edward.[14] Could an account of Óláfr's pilgrimage to the Holy Land have been current at that time, that is, around the middle of the eleventh century? Considering that pilgrimages by Scandinavians to the Holy Land are not reported until the twelfth century, it is more likely that the story of Óláfr's pilgrimage emerged then.

Other aspects of the story also link the pilgrimage segments to a later period. The *Longest Saga* relates that Óláfr is reputed to have met and won favour with the king and the patriarch of Jerusalem, to have turned down their offers of worldly honours and power, and to have finished his days in a monastery in Egypt. These elements further support the notion that the legend underwent transformation in the twelfth and early thirteenth centuries, reflecting the age of crusades and a new emphasis on Jerusalem as the sacred centre of spiritual activity.

One final detail also points to a later period for modification of the legend. The *Longest Saga* mentions that king Edward the Confessor of England used to read to his court the tale of Óláfr Tryggvason out of a book which Óláfr himself had sent from Jerusalem to Edward's father king Æthelred.[15] The author thus traces the origins of Icelandic saga-writing to a period which precedes actual saga composition by almost 100 years. An anachronistic detail such as this can hardly be attributed to so predominantly an oral culture as that of eleventh-century Norway, but seems to reflect and be most relevant to the much more textual society of late twelfth- and thirteenth-century Iceland.

The legend of Óláfr Tryggvason's survival of the battle of Svolder thus appears to have developed in distinct stages. To the story-tellers of the late viking/early Christian period, his destination was probably no further than Byzantium, where he would have joined the company of many other valiant northern warriors in the Varangian guard. The twelfth- and thirteenth-century accounts, however, only hint at this aspect of the legend, burying it beneath stories of a pilgrimage to the Holy Land and a conversion to a monastic lifestyle, stories more relevant to the piety and popular imagination of the crusading age. Doubts about the credibility of such accounts, however, seem to subside as survival accounts evolve and gain momentum.

The time of provenance of the survival story of Harold Godwinson, in contrast to that of Óláfr Tryggvason, is not possible to ascertain. As has been already mentioned, the earliest sources are unanimous on the certainty of Harold's death on the battlefield in 1066; they merely disagree over the whereabouts of his burial. Whether the alternative stories of Harold's fate emerged soon after the battle of Hastings or were the product of twelfth-century imaginations is impossible to assess from the later written sources.

The first source to indicate the dissemination of a story of Harold's survival is Aelred of Rievaulx's *Vita Sancti Edwardi Regis*, completed around 1163. The author affirms that the king was despoiled of his kingdom, but is uncertain whether Harold 'died wretchedly or escaped, preserved, as some people think, for a life of penitence'.[16] Another twelfth-century source, Giraldus Cambrensis, *Itinerarium Kambriae* of *c.*1191, discusses Harold's plight with more certainty: 'Pierced by many arrows, and with his left eye pierced by an arrow and lost, overcome he escaped to Wales.'[17] Gerald then states that Harold completed his life as a penitent hermit in Wales, but again does not mention a final resting place for his body.

Three thirteenth-century chronicles also mention Harold's survival. The Essex native Gervase of Tilbury, whose chronicle, the *Otia Imperialia*, ends in 1216, comments that there was uncertainty in 1066 whether Harold died at Hastings or escaped.[18] The Chronicle of Laôn, written by an English Praemonstratensian *c.*1219, states that many men of good testimony claim to have seen Harold long after his battle with William, and that he lived as a hermit until the twenty-third year of Henry II's reign (1177).[19] Finally, Ralph of Coggeshall, a Cistercian writing in the third decade of the same century, asserts that William deprived Harold of both his kingdom and life, though some people contest that Harold had hid among the slain at Hastings, fled at night, and after many wanderings ended his days as a hermit in Chester.[20]

The most extensive account of this survival legend is a work from the first decade of the thirteenth century, the *Vita Haroldi*, an anonymous piece written apparently by a former regular canon from the Church of Holy Cross at Waltham.[21] The work traces the life of the fallen king through the following stages: one, his pre-regal life, with special emphasis on his pious patronage of the Church of Holy Cross; two, his defeat at Hastings and, with the aid of a Saracen woman, his convalescence; three, his renunciation of the throne in favour of a life of pilgrimage; and four, his pilgrimage on the continent, his return to England, and his migrations from Dover to Wales and to Chester.

Clearly, the *Vita* is an amalgam of all the disparate elements of a story until now transmitted partly through written, but mainly through oral, means. The work, moreover, assumes many of the traits of a saint's Life, even going so far as to claim a place for Harold as Edward's co-heir in heaven.[22] There is in fact additional evidence that Holy Cross may have been interested at this time in perpetuating the report of its famous donor's sanctity. A list of relics found at Waltham and examined in a 1988 article by Paul Gerhard Schmidt mentions Harold as being *iam sanctis connumeratus*.[23]

As a saint's Life, however, the *Vita Haroldi* fails on two important counts: it lacks both a list of miracles, and a specific site of entombment. It does mention that after Harold passed from the world, miracles indicated his entry into heaven, but it fails to specify what these miracles were.[24] Likewise, we are led to understand that Harold died at St John's Church at Chester, but there is no discussion of a site of his entombment or possible translation to Waltham.[25] Indeed, the muddling and continued obscurity of these very important elements would have obstructed any hagiographic aspirations the author may have entertained.

Three other written accounts of Harold's survival legend must not be overlooked, however, as they may clarify the nature of its relationship with the legends of Óláfr Tryggvason. A fourteenth-century Icelandic version of the Life of St Edward the Confessor, *Játvarðar saga*, relates that some Englishmen tell how Harold was discovered alive on the battle-field by some of his men, how he was healed in secret and, deciding not to contend further with William for the throne, survived to the days of Henry the Old (that is, Henry II).[26] Two other Icelandic sources, the above-mentioned *Óláfs saga Tryggvasonar* of Oddr Snorrason, and the thirteenth-century romance *Hemings þáttr*, not only mention Harold's survival but also refer to his alleged sanctity. These two works also make specific reference to the parallels between Harold and Óláfr's penitential lives. Both kings, they note, chose to forgo any further attempts to regain their crowns, and instead opted for lives of penitence, pilgrimage, and holy isolation.[27]

The northern world was thus aware not only of the legend of Harold Godwinson's survival, but also of the parallels between it and that of their own resurrected king, Óláfr Tryggvason. As mentioned earlier, it seems possible that the similarities between these two legends are not coincidental. However, it may be simplifying matters too far to assume that the legend of Harold Godwinson may have been derived from that of Óláfr Tryggvason. While the rumours of Óláfr's escape from battle did precede those of Harold's, reports of Óláfr's pilgrimage and cenobitic lifestyle appear only as early as the late thirteenth century — around the time that the legend of Harold's survival was current in England. Also, while there is documented evidence that the northern world was aware of many aspects of Harold's legend, there is no documentation that the English knew of the stories told about Óláfr. It is possible, then, that Óláfr's legend did not spawn, but drew from, those elements of the legend of Harold which we now see the two legends share: renunciation, pilgrimage, and the adoption of an anchoritic or cenobitic lifestyle. It is just as possible that these elements derive from a third source, though apart from mention of the legend of Harold in the Icelandic material, there is no allusion to an additional source in either the English or Scandinavian accounts.

While their roots may be in the Viking-Age North, the legends of Harold Godwinson and Óláfr Tryggvason's survival and perseverance as holy pilgrims have more in common with the late twelfth- and thirteenth-century world for which they were recorded in writing. Óláfr's pilgrimage and stay in the Holy Land would have had more meaning for the northern world in the late twelfth century, which sent numerous crusaders and pilgrims to Jerusalem, than for that of the early eleventh. The legend of Harold Godwinson, moreover, would have had additional appeal to people in south-eastern and western England, where it may have rivalled the popularity of the sanctity of the recently canonized saints, Edward the Confessor and Thomas Becket, and of the reputed discovery of king Arthur's tomb at Glastonbury in 1191. The elements of pilgrimage and expiation in both stories would find an especially favourable reception from an audience inundated with stories of purgatories, wandering Jews, or Prester John.

Both legends, at each stage of development, give testimony to the self-reflectivity of various cultures in different periods, and to how these cultures borrowed from each other's representations of their misfortunes and tragedies in order to understand and define their own.

References

1 *Anglo-Saxon Chronicles* D. and E. D. Whitelock, ed., *English historical documents*, vol. I, London, 1959, pp.143–4.

2 Jean Marx, ed., *Guillaume de Jumièges, Gesta Normannorum Ducum*, Paris, 1914, VII:15, p.135.

3 Raymonde Foreville, ed. and transl., *Guillaume de Poitiers, Histoire de Guillaume le Conquérant*, Paris, 1952, II:25, pp.204–6: pt ii, sect. 25.

4 Catherine Morton and Hope Muntz, eds, *The Carmen de Hastingae Proelio of Guy Bishop of Amiens*, Oxford, 1972, lines 582–92.

5 Thomas D. Hardy, ed., *Willelmi Malmesbiriensis monachi Gesta Regum Anglorum*, 2 vols, London, 1840, vol. II, p.420.

6 This tradition was recounted by Snorri Sturluson. See Bjarni Aðalbjarnarson, ed., *Snorri Sturluson, Óláfs saga Tryggvasonar*, ch. 112, in *Heimskringla*, vol. I (Íslenzk Fornrit, XXVI), Reykjavík, 1941, pp.367–70.

7 'Vita Haroldi Regis', in John Allen Giles, ed., *Original lives of Anglo-Saxons and others who lived before the Conquest* (*Burt Franklin research and source works series*, CLIV) [repr. of Caxton Society, 5, 16 (1854)], New York, 1967.

8 'An Icelandic account of the survival of Harold Godwinson', in Peter Clemoes, ed., *The Anglo-Saxons: studies in some aspects of their history and culture, presented to Bruce Dickins*, London, 1959.

9 'hætt es til hans at frétta', Snorri Sturluson, *Óláfs saga Tryggvasonar*, p.368, verse 166. All translations are my own, though for the Old Icelandic verse I have consulted Bjarni's Modern Icelandic translations.

10 Enn segir auðar kenni / austr í malma gnaustan / seggr frá sórum tyggja / sumr eða brott of kumnum. / Nú es sannfregit sunnan / siklings ór styr miklum / kannka mart við manna, / morð veifanar orði: ibid., verse 169, pp.369–70.

11 Jacob Langebek, ed., *Historia de Antiquitate Regum Norwagiensium*, ch. 14 (*Scriptores Rerum Danicarum Medii Aevi*, V), Copenhagen, 1783, p.322.

12 Snorri Sturluson, *Óláfs saga Tryggvasonar*, p.368.

13 Guðni Jónsson, ed., *Oddr, Óláfs saga Tryggvasonar*, ch. 78 in *idem* ed., *Konunga Sögur*, I, Reykjavík, 1957, pp.190–1; *Longest saga*, chs. 394–404: *Flateyjarbók*, vol. I, Oslo, 1860, pp.500–16.

14 Ibid., ch. 404, p.516.

15 Ibid

16 'aut misere occubuit, aut ut quidam putant poenitentiae tantum reservatus evasit.' Aelred of Rievaulx, *Vita Sancti Edwardi Regis*, in St Aelred, *Opera Omnia, MPL*, CXCV, Paris, 1855, p.766.

17 'multisque, ut aiunt confossus vulneribus oculoque sinistro sagitta perdito ac perforato, ad partes istas [i.e. Wales] victus evasit.' James Dimock, ed., *Itinerarium Kambriae et Descriptio Kambriae*, in *Giraldi Cambrensis opera*, vol. VI, (Rolls Series, XXI), London, 1868, p.140.

18 Joseph Stevenson, ed., *Gervasii Tileburiensis Excerpta ex Otiis Imperialibus*, (Rolls Series, LXVI), London, 1875, pp.434–5.

19 *Chronicon Laudunensis*, MS unpublished, cited in Christine Fell, 'English history and Norman legend in the Icelandic saga of Edward the Confessor', *Anglo-Saxon England*, 6 (1977), p.234.

20 Joseph Stevenson, ed., *Radulphi de Coggeshall Chronicon Anglicanum* (Rolls Series, LXVI), London, 1875, p.1.

21 The author's association with Holy Cross at Waltham is inferred in the prologue, where he describes his text as having been 'toiled over for the sake of the memorable deeds of our founder', and 'in and about praise of the glorious and deific cross' ('ad laudem et de laude gloriosae ac deificae crucis . . . elaboratum gestis memoriabilibus fundatoris nostri'), 'Vita Haroldi', p.39.

22 Ibid., p.47.

23 '*Veritas naufragatur*: Das Leben und die Taten König Harolds von England nach 1066', *Fälschungen im Mittelalter*, vol. I (*MGH, Schriften*, XXXIII, 1), Hanover, 1988, p.202, n.32.

24 'Vita Haroldi', p.54.

25 Ibid., p.83.

26 *Játvarðar saga*, in Guðbrandur Vigfússon, ed., *Icelandic Sagas*, vol. I (Rolls Series, LXXXVIII, 1), London, 1887, p.397.

27 Oddr Snorrason, *Óláfs saga Tryggvasonar*, pp.196–7; Gillian Fellows-Jensen, ed., *Hemings þáttr Áslákssonar* (Editiones Arnamagnaeanae, series B III), Copenhagen, 1962, p.57.

8

The cult of king Harold at Chester

ALAN THACKER

THE PRINCIPAL WITNESSES were under no doubt about the fate of Harold Godwinson. The main continuators of the Anglo-Saxon Chronicle asserted that he and his brothers Leofwine and Gyrth were slain at Hastings.[1] According to the earliest Norman accounts, the king's mutilated and almost unrecognizable body was buried in unconsecrated ground beside the Saxon shore, which he had guarded so fiercely and with so little success.[2] In the tradition of Harold's own foundation of Waltham (a tradition supported by William of Malmesbury), the king was brought to that house for interment;[3] perhaps, as Freeman suggested, he was buried initially in an unmarked grave and later brought to Waltham with king William's permission.[4] Yet despite this consensus, stories later circulated denying that Harold had been killed and associating him after the battle with a number of places in the south of England and, as we shall see, much further afield.[5] Such survival stories are, of course, a well-attested phenomenon and are frequently attributed to admired leaders by peoples who have experienced some overwhelming disaster. They have, however, their own interest, and in this paper some attempt will be made to provide a context for one of the most extraordinary of those legends, that of king Harold at Chester.

The story that Harold survived Hastings and after various wanderings ended his life as a hermit in Chester occurs in a number of late twelfth- and early thirteenth-century sources.[6] Its fullest treatment is in the *Vita Haroldi*,[7] the Life of Harold Godwinson, composed in the first decade of the thirteenth century, probably 1204/6, by an author connected with the king's favoured foundation of Waltham.[8] The work, which is extant in a single manuscript, written at Waltham abbey in the mid fourteenth century,[9] purports to relate the deeds of Harold, 'illustrissimus ... rex legitimus, ... rite ac legitime coronatus', throughout treated as a saint.[10] Harold is presented as valiant and pious, devoted to the cult of the Holy Cross having been cured of paralysis through the invocation of a miracle-working stone crucifix recently discovered at Montacute (Somerset) and brought thence to Waltham (Essex).[11] He is especially praised for his endowment and adornment of a college of twelve priests at Waltham, a community which grew lax with time and was (in the author's opinion) commendably reformed with the installation of regular canons by king Henry II, 'of blessed memory' ('per dive recordacionis regem Henricum secundum').[12]

The author's main concern is the fate of Harold after Hastings, about which he alleged that he personally had obtained information from a certain Sæbeorht, who had been the king's servant at Chester and who much later in life became a hermit and ascetic at Stanton Harcourt (Oxfordshire).[13] According to Sæbeorht, Harold survived the battle, despite the wounds then inflicted upon him, and spent two years in hiding at Winchester. Restored to health through the ministrations of an Arab woman, he departed for Germany to seek help in regaining his kingdom and after the failure of that mission passed many years as a wandering pilgrim.[14] In old age he returned to England and spent ten years as a hermit in a cave near Dover. Thereafter, he went to Wales, where he lived in disguise, interceding for those against whom he had formerly fought in the interest of his own people.[15] Finally, when his bodily strength began to give way, he sought a last resting-place and was led 'by angelic guidance' to the city of Chester and to the church of St John, where he took the place of a local hermit who recently died.[16]

The author was conscious that his story ran counter to received tradition and that in particular it was challenged by the authoritative history of William of Malmesbury (d. 1143).[17] In its defence he cited the equivocal statement of Aelred of Rievaulx (d. 1166) that Harold had either fallen in the battle or escaped, preserved for repentance ('regno spoliatus Anglorum, aut misere occubuit, aut ut quidam putant poenitentiae tantum reservatus evasit').[18] He dealt with the undoubtedly strong tradition at Waltham — that the king's mangled body had been identified by his former mistress, Edith Swan-Neck, and brought thither for burial — by asserting that Edith had been mistaken in her identification.[19] In support of that contention, he quoted a recent tradition of the community that Walter, first abbot of the reformed monastery (1184–1201), had conversed with Gyrth, Harold's brother, then a very old man,[20] at the court of king Henry II, and received from him an absolute assurance that Harold's remains did not rest at Waltham.[21]

A further witness of extreme importance was the king's successor in the hermitage at Chester. The *Vita* concludes with an appendix based upon his testimony. Citing as his source a certain Moses, who had been Harold's servant for many years and had continued as his own for a further two, the hermit affirmed that after being cured of his injuries the king had journeyed as a pilgrim through many lands. In old age he had returned to England and lived as a solitary in various places, coming eventually to the district of Cheswardine in Shropshire, where he lived for seven years until, afflicted by Welsh robbers, he elected to settle in Chester. There in the chapel of St James, beside the river Dee, outside the city walls and within the cemetery of the collegiate church of St John, he spent a further, final, seven years. The hermit added further details about Harold's asceticism in that last phase of his life: he wore a mail shirt next to his bare skin and kept his identity a strict secret, rarely leaving the chapel and keeping his face veiled. He also provided an account of the king's end. As he lay dying Harold sought the last rites from a priest of St John's called Andrew and confessed to him that although he had taken the name Christian he was truly the last native English king. Upon his death the priest publicly proclaimed that information as a fact. At that point, tantalizingly, the manuscript is defective and the rest of the text is lost.[22]

What are we to make of this story? The *Vita Haroldi* has been generally dismissed as an historically worthless romance, written in obscure and unintelligible Latin.[23] Recently, however, it has been pointed out that an important reason for this disregard is Birch's highly unreliable edition, and that the Life is a largely correct and rhetorically ambitious composition. It is, in fact, the work of a relatively sophisticated clerk, well read in scriptural and other appropriate models, in particular the legend of St Alexius, another ascetic supposed to have lived and died unrecognized among those who had once known him.[24] The author had a well thought-out agenda: he wished to enhance Harold's reputation in so far as it redounded to the credit of Waltham, and to that end chose material from the known events of the king's (pre-1066) life very carefully, restricting himself to three episodes, all of which had to do with Waltham's relic collection, and two of which demonstrated the power of the community's greatest treasure, its miracle-working cross.[25] The story after 1066, of course, takes the reader away from Waltham. There is no evidence, however, that it was intended to promote veneration at any other site: no attempt is made to locate the final resting-place of the king's remains, far less to suggest that they became the focus of miracles. As related in the *Vita*, the story of Harold is scarcely the stuff of an effective royal cult. The tone, as both David Rollason and Henry Loyn have observed, is elegiac and nostalgic rather than mystical and intense: Harold is not depicted as a lost leader who will return to bring victory to his people.[26] In fact, the author's intention is clear: though his work centres on the life of Harold its ultimate purpose was to praise 'the glorious and divine cross' (of Waltham), the reputation of which was enhanced by the merits and virtues of its most celebrated worshipper.[27]

The *Vita* was written with the full approval of, indeed, was perhaps commissioned by, the 'reverend fathers' of Henry II's reformed Augustinian community.[28] The immediate context for its composition was very probably an inspection of Waltham's collection of relics, made on 6 July 1204 by a group of canons headed by Richard, the second abbot, and the occasion of verses which celebrated Harold's donations and asserted his sanctity:

Has huic ecclesie rex reliquias tribuisse
Creditur Haroldus, iam sanctis connumeratus.[29]

Like the *Vita* these verses survive in a single copy in the Harleian manuscript from Waltham, and it seems probable that, as has recently been suggested, the two compositions are the work of a single author, presumably that Geoffrey Rabani who names himself as 'writer' (*scriptor*) of the poem and who was one of the inspecting committee.[30] Certainly both works are marked by a similar devotion to the Waltham crucifix, lauded in a schedule attached to the verses as the 'great and holy cross', the advocate of the community and the principal reason for the honour in which it was held.[31] Significantly, the crucifix had been expensively refurbished and regilded a few years earlier, in 1192.[32]

Undoubtedly, then, for the reformed community Waltham's crucial relic was the wonder-working cross. Possession of Harold's body was not a burning issue. The canons were happy to countenance a story which necessitated the abandonment of their well established claim to house the king's tomb, if it added to his pious image as devotee of their holy crucifix. It should be noted, however, that attitudes may have been different before the reform of 1177 in a community which looked back without interruption to Harold as its founder. Something of the spritual outlook of that community survives in the *De Inventione Sanctae Crucis*, an account of the Waltham cross produced by one of the canons expelled in that year and writing in his enforced retirement.[33] Harold's resting-place clearly mattered to him. In his elaborate relation of Harold's burial, two brethren from the community go to the Conqueror immediately after the battle to request the body, a plea to which the king graciously accedes; they search the field at Hastings and aided by Edith Swan-Neck they eventually identify the royal corpse and bring it home to Waltham.[34] The author of that story is insistent that the remains were still within Harold's church, and his reasons are highly significant: he relates that it had been thrice translated, either because of the reconstruction of the church or because of the devotion of the brethren in showing reverence to the body. He himself could just remember being present at the last of the translations.[35] That sounds rather as if something approaching cultic honours were being paid to Harold in his chief foundation before its reform by Henry II.[36]

In the late twelfth century, however, it was at Chester that interest in Harold for his own sake appears to have been most intense. A version of the survival story was current there before the writing of the *Vita*, and was recorded by Giraldus Cambrensis in his *Itinerarium Kambriae*, compiled shortly after his visit to Chester with archbishop Baldwin in 1188.[37] According to Giraldus the local inhabitants asserted that, despite being scarred by many wounds, the king escaped after Hastings to their territory, where he led a holy and contemplative life as an anchorite attached to a church in their city.[38] It is also clear that the author of the *Vita Haroldi* had access to a source well acquainted with Chester. Unlike the rest of the work, the material in the appendix, attributed to Harold's successor in his hermitage, is very circumstantial and accords with what we know from other evidence: there undoubtedly was a chapel dedicated to St James beside the church of St John in the twelfth century and the church was still associated with hermits in the fourteenth.[39] Especially interesting is the fact that the priest who administered the viaticum to the dying hermit and subsequently publicized his identity was called Andrew; that name is borne by one of the canons of the collegiate church in the third quarter of the twelfth century, by a chaplain who witnesses charters of Ranulph II, earl of Chester, in the 1150s, and by a chaplain of St Peter's, Chester, who died at a ripe old

age in the 1190s.[40] It looks as if one of the crucial figures in the
story was a real person, indeed an eminent local ecclesiastic. It is
perhaps also significant that, like the church at Waltham, the
church of St John was to become a focus of the cult of the Holy
Cross. The relic there was first mentioned in 1256 or 1257
when Fulk of Orby (soon to be justice of Chester until his death
in 1261) made annual provision for votive lights to burn before
it.[41] Enshrined in a golden cross-shaped reliquary adorned with
an image, its reputation extended beyond Chester and into
Wales where it was especially venerated.[42] Indeed, such was its
fame that in the late thirteenth and early fourteenth century St
John's was known as the church of the Holy Cross.[43]

That the story, or something like it, was circulating quite
widely in the early thirteenth century is apparent from a number
of sources. The chronicle of Ralph, abbot of Coggeshall (1207–
18), for example, follows earlier texts in stating that William
deprived Harold of both his kingdom and his life, but adds that
'some say' ('quidam contendant') that the king was borne away
from the battlefield alive, and after many wanderings came to
Chester where he lived as hermit until the end of the reign ('ad
ultima tempora') of Henry II.[44] A similar tale is told by an
English Premonstratensian writing at Laôn shortly after 1219.
In his still unpublished world chronicle, the canon declared that
many reliable witnesses claimed to have seen Harold alive long
after the battle of Hastings and that he died a hermit in the
twenty-third year of the reign of Henry II (1176–77).[45]

It is striking that Ralph and the canon of Laôn place the
episode in the last years of the reign of Henry II, a detail which
occurs in neither the *Vita* nor Giraldus Cambrensis. Their
evidence is confirmed by the treatise *De Inventione Sanctae Crucis*
already mentioned. The anonymous author clearly knew the
story of Harold's survival, his taking shelter in cave near Dover,
and his 'recent' death at Chester, although he dismissed it
as a mere fable ('quicquid fabulentur homines quod in rupe
manserit Doroberniae et nuper defunctus sepultus sit Cestriae').[46]
The date of the *De Inventione* and its relationship with the *Vita
Haroldi* are not entirely clear. The treatise was composed no

later than 1189, by which time the author would have been over seventy, since we know from internal evidence that he entered the community at the age of five in 1124.[47] Undoubtedly, therefore, he wrote before the composition of the *Vita Haroldi*, and is hence an independent witness to the main outlines of the story therein recounted.

In fact, the author of the *Vita* refers to a tract on the finding of the holy cross of Waltham, and some of his material is clearly derived from that earlier work.[48] The most striking episode recounts Harold's visit to Waltham just before the battle of Hastings, during which the image on the crucifix was seen to incline its head in sorrow towards the king, prostrate in prayer before it.[49] That miracle is described in similar terms in the *De Inventione*. The *Vita* also accords with the *De Inventione* in alluding to Edith Swan-Neck's search on the battlefield among the slain for the body of her former lover.[50] On the other hand the two works are at variance on certain matters; in particular, the *Vita* attributes the removal of Waltham's treasures to William I, whereas the author of the *De Inventione* blames William II.[51] It may therefore be that the tract to which the author of the *Vita* had access was somewhat different from the version of the *De Inventione* which survives.

There are then a number of independent sources recording the episode of Harold at Chester and concurring in assigning it to the later years of Henry II. It is tempting, therefore, to assume that in the 1170s and 1180s the city housed a celebrated recluse, who called himself Christian and who allowed himself to be identified with, or was after his death declared to be, king Harold Godwinson, survived to a miraculously prolonged old age and transmuted into a saint.[52] The claims made on the hermit's behalf may well have gained credence from the involvement of Andrew, a senior ecclesiastic associated with St John's. Such a development could have encouraged contact with Waltham and might explain how the church became the home of a venerated relic of the Holy Rood. Probably the whole episode was still fresh in the 1180s, when Harold's brother Gyrth was supposed to have appeared at king Henry's court at Woodstock.

Nevertheless, there are difficulties in assuming that such a story could have been taken seriously, even at Chester. Besides the obvious fact that then as now claims which required a man to have attained the age of about 170 at the time of his death are likely to have excited considerable scepticism, there is also the silence of Lucian, our most important contemporary local source.[53] Lucian, a monk of Chester and author of a remarkable tract in praise of his native city, almost certainly wrote between the years 1180 and 1194, and it might be thought that he would be especially likely to mention events which redounded so much to the credit of the church and the city. In fact, though he alludes (albeit indirectly) to a chapel of St James, and even to an aged priest named Andrew, then vicar of St Peter's, he ignores Harold and his hermitage.[54] One obvious explanation is that he regarded the whole story as a discreditable fable, like those 'bullientes nugae et impudentissima mendacia' brought back by travellers in exotic parts to which he disapprovingly alludes in a passage lauding his own provincialism.[55] On the other hand it is just possible that some reference, hitherto unnoticed, is veiled within Lucian's almost impenetrably allegorical style. Moreover, although he had been educated at St John's, and indeed dedicated his work to a cleric associated with the church, his overriding interest was his own monastery of St Werburgh. His work, which is in reality 'an extended sermon', includes comparatively little hard information about persons and events and it may be that the episode of the hermit was omitted simply because it did not fit his scheme. It should be noted that the visits of archbishop Baldwin and Giraldus are likewise ignored.[56]

That the episode was disregarded at St Werburgh's in the later thirteenth century is apparent from the annals compiled at the monastery in the time of abbot Simon of Whitchurch (1265–91). The sole reference to Harold, in the entry for the year 1066, simply records that he was killed and his army with him.[57] Against this silence, however, must be set evidence that in the early fourteenth century the story retained sufficient prestige and credibility in the city to occasion an *inventio*.

According to an apparently reliable Welsh annal compiled very soon after the event, in 1332 the body of Harold, clad in leather hose, golden spurs and crown, was found in the church of St John smelling as sweetly as on the day that it was buried, allegedly over two hundred years earlier.[58] That episode clearly left its mark on the historiography of St Werburgh's. The abbey's celebrated historian, Ranulf Higden (d. 1364), considered the story of Harold at Chester a matter of *fama publica* within his native city, and implied that it was as likely to be true as the accepted version.[59]

Whether or not we believe the tale to be rooted in an historic event, the fact remains that the concluding sections of the *Vita Haroldi* exhibit considerable familiarity with the city and its environs. There are, moreover, reasons for supposing that Chester in the later twelfth century was a peculiarly favourable centre for the development of such a tale. By then Harold himself seems to have been admired for his military prowess in Wales and the marches. That, certainly, is the implication of a passage in Giraldus' *Descriptio Kambriae*, composed *c.*1194, in which much is made of the Welsh exploits of the last native English king ('Haroldus ultimus'). In particular, Giraldus tells of memorial stones, inscribed in an antique manner with the legend 'Here Harold was the victor', set up in numerous places. Though such an assertion may well rest on mistaken readings of the undoubtedly numerous inscribed stones which adorned the Welsh countryside, they nevertheless suggest a certain reputation. Harold, clearly, was a figure around whom legend could gather.[60]

Chester itself under its powerful earls, Ranulf II (1129–53), Hugh II (1153–81), and Ranulf III (1181–1232), was the administrative focus of a lordship with increasingly strong pretensions to independence.[61] The youthful Hugh II was among the leaders of the unsuccessful revolt against Henry II in 1172–74, and though he lived quietly in his earldom after his release from captivity in 1177, he may have been happy to shelter a figure or countenance a tale whose pretensions afforded comfort to sentiments scarcely sympathetic to Angevin kingship.[62] Significantly, the story was undoubtedly circulating in Chester in 1188 just as Hugh II's son and successor, Ranulf III, attained his majority.[63] Ranulf, whose nurse came from a Cestrian family, was apparently much in Chester in the early years of his manhood, before his departure to Normandy in 1194. He too may have looked with favour on claims which added lustre to the traditions of his native city.[64] While this is not, of course, to claim that Hugh or Ranulf were actively sponsoring a cult for political reasons, it would seem that they presided over a milieu in which the story of Harold as articulated in the *Vita* found a sympathetic audience.

By the late twelfth century Chester was the centre of an active historiographical tradition. At St Werburgh's the monk Lucian expressed a strong sense of his city and shire's particularity in his tract *De Laude Cestriae*, to which I have already referred. Lucian distinguished the 'Cestrienses', the men of Cheshire, from both the Welsh and the English, an attitude which also characterized the diplomacy of earl Ranulf III in his later years, when he aspired to treat with Henry III and the Welsh prince Llywelyn on equal terms.[65] Others, too, exhibited an interest in the local past. At the abbey Lucian's fellow monks were busy recording material about their patron, the Mercian princess Werburg, in a book known in later tradition as the 'third passionary'. Though now lost, its contents can be partly reconstructed from later sources; they included a brief account of Werburg's life and early cult together with a schedule of miracles demonstrating her power as a protector of the city in the eleventh and twelfth centuries.[66] Significantly, among that material were tales of attacks upon Chester by the Welsh king Gruffydd, and by Harald of Denmark, Malcolm of Scotland, and the king of 'Goths and Galwedy'. All that is evidence of a lively interest in the times of Harold Godwinson in late twelfth-century Chester.[67]

The city was, moreover, the source of stories about another recluse with royal pretensions. According to Giraldus Cambrensis, it was claimed locally that the German emperor Henry, after imprisoning his father and pope Paschal, had abdicated in penitence for his sins and gone into voluntary exile to finish his life as an anchorite at Chester.[68] The story relates to the emperor Henry V (1106–25) and his dealings with his father Henry IV (1056–1106) and pope Paschal II (1099–1118). Like Harold, Henry was widely believed to have lived on after the official record of his death, and significantly the most elaborate account of his alleged disappearance was given by an Englishman, Walter Map, writing in the 1180s or early 1190s. In his collection of anecdotes known as *De Nugis Curialium*, Map relates that, overcome by repentance for his misdeeds towards his family and his realm, the emperor feigned death and embarked upon a wandering life. A corpse was found for the imperial funeral, but the deed could not be entirely concealed and many pretenders came forth to masquerade as the royal penitent. Map gives the story of one such impostor, unmasked at Cluny by one of the emperor's familiars, in particularly circumstantial detail.[69] His account is significant because it suggests not only that such tales were in the air in the late twelfth century but that men were prepared to act upon them to the extent of impersonating a dead prince. Although Map makes no mention of Chester as the scene of one of these impostures, it is clear that the story of Henry continued to circulate in the city long after Giraldus's time and indeed became garbled in transmission. The protagonist was deemed by Ranulf Higden to be not Henry V but his father, Henry IV, who having left his English wife Matilda (*sic*)[70] allegedly lived in Chester for ten years disguised as a hermit called Godescallus. Chester may thus have been the home of more than one royal pretender, perhaps the presence of one influenced the other.[71]

The links between Harold and Chester were not confined to the late twelfth century. Sometime after 1063 or 1064, for reasons of political expediency Harold abandoned Edith Swan-Neck, and took as his wife Ealdgyth, widow of Gruffydd ap Llywellyn, king of Gwynedd (1039–63), and daughter of earl Ælfgar of Mercia (d. 1062?).[72] The Mercian earls had links with Chester going back to the days of their ancestor Leofwine, ealdorman in western Mercia *c*.994–*c*.1023, during whose period of office the city seems to have enjoyed considerable significance. Not only did his appointment coincide with a fresh period of activity in Chester and other western mints,[73] but the city served as the main naval base for an attack on Cumberland and Man in 1000[74] and was the destination of Edmund Ironside and earl Uhtred of Northumbria in their attempt to encourage resistance to Cnut in 1016.[75] When in 1023 the descendants of Leofwine succeeded to the whole of the great earldom of Mercia, they seem to have retained an especial regard for the lands which formed Leofwine's western ealdormanry.[76] Before his death in 1057 Leofwine's son, earl Leofric, enriched several important churches and cult centres in the area, including Wenlock, Leominster, Worcester, Evesham and, significantly, the two minsters in Chester itself, St Werburgh's and St John's.[77] When Leofric's son Ælfgar revolted in the 1050s, it was the western marches which became his centre of operations. He brought with him from Ireland a fleet of eighteen viking ships, and after his compromise with Harold in the wake of his victory at Hereford he sent them to Chester to be paid off.[78] Clearly the city was still an important naval base in the control of the comital family.

The rise of the Welsh king, Gruffydd ap Llywellyn, with his seat at Rhuddlan, further focused attention on Chester and its environs.[79] In 1063, after it had been decided to make an end of him, Harold himself came thither and Chester presumably formed a major base for the highly successful campaign which ended in Gruffydd's defeat and death.[80] When as a result the lands beyond the river Dee, which had been conceded to Gruffydd in 1056, were returned to English hands, the main beneficiary was, interestingly, not the king but Eadwine, Ælfgar's youthful son and heir. Clearly by then the king had relinquished all his Cheshire lands to the comital house, and the area held considerable potential for an energetic earl.[81] The continuing close association of Chester itself with the earl's family and indeed with Harold was demonstrated after the battle of Hastings, when the widowed queen, Ealdgyth, was sent thither by her brothers, the earls Eadwine and Morkere.[82]

Ealdgyth's ultimate fate is unknown. She was the mother of at least one son, Harold, by the late king and presumably brought him (or them) with her to Chester.[83] It has even been suggested that she was delivered of posthumous twins in the city.[84] In any event, the fate of the Haroldsons remained bound up with the Irish Sea province throughout the later eleventh century. In 1068 and 1069 Godwin, Edwin (or Edmund) and Magnus, Harold's three sons from his long-standing union with Edith Swan-Neck, sheltered in Ireland, whence they launched attacks on the South-West.[85] In 1098 Harold Haroldson, who had taken refuge in Scandinavia, was to be found fighting with the Norse king, Magnus 'Barefoot' Olafsson, against the Anglo-Norman army on Anglesey; significantly one of the leaders of his foes was Hugh of Avranches, earl of Chester.[86] Such actions by the Haroldsons may have helped to keep alive their father's heroic reputation in the West.

Chester's ties with Harold and the Anglo-Saxon earls were responsible for the city's involvement in the rising of 1069–70, when the Cestrians in alliance with Eadric the Wild and the Welsh besieged Shrewsbury. The Conqueror, then at York, responded by crossing the Pennines and bringing his army to Chester, where he built a castle; resistance collapsed and in Chester Eadwine was replaced by an Anglo-Norman earl.[87] Identified as a centre of disaffection, the city was treated with brutal severity. When Hugh of Avranches received Chester in the 1070s, probably 1071, the value of the farm had been reduced by one third and the city was described as 'greatly wasted'. Of the 508 houses mentioned in the Domesday Survey as extant in 1066, 205 had been lost by the 1070s and had not been rebuilt in 1086.[88]

It would not, then, be surprising if Harold was remembered with affection in Chester. He had linked himself, albeit for reasons of policy, with a family which had enjoyed strong links with the city for well over half a century, and his downfall had dire consequences for the Cestrians. The hermit of Chester, or his advocate, could well have elicited sympathy from citizens conscious of such a past. Interestingly, the author of the *Vita* draws attention to Harold's links with Shropshire and north Wales, precisely the areas which provided the rebels of 1069. Here, in territory where he once was known, the king was first forced to veil his face, lest through recognition he became the object of adoration.[89]

The legend of king Harold at Chester is clearly fantastic. It is debatable whether it was based upon claims made by or on behalf of a real person who died in Chester in last years of king Henry II or whether it was purely a romance. If the latter it was not invented by the author of the *Vita Haroldi*, since it was known to others who wrote before him, including Giraldus Cambrensis and the cleric responsible for the *De Inventione*. Indeed, legends about Harold's survival apparently go back at least to the mid-twelfth century, to the time of abbot Aelred. On balance, it is perhaps more likely that the sudden emergence of the story of Harold at Chester in several different sources in the late twelfth century was indeed based upon a real episode, though one whose subsequent place in Cestrian tradition is difficult to elucidate. Doubtless, the written accounts and perhaps even the hermit's own confession were shaped by traditions already current about Harold and other supposed royal pilgrims and *incogniti*. But whatever the nature of the background to the tale it was certainly propagated by someone who was well acquainted with or had close contacts with late twelfth-century Chester, and who was capable of appealing to local sentiment. With its growing sense of local identity, its interest in its late Saxon as well as its Norman past, and its long-standing and intimate connexion with the Mercian earls, the city was an obvious breeding ground for an elaboration of the legend of Harold's survival. It is no accident that the most locally focused and circumstantial of the stories about Harold after Hastings should be located there.[90]

Acknowledgments

I am most grateful to Dr C. P. Lewis for reading an earlier draft of this paper and offering valuable help and advice.

References

1 Versions 'D' and 'E': D. C. Douglas and G. W. Greenaway, eds, *English Historical Documents*, vol. II, 2nd edn, London, 1981, pp.145, 147.

2 R. Foreville, ed. and transl., *William of Poitiers, Gesta Willelmi Ducis Normannorum et Regis Anglorum* ,(*Classiques de l'Histoire de France*, XXIII), Paris, 1952, pp.204–10; C. Morton and H. Muntz, eds, *Guy of Amiens, Carmen de Hastingae Proelio*, Oxford, 1972, pp.xliii–xlv, 34–8, 116–8.

3 W. Stubbs, ed., *De Inventione Sanctis Crucis in Monte Acuto et de Ductione Ejusdem apud Waltham, The Foundation of Waltham Abbey*, Oxford and London, 1861, pp.30–1; *idem, William of Malmesbury, Gesta Regum*, 2 vols (Rolls Series), London, 1887–89, II, pp.306–7; and see below.

4 E. A. Freeman, *The history of the Norman Conquest of England*, 6 vols, Oxford, 1867–79, III (1st edn), pp.507–22, 754–65, esp. pp.519–20; M. Ashdown, 'An Icelandic account of the survival of Harold Godwinsson', in P. Clemoes, ed., *The Anglo-Saxons: Studies presented to Bruce Dickins*, London, 1959, pp.129–30.

5 M. Ashdown, 'Icelandic account', esp. pp.128–31.

6 They are conveniently summarized by Freeman, *Norman Conquest*, III, pp.758–63. For the Scandinavian and Norse accounts of Harold's survival, which will not be discussed here, see M. Ashdown, 'Icelandic account', *passim*, and M. Cohen, 'From Throndheim to Waltham to Chester', above, pp.143–53.

7 W. de Gray Birch, ed. and transl., *Vita Haroldi*, London, 1885, hereafter *VH*. For a modern translation see M. Swanton, *Three lives of the last Englishmen*, (*Garland Library of Medieval Literature*, X, Series B), New York and London, 1984, pp.1–40. For recent comments on the quality of text and edition see P. G. Schmidt, '*Veritas Naufragatur*: Das Leben und die Taten König Harolds von England nach 1066', *Fälschungen im Mittelalter*, I. (*MGH, Schriften*, XXXIII, 1), Hanover, 1988, pp.189–204, esp. pp.193–5.

8 Its date may be deduced from a number of allusions within the text. It was written after the deaths of Henry II (1189) and abbot Walter of Waltham (1201) and some 140 years after the oath which Harold took to duke William at Rouen: *VH*, cap.3, 9, 18.

9 BL, MS. Harley 3776, ff.1–24v. The *Vita* forms the first item in a miscellaneous volume, which originally comprised portions of MSS 3776 and 3766. Other items include a relic list detailing Harold's gifts to his foundation (ff.31–35v.), and an account of Waltham's principal relic, its miracle-working cross (ff.43–62v.): E.G.M., 'A manuscript from Waltham Abbey in the Harleian collection', *British Museum Quarterly*, 7, 4 (1933–34), pp.112–8.

10 *VH*, cap.1. That the author regarded Harold as a saint is evident, for example, from the statement that 'after his death it was apparent from his miracles that he had gone to heaven' ('ille de mundo recessit, et quia ad Deum abiit miraculorum indiciis patenter declaravit'): *VH*, cap.4. *Cf.* also the reference to the intercession of holy king Harold ('sancti Regis Haroldi intercessio'): ibid, cap.20.

11 *VH*, cap.2, 11-2.

12 *VH*, cap.3. Evidence (as Birch points out) that the author wrote after Henry's death in 1189. On the reformation of Waltham in 1177 see R. Ransford, *The Early charters of the Augustinian canons of Waltham Abbey, Essex*, Woodbridge, 1989, pp.xxiv–xxv, 33.

13 *VH*, cap.4.

14 *VH*, cap.5-8.

15 *VH*, cap.13-14.

16 *VH*, cap.15.

17 *VH*, cap.16; Wm. of Malmesbury, *Gesta Regum*, pp.303, 306-7.

18 R. Twysden, ed., *Ailred of Rievaulx, De Vita et Miraculis Edwardi Confessoris* (*Historiae Anglicanae Scriptores Decem*), London, 1652, col.394.

19 *VH*, cap.17.

20 Even assuming, as the author claims, that Gyrth had been little more than a boy at the time of Hastings, he would have been well over 130 years old by 1184!

21 *VH*, cap. 18. The author claims that his source, Michael, chamberlain (*camerarius*) of the church at Waltham, had been an eyewitness to these events.

22 *VH*, *Narratio inclusi*, pp.94-9.

23 E.g. *VH*, p.x.

24 P. G. Schmidt, '*Veritas Naufragatur*', pp.193-200.

25 *VH*, caps.2-3, 7, 9.

26 D. W. Rollason, *Saints and relics in Anglo-Saxon England*, Oxford, 1989, pp.218-9; H. R. Loyn, 'Harold after Hastings', *Transactions of the Battle and District Historical Society*, 23 (1976, for 1973-74), pp.14-6.

27 'volumen . . . ad laudem et de laude gloriose ac deifice crucis operiosius elaboratum gestis memorabilibus fundatoris vestri, cuius memoria in benedicitone est, cupitis insigniri . . . Crucis sancte ex toto nimirum accedit glorie quicquid in servi sui meritis et virtutibus enituit commendabile.': *VH*, prologue, p.4.

28 Ibid., pp.3–4.

29 'To this church, king Harold, now numbered among the saints, was believed to have entrusted these relics:' BL Harley MS. 3776, ff.31r–v., lines 50–1 of a poem of 70 lines.

30 Ibid., f.31v.; P. G. Schmidt, '*Veritas Naufragatur*', p.202. Note that in his preface the author of *VH* repeatedly addresses the *patres reverendi* of Waltham in the second person plural and refers to Harold as *fundator/patronus/nutritor vester*. Though very closely connected with the college, he was probably not of the foundation.

31 'Crux videlicet magna et sancta, post Deum advocata nostra, totius nostre religionis et honoris huius loci principalis causa:' BL Harley MS. 3776, f.33.

32 Ibid., f.33.

33 For his career, which may be deduced from comments in his text, see *Foundation of Waltham*, pp.xxvi–xxvii, 10–2, 35; A. Gransden, *Historical writing in England* c.550–c.1307, London, 1974, p.271.

34 *Foundation of Waltham*, pp.28–31.

35 '. . . pro certo quiescit Walthamiae: cuius corporis translationi, quum sic se habebat status ecclesiae fabricandi, vel devotio fratrum reverentiam corpori exhibentium, nunc extreme memini me tertio affuisse': ibid., pp.30–1.

36 It should be pointed out, however, that in his text the author of the *De Inventione* does not refer to Harold as a saint. While Edward the Confessor is 'sanctissimus rex', Harold, 'vir ille strenuus', is a Christian hero: 'gloria regni, decus cleri, fortitudo militiae, inermium clipeus, certantium firmitas, tutamen debilium, consolatio desolatorum, indigentium reparator, procerum gemma:' ibid., pp.15, 25, 27.

37 J. F. Dimock, ed., *Giraldi Cambrensis opera*, vol. VI, GCO, 8 vols (Rolls Series, XXI) London, 1861–91, VI, p.140. For the date see ibid., pp.xxxiii–xxxix, confirmed by R. Bartlett, *Gerald of Wales, 1146–1223*, Oxford, 1982, p.216.

38 *Itinerarium Kambriae*, Lib. II, cap. XI: *De fluvio Deiae transcurso, et Cestria cum notabilibus suis*: '. . . Similiter et Haroldum regem se habere testantur: qui, ultimus de gente Saxonica rex in Anglia, publico apud Hastinges bello cum Normannis congrediens, poenas succumbendo perjurii luit; mutisque, ut aiunt, confossus vulneribus, oculoque sinistro sagitta perdito ac perforato, ad partes istas victus evasit: ubi sancta conversatione cujusdam urbis ecclesiae jugis et assiduus contemplator adhaerens, vitamque tanquam anachoriticam ducens, viae et vitae cursum, ut creditur, feliciter consummavit.'

39 A. T. Thacker, 'The Collegiate Church of St John', in *idem* and C. P. Lewis, eds, *Victoria History of Cheshire*, (henceforth *VCH. Ches.*), V, Oxford and London, forthcoming, 1996.

40 J. Tait, ed., *Chartulary of Chester Abbey* (Chetham Society, 2nd series, LXXVIII, LXXXII), Manchester, 1920–23, I, p.94; G. Barraclough, ed., *Charters of the Anglo-Norman earls of Chester* (Record Society of Lancashire and Cheshire, CXXVI), Liverpool, 1988, pp.113, 122, 132 (nos. 99, 109, 117); *idem*, ed., *Early Cheshire charters*, Oxford, 1957, p.12; W. F. Irvine, 'Chester in the 12th and 13th centuries', *Journal of Chester Archaeological Society*, new series, 10 (1904), p.16. Whether Andrew the earl's chaplain is to be identified with the chaplain of St Peter's is unclear. That there were at least two well-connected priests of that name in Chester is apparent from the fact that Andrew the canon and Andrew the chaplain both witness Richard of Wallasey's grant to St Werburgh's abbey: *Chart. Chester Abbey*, II, p.336.

41 J. Brownbill, ed., *Calendar of deeds and papers of the Moore family*, (Record Society of Lancashire and Cheshire, LXVII), Liverpool, 1913, p.146. The grant, which is undated, is attested by the mayor and sheriffs of the city for the year 1256–57: B. E. Harris and A. T. Thacker, 'Lists of Mayors and Sheriffs', in *VCH. Ches.* V.

42 'Gruffudd ap Maredudd ap Dafydd, Odes to the Crucifix at Chester', *Cheshire Sheaf*, 3rd series, 22 (1925), pp.37–40; D. Jones, *The Church in Chester* (Chetham Society, 3rd series, VII), Manchester, 1957, p.51.

43 *Taxatio Ecclesiastica Angliae et Walliae, Auctoritate Papae Nicholai IV*, (Record Commission, 1802), p.258; D. Jones, *Church in Chester*, p.51.

44 J. Stevenson, ed., *Ralph of Coggeshall. Chronicon Anglicanum*, (Rolls Series, LXVI), London, 1875, p.1.

45 'Notandum quod multos vidimus boni testimonij viros qui dixerunt se longo tempore post hoc bellum haroldum regem vidisse. et in heremo usque ad annum xxiij. henrici secundi anglorum regis vixisse:' C. Fell, 'English history and Norman legend in the Icelandic saga of Edward the Confessor', *Anglo-Saxon England*, 6 (1977), p.234. *Cf. idem*, 'The Icelandic saga of Edward the Confessor: its version of the Anglo-Saxon emigration to Byzantium', *Anglo-Saxon England*, 3 (1974), p.181; M. Cohen, 'From Throndheim to Waltham to Chester', pp.143–4.

46 *Foundation of Waltham*, p.30.

47 *Foundation of Waltham*, pp.xxvi–xxvii, 10–2, 35. The author wrote while William de Mandeville, earl of Essex, (d. 1189) was still alive. Ibid., pp.9, 13.

48 *VH*, cap.7.

49 *VH*, cap.11; *Foundation of Waltham*, pp.25–8.

50 *VH*, cap.17; *Foundation of Waltham*, pp.28–31.

51 *Foundation of Waltham*, pp.31–3.

52 There is some divergence about how the story was disseminated in Chester. The main text of the *Vita* presents the hermit himself as suspected of being Harold and when questioned offering ambiguous replies. The appendix, by contrast, makes the priest Andrew solely responsible for the disclosure: *VH*, cap.15, *Narratio inclusi*.

53 M. V. Taylor, ed., *Lucian Liber de Laude Cestriae*, (Record Society of Lancashire and Cheshire, LXIV), Liverpool and Manchester, 1912.. For recent comment on Lucian and the historiography of the period see D. Crouch, 'Administration', pp.71–3; A. T. Thacker, 'Cheshire', in C. R. J. Currie and C. P. Lewis, eds, *English county histories: A guide*, Stroud, 1994, p.71.

54 Lucian, *De Laude*, pp.8–10, 11–2, 37–9, 51–2, 56.

55 Ibid., p.59.

56 Ibid., pp.10–2, 19–20, 30, 37–9.

57 R. C. Christie, ed., *Annales Cestrienses* (Record Society of Lancashire and Cheshire, XIV), Liverpool and Manchester, 1887, p.14.

58 T. Jones, transl., *Brut y Tywysogyon or Chronicle of the Princes*, (Board of Celtic Studies, University of Wales, History and Law Series, XI), Cardiff, 1952, pp.lxxiii, 127, 222. *Cf. idem*, ed. and transl., *Brenhinidd y Saesson or the Kings of the Saxons*, (ibid., XXV), Cardiff, 1971, pp.xiv, xvii–xviii, 270–1.

59 C. Babington and J. R. Lumby, eds, *Ranulf Higden, Polychronicon*, 9 vols, (Rolls Series, XLI), London, 1865–86, VII, pp.244–6.

60 'In cuius victoriae signum, perpetuamque memoriam, lapides in Wallia more antiquo in titulum erectos, locis plerisque in quibus victor extiterat, literas huiusmodi insculptas habentes plurimos invenies, HIC FUIT VICTOR HAROLDUS:' *Gir. Camb. opera*, VI, p.217.

61 For recent discussion see A. T. Thacker, ed., *The earldom of Chester and its charters, Journal of Chester Archaeological Society*, 71 (1991), esp. *idem*, 'The earls and their earldom', pp.11–8, and D. Crouch, 'The administration of the Norman earldom', pp.70–3. See also B. E. Harris, 'Ranulph III, earl of Chester', *Journal of Chester Archaeological Society*, 58 (1975), pp.109–13.

62 On Hugh II see A. T. Thacker, 'Earls and their earldom', pp.13–5; T. A. Heslop, 'Seals of the 12th-century earls of Chester', in A. T. Thacker, *Earldom of Chester*, pp.184–92.

63 From 1181 to 1187 Ranulf was a minor and the earldom was in royal wardship: R. Stewart-Brown, ed., *Cheshire in the Pipe Rolls, 1158–1301*, (Record Society of Lancashire and Cheshire, XCII), Liverpool, 1938, pp.6–25.

64 A. T. Thacker, 'Earls and their earldom', pp.14–5; J. W. Alexander, *Ranulf of Chester: a relic of the Conquest*, Athens, GA, 1983, pp.1–17.

65 A. T. Thacker, 'Earls and their earldom', p.17.

66 This material was used by the 16th-century monk Henry Bradshaw in his vernacular verse Life of the saint: C. Horstmann, ed., *Life of St Werburge* (*EETS* [original series], LXXXVIII), London, 1887.

67 Ibid., pp.154–5, 157–8 (lines 681–729, 758–99).

68 *Gir. Camb. opera*, I, p.186; VI, p.139.

69 M. R. James, ed., *Walter Map, De Nugis Curialium*, revised edn, Oxford, 1983, pp.xxxii, liii, 478–82. For other references to the legend see J. Hinton, 'Notes on Walter Map's *De Nugis Curialium*', *Studies in Philology*, 20 (1923), p.465.

70 Matilda was, of course, the wife of Henry V, not Henry IV.

71 Higden, *Polychronicon*, VII, pp.466–8. The common link could be hostility to Henry II, who would have been bastardized if the emperor Henry V had really survived at Chester. I am grateful to John Gillingham for this point.

72 F. Barlow, *Edward the Confessor*, London, 1970, p.243; M. Chibnall, ed., *Orderic Vitalis, Historia Ecclesiastica*, 6 vols, Oxford, 1969–80, II, p.138.

73 A. Williams, '*Princeps Merciorum Gentis*: The family, career and connections of Ælfhere, ealdorman of Mercia', *Anglo-Saxon England*, 10 (1982), p.171; C. Hart, *Early charters of northern England and the North Midlands*, Leicester, 1975, pp.344–5.

74 J. Earle and C. Plummer, eds, *Two Anglo-Saxon Chronicles Parallel*, 2 vols, Oxford, 1892–9, I, p.133.

75 Ibid., I, 146–8; A. T. Thacker, 'Anglo-Saxon Cheshire', in B. E. Harris and A. T. Thacker, eds, *VCH. Ches.* I, Oxford and London, 1987, p.262.

76 C. Hart, *Charters of N.-W. Midlands*, p.342.

77 B. Thorpe, ed., *Florentii Wigornensis, Chronicon ex Chronicis*, 2 vols, London, 1848–49, I, p.216.

78 F. Barlow, *Edward the Confessor*, pp.206–7; *Two Saxon Chron.*, I, pp.184–6.

79 A. T. Thacker, 'Anglo-Saxon Cheshire.', pp. 262–3; P. H. Sawyer, ed., 'Domesday Survey: Text', in *VCH. Ches.* I, p.344 (no. 7).

80 F. Barlow, *Edward the Confessor*, pp.207–12; A. T. Thacker, 'Anglo-Saxon Cheshire', p.263.

81 A. T. Thacker, 'Anglo-Saxon Cheshire', p.263; *idem* and P. H. Sawyer, 'Domesday Survey: Introduction', *VCH. Ches.* I, pp.316–7.

82 *Flor. Wig.* I, p.228; B. Hudson, 'The family of Harold Godwinsson and the Irish Sea province', *Journal of the Royal Society of Antiquaries of Ireland*, 109 (1979), pp.92–3.

83 *Flor. Wig.* I, p.276. It has been conjectured that she was also the mother of Ulf Haroldson, captured by William I and released by William II, together with Duncan, son of the king of Scots, in 1087: ibid. II, p.21.

84 E. A. Freeman, *Norman Conquest*, IV (2nd edn), pp.142–3, 753–4.

85 Ibid., pp.791–3; B. Hudson, 'Family', pp. 92–100; *Flor. Wig.* II, pp.2–3.

86 Wm. of Malmesbury, *Gesta Regum*, II, pp.319, 376.

87 Orderic, *Hist. Eccl.*, II, pp.228, 234, 236.

88 'Domesday Survey: Text', p.343 (no. 1e).

89 *VH*, cap.14.

90 Since this paper went to press; a new edition of the *De Inventione* has been published: L. Watkiss and M. Chibnall, eds, *The Waltham Chronicle*, Oxford, 1994. The editors' conclusions differ little from those advanced here, except perhaps in their evaluation of the secular canons' attitude to the cult of Harold. It is highly unlikely that the translations of Harold's remains were intended to inhibit veneration, as they suggest (pp.xiii–xiv). The clear sense is that, as we might expect, they were occasioned by reverence for the body and intended to facilitate it. It is only after Henry II's reform of 1177 that devotion to Harold's corporeal remains appears to have been neglected or expressly discouraged.

9

Recognition of worth in
Pearl and *Sir Gawain and the Green Knight*

NICK DAVIS

AT A CRITICAL POINT in the debate over merit and salvation which figures very prominently in *Pearl*, the Pearl Maiden deploys the Parable of the Vineyard in order to remind or convince the dreamer of the distance that separates divine action from human understanding. It is an exposed moment in the argument of the poem where structures of explanation could readily break down altogether. The parable is retold substantially from the viewpoint of the vineyard labourers (in Matthew xx there is no comparable effect of 'viewpoint'), whose sense of rightful dealing is understandably affronted when those latecomers who have not seen through a whole day's work in the vineyard receive exactly the same wages as they do. Their 'Uus þynk uus oȝe to take more' (line 552)[1] would have had considerable resonance in an era of widespread labour scarcity when the levels of remuneration due to agricultural workers were commonly a matter of fierce dispute. Nevertheless, the Lord of the Vineyard sends the protesting men on their way, informing them from an unassailable position that he has dealt with them justly and that their objections are quite out of place; the men's assessment of the worth of their labour is not met by a corresponding recognition of its worth. In this passage and elsewhere the *Gawain* poet[2] engages with a set of preoccupations — implicitly philosophical, though practical enough in their immediate import — which often emerge into the foreground of fourteenth-century writing: given that human beings' ordinary dealings with the world produce a reliable sense of what things in it, including their own activities, are worth, how far does this estimation reveal the value that things genuinely possess? A case in point would be that of an agricultural hand in a late feudal society conscious of the market value of his labour; his ordinary truck with people supplies him with an understanding of just dealing, resting on agreed quantifying procedures, which will in its turn tend to form part of his more generalized conception of Justice and its workings. The cited passage from *Pearl* conveys, however, in very unpalliated form the notion that absolute justice and the sense of justice at which the vineyard labourers have arrived by being vineyard labourers stand in no necessary correspondence whatsoever.

Thinkers of the thirteenth and fourteenth centuries possessed, by comparison with their predecessors, a sharply defined sense of what a later era would call 'rational method', where rationality is a matter of evaluating things by publicly available criteria, or of assigning things accurately to relative positions on a specified conceptual grid. The historian of science A. C. Crombie writes of 'a general movement in practical life to quantify space, time, weight, and other aspects of the world as experienced and used'.[3] Typical manifestations of this diffuse cultural tendency are the later medieval adoption of the comparatively efficient Hindu-Arabic numerals, and an associated positional arithmetic, for the construction of calendars and astronomical tables as well as for some commercial reckoning, and changed practices of timekeeping associated with the gradual introduction of mechanical clocks; a revealing example would be the clock of Henri de Vick set up on the Palais Royale at Paris in 1370, which divided the day into twenty-four equal hours and with which the bell-ringing of the city was synchronized by royal edict. Developments of the kind yielded apprehensions of a world whose processes were at least partly available for calculation. These apprehensions were probably lent further strength by consonant developments in academic thought which suggested that truth, unchanging and absolute in the familiar philosophical conception, might be made the object of a purely logical enquiry. To bring out the distinctiveness of this phase or tendency in later medieval academic reasoning, Crombie compares the case of two eleventh-century clerks who are attempting to demonstrate the truth of the already-known fact that the internal angles of a triangle add up to two right angles; their final recourse is to test the proposition by experimenting with shapes cut from parchment. By the thirteenth century, however, western thinkers had become acquainted with Graeco-Arabic scientific method, and with classical texts (principally the *Elements* and Aristotle's treatments of logic) which very fully expounded the nature of logically formalized deductive reasoning, which together suggested that mathematical reasoning held massive philosophical promise. Among the fruits of this acquaintance are Grosseteste's installation of mathematics as the meta-science ('All causes of natural effects have to be expressed by means of lines, angles and figures'), and the Oxford Calculators' mathematical charting of evenly accelerated or decelerated motion, as applicable in their view to the operation of divine grace on the movement of natural objects.[4]

These cultural developments posed a cognitive problem which had two principal dimensions: first, how far does (what I am calling) 'rational method' reach? What precision in quantification and deductive reasoning have in common is that they are powerful mechanisms for producing agreement about the nature of things; their results are, in their own presented terms, difficult to controvert. Does such agreement, however, give human beings a conceptual purchase on the reality of things? Later medieval academic philosophy was shaped in important respects by an attempt to impose limits to a confident, expansive rationalism whose most powerful avatar was new Graeco-Arabic science. 219 propositions associated, broadly, with the new science were condemned at Paris in 1277; the general effect of this influential condemnation was, as Edward Grant puts it, to assert 'God's infinite and absolute creative and causative power against those who thought to circumscribe it by the principles of natural philosophy'.[5] In the course of a discussion of angels' spatial location Henry of Ghent voiced widespread suspicion of a mathematically-founded rationalism in declaring that the best mathematicians often make the worst philosophers, since 'they cannot raise their minds above the spatial notions upon which mathematics is based'.[6] Second, what in any case counted as rationality's proper object, given that academic practice tended to sustain the traditional (ultimately classical) perception that authentic mathematical reasoning and ordinary, workaday calculation were two quite different things? According to Boethius's standard textbook, the *De Arithmetica*, mathematics conducted with a properly philosophical set of mind yields intuitions of transcendental order, furnishing the means by which one knows truth in its absolute, unchanging form. By the same token the practice of philosophical ('Pythagorean', 'speculative') mathematics cannot be expected to serve worldly needs; Boethius transmits, implicitly, his culture's well-established working distinction between *arithmetica*, or disinterested investigation of the properties of number, and base numerical reckoning (*logistica*), the exclusive concern of merchants and slaves. The pure, stable forms which are *arithmetica*'s objects of study are not, in principle, to be encountered in ordinary experience: as Boethius' textbook puts it, they 'pass into a condition of inconstant changeableness' ('in vertibilem inconstantiam transeunt')[7] when joined to any form of corporeal existence.

These are emergent problems for fourteenth-century poetic writers, as for other thinkers of the period. The poetic writers often address them, however, and perhaps surprisingly, through reflection on relations between men — and women as they figure in men's thoughts — so delving into the cultural foundations of Western rationalism itself. By deeply-laid traditions of classical thinking, whose most powerful articulation is to be found in Plato and later Platonists, the touchstone for attainment of reason (*nous, logos, ratio*) is that reason should be seen to have submitted man's (male) relations with woman to a regime of precise and logically ordered deliberation.[8] A common, if somewhat elliptical, expression of the principle across a wide range of philosophical writing was the contention that reasoning is a matter of submitting the female or more 'disorderly' part of one's mind to the control of the male or more 'orderly' part; the philosophical contention both appealed to and, as one would expect, was also used to justify, normative practices of social authority.[9] Reflection on what women are to men, familiar enough as a focus of interest in fourteenth-century writing, is thus intimately bound up with reflection on the nature and limitations of reason itself.

Reference to Langland and Chaucer will help to make the point clearer. *Piers Plowman* is developed partly out of, and as a critique of, the core idea that the life of a ploughman who works for a lord and owns a half-acre of land, dealing rightly with fellow human beings on a basis of concrete obligation and need, may already yield the thinking required for recognition of truth in its absolute form; as Piers puts it, he is truth's servant: 'I know him as well (as 'kyndely') as a clerk knows his books' (B-Text: Passus V, line 538).[10] On the way to encountering Piers, however, Langland's dreamer encounters Meed, a fine-looking and eloquent woman who manipulates the men who think they have power over her, and who is associated with whatever circulates in excess of rightful, justly measured dealing (see especially the beginning of Conscience's speech, Passus III, lines 230–58; 'bribery', for example, would be far too narrow a term to encompass Meed as perceived threat to orderly thinking). The poem's difficulties in settling conceptual accounts with Meed (see the endings of Passus III and IV) thus enforce a first apprehension of the irreducible difficulties that it faces in constructing a logical, step-by-step exposition of truth; 'woman' here is precisely that of which reasoning cannot render a self-validating and consistent account. To somewhat different effect but deploying a similar form of thinking, Chaucer's poems often invite reflection on the difference between what reasoning, in a broadly Graeco-Arabic conception, illuminates or constructs, and kinds of worth which are conferred, for good or ill, by male perceptions of or responses to desired women, and which seem to require instatement outside structures of reasoning. *The House of Fame*, in this respect a kind of Chaucerian poetic manifesto, accordingly contrasts the rational architecture of the *Aeneid* with the passionate self-declaration of the wronged Dido (in this passage the reference shifts from Virgil to the Ovid of the *Heroides*) for which this architecture can find no satisfactory place; it then goes on to contrast the mechanical and stochastic operation of fame, whose explicability seems to be in inverse proportion to its claims on our interest (the dreamer's eagle-instructor is a pedant, the chance dealings of fame are tracked at tedious length to show precisely that they are chance dealings), with the sheer, incalculable attractiveness of those 'love-tydynges' which a 'man of gret auctorite' (lines 2143, 2158)[11] seems to be on the verge of delivering at the point where the poem breaks off. In both cases the proposed rational frame proves inadequate to an object that it supposedly enframes. The Knight's Tale similarly sets the malign cunning that Saturn brings to the resolution of a logical problem at the expense of Arcite's life against the significance with which Arcite invests his dying words to Emily, in defiance of available rational schemata ('Foryet nat Palamon, the gentil man'; line 2797).

Troilus and Criseyde provides what may be a still more pointed exposition of the idea. At a foregrounded moment in the poem Chaucer's heroine startlingly invokes Euclidean deductive reasoning as a means of standing out against Pandarus's insistence that she admit Troilus to her bedchamber (we are at the centrally-placed pivot of the poem's action: Criseyde and Troilus are about to become lovers):

> [W]hether that ye dwelle or for hym go,
> I am, til God me bettre mynde sende,
> At dulcarnoun, right at me wittes end.

> (Book III, lines 929–31)

'Dulcarnoun', deriving from an Arabic phrase meaning 'The two-horned', was the name commonly given to the visual demonstration of *Elements*, Proposition I.47, now better known as Pythagoras' theorem. This theorem is the most important building block of many in the massive structure of Euclid's work. As well as being difficult, I.47 forms part of an exemplary structure of logical demonstration: its validity is borne out by reference to the already-established validity of foregoing propositions, and it will in its turn be incorporated into the proof of propositions that follow. Criseyde is thus stating plainly enough, within the limits of tact, that she can find absolutely no reason for admitting Troilus to her bedchamber, where reason is a matter of proceeding to a consequence that follows logically from what she and other parties to the transaction have done before. The tact is present in the concession that there *might* be a logic to her uncle's proposal, but that she really cannot see it: the way is open for Pandarus to explain through cogent reasoning why she should yield to this latest and most unreasonable-looking demand of Troilus's love. Pandarus, however, getting the Euclidean reference wrong,[12] goes on flatly insisting that Criseyde do what is required of her, whereupon she simply passes the initiative back to him ('"Than, em", quod she, "doth herof as yow list"'; line 939). The burden of the passage seems to be that the validity claimed for matters of love, where 'love' = 'male desire', is not something that Criseyde is going to be in a position to establish through the application of any available process of reasoning.

All four of the poems ascribed to the *Gawain* poet show a will to probe the nature or natures of reasoning, and to assess reasoning's powers of objective evaluation. The two poems that have had the widest modern currency, *Pearl* and *Sir Gawain and the Green Knight*, test out forms of inherently valid reasoning in actions given shape by the pressure of male desire. Their companion pieces adapt and reframe Old Testament narrative in such a way as to foreground anomalies in human processes of reasoning as such. *Patience* and *Cleanness* are, among other things, very clear narrative statements, in the spirit of the 1277 Condemnation, of the principle that God's absolute and infinite creative power is not to be circumscribed by human efforts of intellectual understanding. Jonah's retention of life when the whale swallows him in *Patience* (see esp. lines 258–9), and the universal Flood and destruction of Sodom and Gomorrah in *Cleanness* (see esp. lines 363–72, 947–1052) are presented as drastic affronts to an envisaged order of things of the kind that a natural philosophy might construct. At the same time, however, these poems give a prominent role to logical reasoning as a necessary aid to reflection on the relationship between human thinking and a transcendent God. In two revealing episodes, and by an irony that seems characteristic of the whole Cotton Nero group, this reasoning operates outside the volitional control of its human bearers: what it articulates for them is virtually the opposite of what they want to find themselves saying. *Cleanness* develops Abraham's pleading with God for the preservation of Sodom and Gomorrah at Genesis xviii:16–33 as an elaborate request for mercy made as a reasoned case which of its nature solicits justice. Abraham's reasoning here, unlike its scriptural counterpart, explicitly breaks down in a final, desperate appeal to mercy as such: in effect, 'Temper your anger and save my kinsman Lot' (see lines 713–78). Reasoning has, in other words, genuinely clarified the nature of a plea which cannot, however, be made adequately within its terms. In *Patience* Jonah, infuriated by God's failure to destroy Nineveh as promised, constructs — accurately in context — the image of a 'courteous' God for whom both justice and mercy are available modalities of action (see lines 413–28). What Jonah cannot do (indeed, by his own heartfelt declaration cannot do), however, is live the state of unconditional acceptance or patience *vis-à-vis* the actions of a transcendent God which his reasoning logically recommends: he lays no claims to the 'courtesy', or graceful spontaneity of behaviour, which he attributes to the God who has singled him out as a prophet. Laurence Eldridge has suggested that in characterizing patience as a 'poynt' — usually glossed as 'virtue' — which often displeases those who exhibit it, the poem's opening and closing lines allude to contemporary reflection on the nature of the mathematical *punctus* or point on a line.[13] Although philosophers disputed the

question of whether the *punctus* exists *in re* or only as a creature
of the mathematical imagination, there was general agreement
that the notion of a *punctus* is to be arrived at solely through
logical inference and construction.[14] It is not, then, an entity
which one can meet or whose place one can occupy in
experience; hence the disconcerting precision of Julian of
Norwich's 'I saw God in a poynte'.[15] Patience as mathematically-
conceived 'poynt' would be a virtue which is imaginable, and
(in context) real, but not available for the sort of scrutiny that
one brings to an object that one can straightforwardly encounter
in one's own experience or anyone else's. The poems of *Patience*'s
group show, I suggest, a continuing concern with possible
dislocations between what reasoning posits and what experience
can substantiate for thought.

Structured as romances, *Pearl* and *Sir Gawain and the Green
Knight* bring this epistemologically uncomfortable state to very
full narrative definition. What I am calling 'romance' has as its
premise fixed engagement of a male protagonist's desire with a
valued woman, and depends for much of its interest on a complex
play of recognition which inherently involves more than one
figure: desire so characterized draws a male figure into an
action where a sense of identity is conferred on him by his
relations to a commanding female other, and to male or female
others with whom his desire for the valued woman embroils
him. *Sir Gawain and the Green Knight* stands, as is often pointed
out, in a somewhat parodic relation to romance form so
defined: Lady Bercilak plays the role of the commanding female
other, *vis-à-vis* Gawain, under circumstances in which Gawain
is more or less obliged to accept her as such, whatever else he
may think or want (see esp. lines 1195–9, 1282–5, 1658–63). At
one point she even provides Gawain with a potted summary of
a typical romance narrative (see lines 1512–9), apparently in
order to keep him in the right frame of mind. The generic
attribution may seem considerably odder in the case of *Pearl*,
given that the identities which crystallize out for the two main
speakers are those of grieving father and daughter lost through
death.[16] Nevertheless, *Pearl* in its opening stages directly

evokes the idea of romance adventure (see lines 63–4), and of male longing for a female loved one in its most generalized cultural form (*cf.* the 'luf-daungere' of line 11, and the erotically-inflected language of line 6). Both poems mobilize the energies of romance in order to open up and maintain a gap between acts of recognition performed spontaneously by the hero, and contrary, often disconcerting recognitions precipitated by the action as a whole.

The dreamer in *Pearl* is introduced into the poem as one who possesses a kind of certainty in his estimation of the lost one's worth:

> Queresoeuer I jugged gemmes gaye
> I sette hyr sengeley in synglure.
>
> (lines 7-8)

In this first perspective the pearl, when his, accordingly conferred certainty of worth on the dreamer himself. Given that she was a singularly precious gem, even a prince — he observes — would have acknowledged her worth and used it to manifest his own by having her displayed in the setting that his wealth and status could provide (here the poem deploys a common formula from the period's lapidaries):[17]

> Perle plesaunte, to prynces paye
> To clanly clos in golde so clere:
> Oute of oryent, I hardyly saye,
> Ne proued I neuer her precious pere.
>
> (lines 1-4)

This is not the same as saying, 'The pearl was precious *to me*', as one on whom the dreamer has subjectively conferred the highest value. On the contrary, the poem persistently places the dreamer in the position of a 'jeweller' (see the refrain of section V, lines 241–300, and the invocation of the Parable of the Pearl from Matthew xiii at lines 729–44), who would occupationally assess the worth of jewels by publicly recognized standards. Jill Mann has pointed out the relevance of concepts of assaying, or exact assessment of the material constitution of precious metals or gems, to the design of *Sir Gawain and the Green Knight* (this will be discussed in due course),[18] and they are also of considerable relevance to *Pearl*. Historians have argued that assaying was the medieval technical practice in which quantifying procedures were brought to their highest development;[19] professional assessment of the worth of a coin, or a gemstone, or a pearl, was in this sense a highly rational business, producing what were generally accepted as being objective standards of certainty. Different physical techniques were brought to the assaying of different substances (metal alloys were heated, pearls were encased in earth as a test of purity, which no doubt has a bearing on the thought of *Pearl*; see esp. lines 271–2), but a basic resource of the assayer was precise measurement of weight, effected by means of technically sophisticated scales which are recognizable ancestors of the modern chemical balance (the best were, in modern terms, sensitive to about 0.1 milligram). The assessment of individual jewels no doubt retained a subjective or unquantified component over which connoisseurs might argue. Nevertheless the dreamer, *qua* 'jeweller', primarily assigns the worth of his lost pearl to a domain of public, objective evaluation where it ought to be beyond controversy.

The dreamer's identity as mourner of the lost pearl is anchored in a series of reciprocally confirming and in their own terms secure recognitions. He has objectively assessed the pearl's worth. Familiar acquaintance with the pearl gave a worth to his life that has now been lost with her loss. His claim to relationship with the pearl is not so vitally one of ownership as one of knowledge: he knew that she was fitted to please a prince, or, in other words, that he knew the place to which her worth properly assigned her. A tomb is precisely her wrong place ('O moul, þou marrez a myry juele'; line 23). A good deal of the emotional and intellectual astringency of *Pearl* has, therefore, to do with the Pearl maiden's continuing capacity to elude the dreamer's convincing, in their own proffered terms genuine, claims to relationship through knowledge. Purely as perceived object, the maiden in her pearl-embroidered dress radically exceeds the human capacity to assess worth; the dreamer notices that her tunic centrally displays a pearl whose properties he must however declare unquantifiable:

Bot a wonder perle withouten wemme
Inmyddeez hyr breste watz sette so sure;
A mannez dom moȝt dryȝly demme
Er mynde moȝt malte in hit mesure.

(lines 221-4)

The last two lines apparently imply a (more or less Aristotelian) theory of cognition. The receptive part of the mind would normally 'melt' (and recompose) its properties in conformity with those of the object perceived; but the huge, blemishless pearl is not by these criteria an object, and resists the ordinary process by which the mind forms a judgement ('dom') about what something is. More than this, however, what the dreamer sees and hears under the maiden's tutelage points towards a thorough dismantling of the principle of objectivity as such. The landscaping of the dream has the dreamer address the maiden, as inhabitant of the Christian heaven, across a river (the barrier of physical death) which represents among other things the inherent limits of human rational comprehension. What he can see on his side of the river is, though strange enough (the trees have indigo trunks and silver leaves, the flame-coloured birds sing an improved human music, and so on; see lines 67-120), entirely amenable to human thinking; it is the Earthly Paradise, here a version of the highly exotic.[20] What is on the other side of the river is not, however, and as the Pearl maiden unflinchingly explains, amenable to human thinking at all: mortal human beings can attempt to think it, and are perhaps enjoined to make such an attempt, but the thinking in question generates baffling and interminable paradoxes. Here, says the maiden, there is absolute hierarchy and absolute equality, projected in the fact that my companions and I all have the rank of queen. Here 144,000 virgins including me are simultaneously married to a lamb ('Quat kyn þyng may be þat Lambe?' (line 771), asks the dreamer, a not unreasonable question under the circumstances).[21] I as entity am quite different from what you can possibly imagine — a proposition that the dreamer formally embraces in stating that Pygmalion could not have succeeded in portraying the maiden, and Aristotle could not have incorporated her properties into his philosophy of nature (see lines 750–2).

What this presentation of Heaven seems to challenge most specifically is that idea of quantifying method which initially gave the dreamer, outside the framework of the dream, his secure sense of what he and the Pearl maiden were. Assaying had, as has been said, measurement of weight as its core procedure (the word is derived *via* French 'assayer' from late Latin 'exagere', 'to weigh'), and weighing is inherently a matter of comparison between given objects. The period's assaying achieved very high standards of objectivity, but through dealing in comparative, not absolute, ascriptions of worth: it assigned objects to a position on a scale of worth on the methodical principle that worth can be relationally established. Similarly, a queen objectively assessed might be said to be someone who ranks higher than, for example, a countess (as the dreamer points out at lines 489–92); a principle of comparison seems to be intrinsic to the idea of 'queen' in its ordinary currency. To this going objectivity, however, the poem counterposes an absolute arithmetic which appears not to correspond to any reliable or familiar calculus of worth; the maiden's worth moves as it were off the scale now that she defines herself as belonging properly in Heaven.

It may be possible to give this 'absolute arithmetic' a more precise cultural form. At certain points in the poem it is suggested that the mathematics of heaven is simply not subject to the constraints of earthly mathematics: God can, at will, create a world in which quantity is not reduced by subdivision (all the brides of the Lamb are said to wish that he had five times as many brides; line 849, and see line 451).[22] At other points, however, God's power to place ordinary processes of calculation in disarray is apparently associated with similar powers attributed to the period's new-style positional arithmetic. The Roman numerals still most commonly used in the poem's era to represent numbered quantity are a weakly or slightly positional form of arithmetical notation. Their component figures — I, V, X, and so on — always possess the same numerical values, but in a given representation of number these values are added to or subtracted from one another according to the figures' relative placing. The new Hindu-Arabic numbering ('algorism'), accepted very gradually into European calculating practice during the medieval and early modern period,[23] is, by contrast, entirely positional: the '7' in '702' has an entirely different value from the '7' in '207'. Although the imported algoristic system is, as modern Europeans have found, inherently simple to use, it tends to look difficult and even perverse from the standpoint of one whose idea of notation has been formed by the Roman system; a good deal of later medieval documentary evidence shows how strongly algoristic procedures could be felt to challenge the clear dictates of common sense.[24]

The anxieties that the new system generated were often focussed on the figure '0', for which the Roman system and, just as importantly, the classically-derived philosophy of number studied in the schools had absolutely no counterpart. How was it that a figure representing 'nothing' could (depending on the way in which it was construed) multiply the value of, or hold a place of value in relation to, the numbers that adjoined it? To many contemporaries of the *Gawain*-poet the zero was a distinctly uncanny figure, sinister or possibly embodying a sacred mystery, but at any rate resistant to satisfactory logical placing. In the dreamer's perspective one of the most challenging doctrines that the maiden has to impart is that her worth is entirely a function of her place, in a context where mortal human beings cannot perceive place accurately. As she expresses it, to the dreamer-Jeweller, and when alive, she possessed worth through a kind of wishful projection, but her absolute value is and always has been fixed by her relationship to God:

Me þynk þe put in a mad porpose,
And busyez þe aboute a rayson bref;
For þat þou lestez watz bot a rose
þat flowred and fayled as kynde hyt gef;

Now þur3 kynde of þe kyste þat hyt con close
To a perle of prys hit is put in pref.
And þou hatz called þy Wyrde a þef,
þat o3t of no3t hatz mad þe cler;
þou blamez þe bote of þy meschef;
þou art no kynde jueler.

(lines 267–76)

Although it will appear to the dreamer that her value has been transformed, death has merely put it 'in pref', or to the test. The pearl of inestimable worth that stands in the middle of the maiden's tunic might be considered to evoke the form of numerical zero, the 'no3t'[25] already paradoxically endowed with a value ('o3t') which God alone determines, and which the dreamer, even under the maiden's expert instruction, now has the greatest difficulty in reading off. *Pearl* and *Sir Gawain and the Green Knight* both have one hundred and one stanzas, a numerical quantity unlikely to have been arrived at by chance, and — given the tail-in-mouth structure of the poems — one more satisfactorily expressed in the symmetrical form of '101' than in the asymmetrical form of 'CI'. More generally, *Pearl* seems to deploy concepts derived from positional arithmetic in order to point to the idea of a divine rationality that exceeds ordinary human powers of comprehension, or of a divine power to dispose things in their proper place that eludes ordinary human vision.

In discussion of *Pearl* it seems helpful to distinguish between two ways of ascribing worth; through a generally accepted objectivity, as represented in particular by the procedures of assaying, and through a quite differently founded perception of absolute worth, or relation to what Augustine calls 'that [divine] Law which is called the highest Reason'.[26] These polarities are also of considerable importance to the narrative design of *Sir Gawain and the Green Knight*. As I have argued elsewhere,[27] the arming passage from this poem (lines 566–669), which climaxes in the exposition of Gawain's heraldic device, the Pentangle (in more mathematical language, the regular starred pentagon), shows how ethical decision-making can be brought into working conformity with an absolute pattern of truth. This passage from the poem elaborates what amounts to a theory of the moral life, making particular reference to the choices that recurrently confront the male member of a courtly culture. As in the 'Maying' passage from Malory's *Morte D'Arthur*,[28] the 'gentle' man is regarded as having three different kinds of inalienable ethical commitment, to woman (in Malory's version, to one woman) through sexual love, to fellow males in a context of social and political obligation, and to God. Self-evidently these commitments can pull in contrary directions, as in the conspicuous case of Malory's Lancelot. But where the Malorian narrator recommends in broad terms that the commitments be, as far as possible (see the extreme delicacy of the situation in which Guinevere and Lancelot find themselves), thought of as an interrelated whole and honoured simultaneously, *Sir Gawain and the Green Knight* offers what seems to be far more precise guidance in reconciling aspects of life that can well be at odds with one another. As anyone moderately familiar with Euclidean geometry would have recognized (allusions to mathematical discourse in the language of the passage help to establish this as an available context), the Pentangle is built at every level out of that intriguing mathematical proportion, known in our own time as the 'Golden' proportion, where the ratio between the larger section and the smaller section of a cut line is repeated in the relation between the larger section and the whole. This mathematical proportion (a decimal approximation is 0.618), for which Euclid uniquely supplies a verbal definition (see *Elements*, VI, def. 3), has huge suggestiveness in a context of ethical reflection (especially Aristotelian ethical reflection in the period's familiar style) since it is the proportion that encodes the very principle of achieved proportionality across a number of different magnitudes: the relation of commitment A to commitment B already yields the relation of commitment B to commitment C. In the terms of the arming passage, Gawain is an exemplary knight because, through a good disposition of mind, he sets his three kinds of obligation in a proper ordering by relative importance, and in so doing brings them into a harmonious and mutually supportive arrangement. As a good deal of the action of the poem demonstrates, Gawain is amorously committed to woman (an important obligation) as one already committed by loyalty (treated as being of greater ethical significance) to fellow males, and committed to fulfilling obligations to males, where obligations to woman are also at stake, as one already devoted to fulfilling his obligations to God, the most binding of all.

The whole span of action in which Gawain is involved amply demonstrates the worth of this moral theory, and thereby demonstrates Gawain's worth in adhering to it; here I would wish to part company with those modern commentators on the poem who see it as questioning the practical utility of Gawain's moral idealism. Any knight with a less exacting and well-reasoned disposition of mind would have succumbed to the advances of Lady Bercilak, so departing fairly drastically from Christian rectitude, before losing his head more literally to her husband. At the point of crisis, however (see lines 1770–8), Gawain places his relations with the lady in the context of his relations with Bercilak, and of his relations with God, so preserving all three relationships simultaneously, or according to the conception of the Pentangle maintaining a harmony between these entirely disparate moral commitments. Gawain's self-excoriation in the concluding passages of the poem is not, however, that of one who believes that he has given demonstration of his worth as an ethical being, and examination of Gawain's performance in another, less serious transaction into which he is drawn — the formal exchanging of the kisses that he has received against the products of Bercilak's hunting — may help to explain why this should be so.

Gawain's absolute worth as the poem defines it is the approximation of his behaviour to an absolute pattern of truth: what one is invited to see in the elaborately-glossed spectacle of Gawain's arming is not exactly Gawain himself but the clarified pattern, a pure structure apprehensible by rational thought. Gawain similarly looks at the Pentangle emblem before placing the shield on his arm, presumably recalling to mind the pattern to which he shapes — as far as one could — his ethical choices. The narrative, however, in the manner of romance narratives, draws Gawain into structures of recognition where he becomes known to others, and in the same process known on this new basis to himself; here the most psychologically compelling, and at the same time least cognitively assimilable, recognitions accrue in Gawain's dealings with women. Superficially viewed, Gawain's exchanges of 'winnings' (kisses, parts of animals) with Bercilak, like the whole action of which they form a subsidiary part, show the possibility and value of bringing different kinds of ethical commitment, possessed of different degrees of importance, into a mutually supportive relationship: Gawain's courteous and rationally constrained dealings with a woman have provided him with the means to acquit himself well in his public dealings with a fellow-knight (he has 'winnings' of his own to exchange for the objects that Bercilak has more palpably won); the exchanges are carried through with a calculated precision (see Gawain's offer at line 1391: 'I wowche hit saf fynly, þaȝ feler hit were') evoking that of the Pentangle as geometrical 'bytoknyng' (line 626) of an absolute truth. The problem with this assessment, however, is that the kisses which Gawain has received from the lady cannot really be drawn into a structure of exchange. Gawain can kiss Sir Bercilak, but he cannot hand over the kisses as received: though the original kisses are in some sense 'things of value', they are not available for circulation and public appraisal in the manner of valued commodities (I might similarly say that my memories have value, but this is not a value which I can test adequately by comparing them with other people's; still less can I exchange them with other people's). Gawain and Bercilak extensively deploy a mercantile language as they hand over their respective winnings;[29] partly, it seems, to maintain a friendly pretence that objects really are being exchanged — one might say that friendly words here are the items that the parties to the transaction more genuinely trade, in that the men constantly profess admiration for one another's achievements; and partly — given that no one is

fooled — to mark the ironic distance between what takes place
and actual market dealing involving public arbitration of
value.[30]

A carefully inflected compliment that Bercilak produces on
the second day takes suitable measure of this distance:

> þe lorde sayde, 'Bi Saynt Gile,
> ȝe are þe best þat I knowe!
> ȝe ben ryche in a whyle,
> Such chaffer and ȝe drowe.'

(lines 1644–7)

— 'You'll soon be a rich man if you carry on like this.' Gawain as
'merchant' is becoming richer with each exchange (which
already negates the idea that a rightful exchange in the going
Aristotelian conception is taking place), apparently in a double
sense: first, Gawain is getting something for nothing: Bercilak
has said that the transferred kisses *might* be worth something, to
him, if he were told where they came from, but Gawain has
pointed out that this is not part of the contract (see lines 1391–7);
what Bercilak produces, on the other hand, manifestly
possesses some value (it displays the huntsmen's art, much of it
can be eaten), even if a large part of its value to Bercilak (the
excitement of a day's hunting) cannot genuinely be transmitted.
Second, given that the original kisses cannot be handed over,
Gawain is in effect keeping to himself these things of value: by
the end of day three he 'has' six of them. The enrichment is not
at one level a purely notional matter, since Gawain is being
frankly admired by Bercilak as one who has shown his ability to
win kisses: under this approving male gaze their value transfers
itself to him. Gawain's literary reputation was, among other
things, that of an adroit sexual opportunist (see Malory's reception
of the Gawain of French romance), and on his arrival at the castle
Bercilak's retainers have expected him to show special skill in
'luf-talkyng' (line 927). In this context the supposed exchanges
with Bercilak least ambiguously reveal Gawain's worth as that
of one on whom a woman or women have bestowed kisses.

Before God, Gawain maintains his worth by an honesty in
straightforward dealing which the poem apparently endorses.

Preparing himself to meet the Green Knight and, with a fair
degree of certainty, death, Gawain goes to a priest, confesses all
of his sins, and in a properly penitential spirit asks for mercy; on
which the priest 'asoyled hym surely and sette him so clene/As
domezday schulde haf ben diȝt on þe morn' (lines 1883–4).
There seems to be no point in the action at which we are given
reason to doubt Gawain's Christian scrupulousness, or the
possibility that a good knight can be a good Christian. The present
passage, grave and measured in tone, shows a Gawain behaving
very much unlike his French counterpart, and appears to mean
exactly what it says: Gawain made a good confession, and was
entirely absolved of his sins.[31] In his dealings with Bercilak
Gawain is less scrupulous by a small and measurable quotient
(retention of the Green Girdle). Nevertheless, dealings between
the two knights (for convenience Bercilak may be divorced
from his hostile, Green Knight *persona*) are generally characterized
by ready admiration, bonhommie and unwillingness to find
fault with a being whom one esteems on much the same basis as
one esteems oneself; Gawain obviously gives some offence to
himself in witholding the girdle (witness his wish to make that
day's exchange as quickly as possible), even though he has
decided that this is a necessary act, and at the poem's dénouement
Bercilak is quick to pronounce forgiveness on a friend who has,
under duress, mildly and locally deceived him (as it might be
worth pointing out, Bercilak is at the same time explaining that
he has deceived Gawain). In women, by contrast, Gawain
encounters a human other before whom he can retain a sense of
worth, if at all, only through what are felt to be extraordinary
feats of vigilance and cunning; by a logic that Gawain cannot
avoid, therefore, it is in dealings with women that the most
compelling, and possibly disconcerting, recognitions of worth
necessarily accrue. In the concluding action of the poem he
quickly mends relations with Bercilak where relations seem never
to have been severely damaged. Despite Bercilak's invitation,
however, he has no stomach for a further encounter with the
Lady of the Castle, before whom he was not capable of being
the person whom he took himself to be.

Gawain's much-discussed diatribe against women and their wiles (see lines 2407–28), which attempts to classify serious male dealings with women as acts of folly *tout court*, seems a desperate recourse under the circumstances, and a poor excuse for declining Bercilak's suggestion. Bercilak's final revelations concerning what has been hidden from Gawain, on the other hand, define the kind of recognition that the action now being formally brought to a close potentially has to offer. When set beside Gawain, bearer of the Pentangle, Bercilak can be heard as speaking for a different sense of ethical priority. In Fitt IV of the poem he takes on some of the inexorable judgemental authority of God as represented in other poems from the Cotton Nero group (see in particular lines 2338–40, and compare *Pearl*, lines 341–7, *Patience*, lines 525–7); the tone of his final speeches is that of an elder knight who has conducted a younger knight through a painful though necessary rite of initiation. At the same time, however, Bercilak would count in Aristotelian terms as an ethical primitive: he recommends a simple honouring of reciprocity in moral dealing (see lines 2354–7), which would imply that he has no use for or understanding of the cultivation of good proportionality in the fulfilment of varied moral commitments as recommended by the Pentangle passage; it is probably significant that Bercilak's castle is, though impressive and cunningly designed, marked out by a profusion of detailing that shows no concern for absolutes of architectural proportion (see lines 785–802, which compare it to the sort of fanciful decoration one would cut out of paper). But for this writer, it seems, unfolded narratives are also entities that violate absolutes of proportion: the precisely ordered moral theory of the Pentangle passage is thus preceded by dark warnings about the general fate of human intentions, approximately summed up in the gnomic 'þe forme to þe fynisment foldez ful selden' (line 499). I would suggest that Bercilak at the end of the poem speaks for those insights which become available specifically in the working out of a narrative, as distinct from an abstractive mapping of the moral life of the kind that the arming passage presents; within this narrative, as Bercilak now explains, women — including, in the 'goddes' (line 2452) Morgan, a woman of ultimately undefinable powers — have carried out the most serious probing of Gawain's worth.

The insights that this probing potentially brings would not be assimilable to the structure of thought projected in the Pentangle passage; hence, it seems, Gawain's difficulty in coping with them. In one respect the knowledge concerning Arthur and his knights that Morgan is capable of bringing to light lies below the threshold of ordinary cognition:

> þe maystrés of Merlyn mony ho hatz taken,
> For ho hatz dalt drwry ful dere sumtyme
> Wiþ þat conable klerk; þat knowes alle your kny3tez
> At hame.

(lines 2448–51)

By means of love-dealing with Merlin, Morgan has acquired a — to them — alarming psychological intimacy with the members of Arthur's court; she knows them 'at home', or more closely and invasively than they would usually be obliged to know themselves. In another respect, however, the assessment of Gawain over which Morgan presides yields objective results, of the kind that *Pearl* similarly counterposes to absolute revelations of worth. Bercilak characterizes the Lady's and Morgan's evaluations of Gawain, and finally of the whole court, as acts of assaying, defining his own agency in the testing of Gawain thus:

> And the wowyng of my wyf, I wro3t hyt myseluen;
> I sende hir to asay þe, and soþly me þynkkez
> On þe fautlest freke þat euer on fote 3ede.
> As perle bi þe quite pese is of prys more,
> So is Gawayn, in god fayth, bi oþer gay kny3tez.

(lines 2361–5)[32]

Gawain has emerged well from this testing, which is still, however, a matter of comparison: he has done well in the sense that other knights would have done worse. Behind Bercilak, meanwhile, stands Morgan, who has given Bercilak a role in a larger strategy of assaying:

Ho [i.e. Morgan] wayned me upon þis wyse to your
                                        wynne halle
For to assay þe surquidré, ȝif hit soth were
þat rennes of þe grete renoun of þe Rounde Table.
                                        (lines 2456-8)

Bercilak seems, moreover, to be one who fully accepts the name
and perceived worth that Morgan's powers bestow on him.
When Gawain asks for his 'right name', he responds thus:

'þat schal I telle þe trwly,' quoþ þat oþer þenne:
'Bertilak de Hautdesert I hat in þis londe,
þurȝ myȝt of Morgne la Faye, þat in my hous lenges.'
                                        (lines 2444-6)[33]

Modern editors have chosen to place a full stop after 'londe' in
this passage, but that leaves the next two lines awkwardly floating:
Bercilak here seems to be stating clearly enough that Morgan is
the one who sustains his name and reputation. There are, in the
poem's terms, declarable absolutes of worth, and also a going
currency of worth which has the objectivity of comparison and
the compellingness of humanly-exchanged recognition; the
second is what Bercilak here emphatically embraces.[34] It is hard
simultaneously to think the abstracting philosophical idealism
of the Pentangle, and the penetrating empirical enquiringness
of Morgan and her agents, but the narrative design of *Sir
Gawain and the Green Knight* calls for such an effort of
thought.

References

1 *Gawain* poet references are to M. Andrew and R. Waldron, eds, *The
poems of the Pearl manuscript*, London, 1978. 'U' and 'v' are, however,
treated according to the modern convention.

2 I accept the current view that the poems preserved in BL Cotton Nero
A.x are the work of a single writer, and that they probably belong to the
second half of the fourteenth century.

3 A. C. Crombie, *Science, optics and music in medieval and early modern thought*,
London, 1990, p.85.

4 See ibid., pp.85, 118–9, 128, 142–3. For the Calculators, see Marshall
   Clagett, *Science of mechanics in the Middle Ages*, Madison, WI, 1959, and,
   for a brief treatment of their influence which references recent work in
   the field, my 'The *Tretise of myraclis pleyinge*: on milieu and authorship',
   Medieval English Theatre, 12 (1990), pp.124–51.

5 In N. Kretzmann, A. Kenny and J. Pinborg, eds, *The Cambridge history of
   later medieval philosophy*, Cambridge, 1982, pp.537–8.

6 Cited in R. Klibansky, E. Panofsky and F. Saxl, *Saturn and Melancholy*,
   London, 1964, pp.338–9.

7 M. Masi, ed., *Boethian number-theory*, Amsterdam, 1983, p.71;
   G. Friedlein, ed., *De Arithmetica*, Leipzig, 1879, p.8.

8 For the Middle Ages and Renaissance the definitive expression of the
   idea was probably found in the *Timaeus*, Plato's elaborate cosmological
   myth which explains how a male creator-god submitted female inchoate
   matter to an optimal ordering in forming the cosmos that we have, so
   making it possible for human beings to come into possession of reason
   by a similar process. The *Timaeus* was the only text of Plato's available
   for study (in Latin translation) throughout the Middle Ages.

9 For a concise account of the philosophical tradition see Genevieve
   Lloyd, *The man of reason*, London, 1984, esp. pp.1–37.

10 References are to A. V. C. Schmidt, ed., *The vision of Piers Plowman*, London,
   1978.

11 References are to L. D. Benson, ed., *The riverside Chaucer*, Oxford,
   1987.

12 'Quod Pandarus, "Yee, nece, wol ye here? / Dulcarnoun called is
   'flemyng of wrecches' " '; lines 932–3. 'Fuga Miserorum' was the name
   properly given to an earlier proposition in *Elements* I; for these Euclid
   references see T. E. Hart, 'Medieval structuralism: Dulcarnoun and the
   five-book design of Chaucer's *Troilus*', *Chaucer Review*, 16 (1981),
   pp.129–70 (pp.162–3, notes 23 to 25). Pandarus is in any case not listening
   very closely to what Criseyde is saying: in his handling of the conver-
   sational exchange Criseyde tells him that admitting Troilus is difficult,
   on which he informs her that it is not difficult at all.

13 See L. Eldridge, 'Late medieval discussions of the continuum and the
   point of the Middle English *Patience*', *Vivarium*, 17 (1979), pp.90–115.
   I differ from Eldridge, however, on the application of this mathematical
   concept to the poem.

14 For more on the background to the debate, see A. G. Molland, 'Continuity
   and measure in medieval natural philosophy', in A. Zimmermann, ed.,
   Mensura. Mass, Zahl, Zahlensymbolik im Mittelalter, Berlin, 1983, pp.132–44.

15 M. Glasscoe, ed., *Julian of Norwich. A revelation of Love*, 3rd edn, Exeter, 1986, p.13.

16 The most direct identification comes at the very end. Norman Davis points out that the last stanza of *Pearl* uses a formula, 'In Christ's blessing and mine', typically found in parent's letters to children; see 'A note on *Pearl*' and the subsequent letter in *Review of English Studies*, new series, 17 (1966), pp.403–5, and 18 (1967), p.294.

17 See W. H. Schofield, 'Symbolism, allegory, and autobiography in *The Pearl*', *PMLA*, 24 (1909), pp.585–675, esp. pp.600–2.

18 See J. Mann, 'Price and value in *Sir Gawain and the Green Knight*', *Essays in Criticism*, 36 (1986), pp.294–318.

19 See C. S. Smith and R. J. Forbes, 'Metallurgy and assaying', in Charles Singer *et al.*, eds, *A history of technology*, III, Oxford, 1957, pp.27–71 (pp.59–68).

20 M. Andrew and R. Waldron, *Poems of the Pearl manuscript*, lines 113–6n, point to the influence of literary representations of the exotic including those found in Mandeville's *Travels* and the romance *Floire et Blancheflor*.

21 A. C. Spearing, '*Purity* and danger', *Essays in Criticism*, 30 (1980), pp.293–310, which draws on the anthropological enquiries of Mary Douglas, has very pertinent comments on the *Gawain*-poet's pervasive interest in entities of anomalous conceptual status.

22 There may be a reference to five's identity as a Boethian 'circular' number: however often five is multiplied by itself, the last digit of the sum produced is always five. In these terms the 'fiveness' of numbers generated out of five might be said not to be alterable by division or multiplication. The relevance of this concept, outlined in the *De Arithmetica*, to the Pentangle passage from *Sir Gawain and the Green Knight* is argued in Ross Arthur, *Medieval sign theory and Sir Gawain and the Green Knight*, Toronto, 1987, pp.31–45, and in my 'Gawain's rationalist Pentangle', *Arthurian Literature*, 12 (1993), pp.37–61 (p.46).

23 Arguably, the 'capture' of Europe by the new system was only completed in the Napoleonic educational reforms. Until that time calculation was still carried out in many localities by means of the abacus, and its results recorded in the Roman notation.

24 See Karl Menninger, transl. Paul Broneer, *Number words and number symbols*, Cambridge, MA, 1969, pp.422–8.

25 The *Middle English Dictionary* records early fifteenth-century use of 'nought' to mean 'numerical zero'.

26 'Illa lex quae summa ratio nominatur', *De libero arbitrio*, I, 6; *MPL*, XXXII, (Paris, 1877), col.1220.

27 See N. Davis, 'Gawain's rationalist Pentangle', p.46.

28 E. Vinaver, ed., *Malory: Works* 2nd edn, Oxford, 1971, pp.648–9.

29 For the extent and importance of mercantile linguistic usage in the poem as a whole, see R. A. Shoaf, *The Poem as Green Girdle: Commercium in Sir Gawain and the Green Knight*, Gainesville, FL, 1984, and J. Mann, 'Price and value'. Mann's analysis in particular brings out the instability of mercantile language as pressed into service by Gawain, Bercilak and the Lady of the Castle.

30 I fully concur with Mann's view that the poem does not evoke the idea of mercantile dealing in a spirit of aristocratic disdain; my argument is that the idea is introduced here quite seriously to evoke standards of rightful dealing to which the 'exchanges' between Gawain and Bercilak manifestly fail to conform.

31 I dissent from the widely-held view, most forcefully argued in J. A. Burrow, *A reading of Sir Gawain and the Green Knight*, London, 1965, pp.104–9, that Gawain cannot make a full and valid confession while intending to keep an item that he has 'won', the Green Girdle, from Sir Bercilak. It goes against the grain of the era's penitential instruction to treat cheating in a game as a matter of spiritual significance: the manuals characteristically distinguish between *kinds* of game which were dangerous to the soul (e.g. because they characteristically involved swearing or acts of violence), and kinds which are intrinsically harmless, taking no further interest in the conduct of the latter.

32 M. Andrew and R. Waldron's punctuation has been adapted.

33 As above.

34 J. A. Burrow, *A reading*, p. 134, similarly distinguishes between an absolute form of evaluation associated with Gawain, and a relativizing form of evaluation associated with Bercilak.

10

Constructing bliss:
Heaven in the *Pearl*

E. RUTH HARVEY

But, as it is written: 'Eye hath not seen, nor ear heard,
neither have entered into the heart of man, what things God
hath prepared for them that love him.' I Cor. ii 9.

THE TEXT, St Paul's quotation of Isaiah lxiv 4 in the first epistle
to the Corinthians, says it all: heaven is beyond human description;
the only official words we have on the subject say it is indescribable.[1]
Of course heaven has been described, but it often seems that it
was rather rash of the author to make the attempt.[2] It is in the
the third book of *Paradise Lost* that Milton traditionally loses
his readers; and more than one person has admitted to failing to
make it through Dante's *Paradiso*. But, somewhere in the
fourteenth century in the north-west of England, the *Pearl* or
Gawain poet situated most of his nameless poem about a lost
pearl in a landscape which provided at least a distant prospect of
the celestial city, and from that vantage-point tried to grapple
with the nature of heavenly bliss.

The medieval alliterative poets of the north-west of England
are famous for their mastery of elaborate specific vocabulary:
the correct technical terms for bits of armour or the parts of
ships, the terminology of the hunt and heraldry, skilful
variations on the innumerable rare words for battle scenes or
storms or topographical features. Yet this skill is not ideally
suited to descriptions of heaven. Dante conjures up a magnificent

symbolic planetary perspective where heaven is suggested by such ethereal images as light, Beatrice's smile and the celestial rose; Milton falls back on paradox: 'Dark with excessive bright thy skirts appear'[3] and lots of busy, if rather pointless, angels. The unknown poet of *Pearl* is more matter-of-fact: his heaven is a city in plain view, set in a paradisal landscape; but while the precise details, so dear to alliterative poets, must be read symbolically, it is the confrontation of the two characters in the poem which attempts specifically to define the meaning of heaven.

The poem now called *Pearl*[4] is the speech of a 'jeweller', grieving for a prized pearl he had lost in a garden, on a mound where beautiful flowers now grow. As he lay mourning, the grief in his heart fighting with his reason and faith, he fell asleep and had a vision. He dreamed that he was in a wonderfully beautiful landscape, full of jewels and light; the trees had indigo trunks and silver leaves; flame-coloured birds sang more beautifully than any instrument. He was led on by ever-increasing delight, comforted and joyful, until he saw across a stream a beautiful maiden, whom he recognized as his lost pearl. He thought to join her and stay with her for ever, but she, after her first courteous gesture of welcome, pointed out that he had completely misunderstood the situation: he was judging entirely by appearances and did not understand that the stream could not be crossed by the living. In answer to his questions, the maiden tried to explain that she was now in bliss; she told him about heavenly rewards, the value of innocence, and her own status as one of the 144,000 brides of the Lamb. When the baffled dreamer asked her to show him where she actually lived, she told him to walk upstream a little so that he would be able to see the New Jerusalem across the river. After a long description of the city, which appears very much as St John described it in the Apocalypse, the dreamer became aware of a procession: the brides of the Lamb and the Lamb himself, the biblical elders and the angels all moved towards the throne in the city. But when he saw his own Pearl, whom he had thought to be standing near him across the stream, taking her place within the procession,

he was so overwhelmed with emotion that he plunged into the
water to try to reach her, and woke up. In the brief conclusion
to his dream the speaker commended his lost pearl to God in
the conventional words of parental blessing. The poem is
perhaps the most elaborate surviving example of the whole
English alliterative tradition. Its 1,212 lines have both alliteration
and rhyme, concatenation and intricate numerical symbolism; it
is a thoroughly detailed and precise attempt to contain the
uncontainable, and describe the indescribable.

The exact nature of the relationship between the dreamer
and his lost pearl has provided the stuff of lively critical argument.
The dreamer never identified her any more precisely than as
one 'nerre than aunte or nece', who had left the world before
she had been in it two full years, but his parting commendation
of her to God, 'in Krystes dere blessyng and myn' implies that
she is his daughter. But this imprecision focuses attention on
what is surely the crucial point about the maiden: she is not just
a dead girl of uncertain age but the soul of a baptized child who
died in indubitable innocence, before she was capable of
committing any sins — the soul, in other words, of a human
being who is, by the Christian promise, guaranteed heaven. The
jeweller's problem is that a believing Christian should rather
rejoice than mourn for the death of such a child; heaven, by
definition, is the longed-for goal of every Christian soul, and a
baptized but sinless child would be entitled to immediate entry.
The dreamer acknowledges this himself at the beginning of the
poem: though reason and Christ offered him comfort for the
loss of his pearl, his 'wreched wylle' kept him in sorrow. *Pearl*
has often been described as a consolation poem, but its consolation
is addressed to the obstinate human conviction that the death
of a beloved person, even with the belief in 'going to heaven', is
not a joyful thought. The dreamer knows what he should
believe about heaven; he just has great difficulty in feeling the
correct emotions which should arise from that belief.[5]

To say that a small Christian child is better off dead sounds
extraordinarily brutal to us. We would, I think, hesitate to offer
any bereaved parent comfort by saying, 'well at least she is happier

where she is now' — not least because it has become rather unfashionable, even for believers, to be very specific, or even confident, about the joys of heaven. But it is also because to say such a thing would not address what we would see as the real issue: not the state of the child's soul, but the emotions of the parent. We have perhaps more belief in the survivors' grief than we have in the child's immortality. In the deeply Christian medieval world inconsolable grief was the more reprehensible in proportion to the degree of faith in heaven. *Pearl* presents, in its two protagonists, the direct confrontation of a rational faith in heaven with the human emotion which will not be comforted; the maiden is the product of medieval belief about the nature of heaven, and the dreamer embodies the earthly human response to that belief.

If our ideas about heaven have become rather murky, so that descriptions of heaven now seem to be foolhardy and naive, if not in poor taste, medieval authorities were much more definite. They did not, however, always agree. There are several kinds of medieval heaven. They can, in a rather simplifying schema, be polarized between two extremes: vulgar heaven and intellectual heaven. Vulgar heavens are inhabited by roving herds of freshly-roasted pigs; they feature rivers of wine, and birds that fly around fully cooked, shouting, 'Eat me!'. Such heavens are often explicitly parodic, like the one invented in Boccaccio's *Decameron* as part of a horrible practical joke: it is a land consisting of a mountain of grated parmesan cheese with free ravioli thrown in, where the vines are all tied up with sausages.[6] The English (or Irish) land of Cockaygne has a river of milk with skinny-dipping nuns to add to the general jollity.[7] Such fantasies provide a grosser gloss on the fundamental prerequisite of heaven: it ought to be the place where every desire is satisfied.[8] It just depends on your desire. In the Big Rock Candy mountains 'you never change your socks / And the little streams of alkyhol / Come a-trickling down the rocks'.[9] There is a pleasing concreteness and solidity to the imagery of vulgar heaven.

Intellectual heaven, on the other hand, satisfied the desires of the theologians, which were naturally austere and cerebral. Intellectual heaven (which was of course the official heaven of the Middle Ages) consisted of the ultimate satisfaction of the highest (though sometimes unrecognized) desire of the human soul: the desire for God. The vision of God 'face to face' in heaven comprised all truth, beauty, pleasure, riches, knowledge and love;[10] heaven consisted in the uninterrupted and ceaseless contemplation of God known as the Beatific Vision.[11] Within this vision all other joys found their place: the blessed would have a comprehensive knowledge of all the arts and sciences, and would top off their pleasure by contemplating, unmoved, the tortures of the damned.[12] Where vulgar heavens are charmingly specific with their lists of satisfying, if unlikely, pleasures, intellectual heavens tend to lean on St Augustine,[13] and place a heavy reliance on abstract nouns.

There are heavens in between these two extremes, of course. There are accounts offered by medieval visionaries which tend towards vulgar heaven in their concreteness but avoid its grossest manifestations. The naked nuns find a more elevated counterpart in the rather embarrassing sublimated eroticism of the female mystics;[14] the roasted pigs and pasta are most often replaced by ever-bearing fruit trees;[15] the rivers of wine and milk are joined by rivers of oil and honey, which somehow renders the effect biblical rather than alcoholic.[16] Heavens of this kind may be called 'conventional heaven': much of the imagery lingers on vaguely today: thrones, streets of gold in the holy city, blessed souls wearing white, fragrance, flowery meadows, beautiful music of voices, instruments (not harps) or sometimes birds. The pleasures are defined in sensory terms, but the whole effect is refined and rather restrained. *Pearl* preserves the beautiful landscape, delicate sensory pleasures, white robes and holy city which are characteristic features of conventional heaven.

If conventional heaven leans in the direction of vulgar heaven in imagery, the corresponding realm leaning towards intellectual heaven might be termed 'academic heaven'. Academic heaven is what you get when you accept the fundamental given of intellectual heaven, the Beatific Vision, but cannot let well alone. Academic heaven was constructed by the curious, who wanted to know more details about celestial bliss, and were not embarrassed to ask. It can be found in textbooks and compendia made for the purpose of instruction, such as the dictionary-cum-encyclopaedia the *Catholicon*,[17] or the late medieval encyclopaedia, the *Margarita philosophica*.[18] Here the interesting ramifications of the idea of heaven are thoroughly explored, sometimes with rather surprising conclusions.

For instance, do you enjoy the Beatific Vision immediately after death, or do you have to wait until after the Last Judgement?[19] If the souls of the righteous go directly to heaven after death, what difference will it make when they are given their bodies back after the last day? These were very obscure areas of enquiry, but it was usually accepted that the souls of the righteous deceased were already in heaven and enjoyed some kind of vision of God. In contemplating God they would enjoy knowledge of past, present and future, and read the secrets of the Trinity in the book of life.[20] They would have no bodies of any sort, but after the Judgement each soul would be given back its own body, to share in beatitude or damnation for eternity. Visionaries who reported on the state of the blessed not surprisingly tended to ignore the fact that separated souls are entirely invisible, and gave them their risen bodies in advance of the fact.

The nature of the risen body gave rise to much earnest discussion. If, for instance, heaven is (as Augustine said) the fulfilment of the individual human being in the love of God, then the fulfilled being must be perfected. Hence in heaven we cannot be resurrected just as we died in feeble infancy or decaying old age: the most widely held belief was that the just will all be resurrected at the age of thirty-three. There will be, therefore, no children in academic heaven, and no old folk; it is possible that the pre-Christian patriarchs will be resurrected in their aged dignity, but all those born in the Christian era will definitely be no more than thirty-four.[21] Knowledgeable medieval believers did not expect to meet their children in heaven: or at least, meet their children as children; they would meet perfected souls: the fulfilled potential of what their children would have been had they reached sinless adulthood.

The bodies of the blessed will be endowed with impassibility, clarity, subtlety and agility.[22] That is, they will not be subject to any suffering, they will be beautiful, with a brightness they can veil at will, they will be able to penetrate matter (walk through walls), and they will be able to move instantly from place to place. There will be no defects in the inhabitants of heaven. All physical disabilities will be corrected, missing limbs and wits supplied. It does not matter if your original body had been cremated or eaten by animals: it will still be restored in glorified form in heaven.[23] Every hair on the head is numbered (Luke xii; Matt. x) and will be restored. This gave rise, in academic discussion on heaven, to the awkward question: will not celestial bodies be rather unsightly if they get back all the hairs of their heads, and all their fingernails? The answer is that we can safely leave our future beauty to God, the supreme artist. What happens to bodies that have been eaten by cannibals — which party do they belong to? If all bodily matter goes back to the person it first belonged to, does that mean the child disappears into the seed of its father? For a moment a marvellously fantastic picture of the entire human race telescoping itself at lightning speed backwards into Adam, like something out of Hawking's universe, flashes before the mind. For that matter, what about Adam's rib? If he gets it back, where will Eve be? But the academic answer is no: the father's seed belongs to, and becomes the child, and Adam's rib was not really part of him; it was deliberately created as an extra.[24] But speaking of Eve, another awkward question arises: women are less perfect than men; if we are all raised perfect, will there be any women at all in heaven, or will we all face eternity as men?[25] Questions like these, and the thoughtful answers to them, create academic heaven.

The blessed souls will know all the arts and sciences, and all the secrets of creation and nature. But this does not mean that we should put off studying such things now because we will have complete knowledge of them later on: there will be degrees of knowledge in heaven, and those who develop their gifts here will be in a better state when they get there. Although the souls now in bliss can look down upon us here on earth, they cannot be grieved by anything we do, or moved in any way by our fates. They are in bliss, and invulnerable.

The root problem with almost all kinds of heaven, except perhaps for the supremely vulgar — the mental capacities of whose inhabitants are not up to grasping any sort of problem — is that of duration. Eternity is outside time, a continuous, simultaneous present. Very few human joys take us out of time, and they are mostly solitary, or at least very private ecstasies. For the mystic, the contemplative, the intellectual, the moment of rapture provides an excellent foretaste or analogy to eternal bliss; but even if a whole society could go into a state of collective rapture, the relationship of each soul would be with its God, not with its fellow-souls. There is a medieval philosophical text written in Arabic in which the protagonist achieves an intellectual state of ecstasy: he perceives himself as if he is a mirror turned towards and reflecting the flood of light from the Active Intellect of the universe; he is aware of other souls, like other mirrors, turned towards the same light,[26] but there is no relationship between the mirrors, except perhaps a remote sense of unity. This is in fact rather like the strictest interpretations of the Beatific Vision, although it is not Christian. For those who aspired to intellectual heaven, such bliss was entirely desirable, and the problem of duration — responsible for so much of the boredom of heaven — does not arise.

To more pedestrian souls, such a heaven, such bliss, is well-nigh incomprehensible. The very human desire to 'meet again' in heaven, the difficulty of the idea of eternity, the biblical image of the celestial city, all suggest a friendly heaven where we will have some interaction with those we love; some even argued that Aristotle's dictum that man was fundamentally a social animal required that we should eventually take our places within a heavenly society. But what kinds of relationship could blessed souls possibly have with each other? If we are all going to be citizens of the heavenly Jerusalem, what sort of dealings will we have with our fellow-citizens? There are very few medieval answers to this question. Even St Augustine, whose own mystical experience confirmed the idea of the individual soul finding beatitude in God,[27] was very unclear about the saved soul's relationship with other saved souls. Intellectual heaven is not a sociable place. We do know that there will be no sex there, for a start: we have that on divine authority, 'there will be neither marriage nor giving in marriage' (Matt. xxii 30). (At least one medieval poet is on record as saying that, in that case, he was not interested.)[28] There will be no children, and presumably no parents: all human relationships will be cancelled. I do not think there are going to be any animals in heaven, although there are birds in the *Pearl* landscape. The only thing in heaven that could be called work is the contemplation of God, and everybody knows everything, though some seem to know more than others. But no-one will be envious: we have that on Augustine's authority. We will have our glorified bodies: beautiful, agile, strong and free; but it is very unclear what use our bodies will be to us, since our intellects will be able to apprehend everything directly without recourse to the senses. Even if our nearest and dearest are in hell, we will not grieve for them; indeed, we will contemplate their sufferings with satisfaction, as evidence of the perfection of divine justice. In short, in any ordinary human terms, 'heavenly society' is an oxymoron. Most medieval visions expend far more energy on the description of the pains of the damned, which pay better emotional dividends.

The nature of heavenly society continued to be a problem after the Middle Ages. There is an anxious meditation on the subject in a seventeenth-century manuscript in the Harley collection; the author, in his little treatise entitled 'That mutuall knowledge and rejoyceinge with one another may consist with our blessednes in heaven', puts the problem rather nicely:

> But some may say, with what affection shall the parent and the child, the husband and the wife, and one freind

greet another? Wee must not surely ymagine that anie of
these conjugall or paternall affeccions which had their
consummation on earth can be of anie use in heaven, nor
that there shal bee anie retourne of foregone and mortall
affeccions towards freinds, kindred and children; but as
the bodie must put on incorruption and immortallity ere
it can bee a fitt companion for the soule, soo must the
soule bee divested of all such desires as are apt again to
wedd it to earthly and transitorie delights before it can
bee received into the blessed communion of the saints.
And as the soule shall assume the eye, the hand and every
member of the bodie unto a participacion of glorie
without sollicitynge them againe to undergoe the forepast
drudgeries of the flessh, soo the father and the child, the
husband and the wife, and one freind may behold another
without the intimacion of such duties or anie resultance of
such mortall desires as are ymplied in those relacions.[29]

The image of the golden city, or even the groups of souls
wandering in beautiful meadows hint dimly at celestial social
pleasures, but on closer examination the imagination (except in
very vulgar heavens) shies away from any detailed picture of
what this interaction is like. The sad truth is that almost none of
our earthly pleasures is fit for heaven. That is why it is such a
dull place.

The *Pearl* poet presents an unusually tough-minded and
questioning confrontation between a grief-filled hope in the
literary conventions of heaven and the standard academic
teaching on the same subject. Poets, practising what Thomas
Aquinas called 'the lowest of the academic subjects',[30] dealt in
the concrete images of the material world used symbolically, to
appeal to and stir up the human emotional faculties in the cause
of truth. But heaven is one of the subjects, where, as we have
seen, the known doctrine is emotionally incomprensible. In
presenting the dramatic confrontation between a grieving
mortal and a soul in bliss the poet's base in the emotional and
concrete weighs in heavily on the mortal side; the abstractions,

reason and faith, can produce only a rather stern form of comfort.

The bliss needs little elaboration: the dreamer finds the beautiful landscape and the golden city;[31] he is transported with delight in one and moved to rapture by the other; the happiness of the maiden, the glory of the celestial marriage, the jewels and light and music are all part of the heavens at the more colourful end of the medieval spectrum. But against this, the conversation between the dreamer and the maiden highlights the difficulties of academic heaven: almost everything the jeweller says reveals the limitations of love as we know it, and the losses we will suffer by going to heaven. The dreamer's first words to the maiden are revealing:

> 'O Perle', quod I, 'in perles pyght,
> Art thou my perle that I haf playned,
> Regretted by myn one on nyght?
> Much longeyng haf I for the layned,
> Sythen into gresse thou me aglyghte.
> Pensyf, payred, I am forpayned,
> And thou in a lyf of lykyng lyghte
> In Paradys erde . . .'

(lines 241–8)

The natural expressions of human love are possessive, singular and not unselfish: *my* pearl, he says, and 'I've missed you so' and 'now that I've found you, I'll never let you go'. He wants her to know he has been miserable without her, even though she is perfectly happy without him. She is not moved. She replies, 'Sir, ye haf your tale mysetente'; he has got it all wrong. She says, in effect, that she is not his pearl any more, and no, she is not in the least unhappy without him. To his natural concern over who is looking after her and providing her with beautiful clothes she replies that she has found herself a powerful husband, and then to his increasing bewilderment she explains that she is one of 144,000 'pearls', all brides of the same husband. His concerns as a father — one whose duty it would have been to find her a husband — are obsolete; his private and stifled grief is countered by her incomprehensible joy at her lack of singularity in heaven: the brides of the Lamb all rejoice the more of them there are. Every connection he had with Pearl before her death — the authority of a parent, the knowledge and book-learning of a literate man in comparison to a little girl barely able to talk — is reversed: as a soul in bliss she is no longer a child, no longer his in any sense, and is possessed of a knowledge and authority far beyond anything he can comprehend. What he is desperately pleading for, in our terminology, is a 'relationship' — something that has no place in heaven.[32] She does not need or want his love: she only advises him coolly to work on his own salvation:

> I rede the forsake the worlde wode
> And porchace thy perle maskelles.

(lines 743-4)

For the truth is that, according to medieval theology, the jeweller has lost the Pearl he knew forever: there are not only no children in paradise, but love there will be devoid of singularity and protectiveness, and those we love will be in no need of our care, attentiveness, devotion, or company — indeed, they would be just as happy if we were in hell. There will still be love, we are assured, and it will be better than anything we can understand, but the point is that such love is quite impossible for us to imagine, and even more impossible for a poet to describe.

The *Pearl* poet confronts this truth unblinkingly. The alliterative arsenal of skills is deployed to render the symbolic details of his heaven as gloriously as possible, but the heart of the poem, the encounter between the jeweller and the maiden, dramatizes the bafflement of the human imagination trying to come to terms with the joys of heaven. He has his dreamer conjure up the blessed soul of his beloved Pearl, and confront the irrevocably changed nature of their relationship. Boccaccio's *Olympia*, a poem once thought to be the source of *Pearl*, is sentimental in comparison: the child Olympia tells her father how she was welcomed into heaven by her grandfather, and spends her time there playing and singing with other children.[33] The *Pearl* poet knew too much about heaven to offer any such consoling family pictures; instead he gives us a scene of human love rebuked at almost every turn, its possessiveness and selfishness exposed in nearly every word the jeweller says. For example, the ancient topos of mourning, the lament that the young girl died still unmarried — as old as the story of Jephtha's daughter or the Greek epitaphs, and recognizable in Gertrude's words at Ophelia's funeral: 'I thought thy bride-bed to have decked, sweet maid, / And not have strewed thy grave' — is reworked in *Pearl* to show its limitations. In answer to the mourner's grief, the Pearl maiden appears as a bride: one who has won the best husband in the universe; and the jeweller's incredulity ('And quen mad on the fyrst day!') provides a touch of sardonic humour. It is after all what Christians believe: why should he have such trouble accepting it? Her glory as a bride of the Lamb surpasses beyond comparison anything the world could provide, but it does not entirely erase the purely human sense of regret for a life, in our terms, unfulfilled.

What kind of heavenly society or reunion does the *Pearl* poem offer? When the jeweller sees the New Jerusalem he is dazzled by the splendour and glory of the holy city, with its jewelled foundations, the gleaming river that runs through its streets, the trees of life that bear fruit twelve times a year. But the inhabitants of the city appear before him not as a society but as a mighty procession, all moving towards the throne of the Lamb. They are partakers of unimaginable bliss, their delight cannot be expressed in words, but they are all facing one way: they look to the throne of the wounded Lamb, whose flowing blood is the occasion for celestial rejoicing. It is the sight of his Pearl's joy 'among her feres' in the procession that drives the dreamer to the mad plunge into the river that breaks his vision. What does he want to join: the society of heaven or that of his Pearl? It is the custom of critics of the *Pearl* to treat the jeweller with contempt: he is stupid, earthbound, and according to the latest article on him, a fine example of the evils of patriarchy in his lust to possess, control and dominate the maiden.[34] I think this is a bit hard on the jeweller. It is true that he does not comprehend very well, but he is trying to comprehend the incomprehensible. His love for his Pearl produces a paradoxical result: moved by his desire to be with her, he throws himself into the stream and loses his vision: but how better could the poet express the overwhelming attraction of such an unattractive place as heaven? What the dreamer hears is beyond understanding, but the instinctive and uncontrollable desire to be there demonstrates more clearly than anything else that heaven is his natural home. In the same way, but more quietly, the beauty of the dream country is unspeakably comforting to the dreamer, but its strangeness (indigo trees with silver leaves) constantly asserts its difference from anything in our world. Heaven is home, but not here; like our world, but quite different. The jeweller's love for Pearl might have its limitations, but it is at least recognizable, paralleled by songs and poems of all periods; the kind of love he is to enjoy in heaven, if he gets there, is beyond understanding or comparison. But even if his love is mostly too earthbound, too vulgar, crude and particular for heaven, it still provides a link: after all, however faulty it was, it brought him his vision and gave him a hint of understanding about celestial truths. It is like his recognition of the maiden: she is entirely changed, but he still knows her. Particular love for unique objects, what we have here, must become universal love for everything and everyone on God's side. We might find this heaven an unattractive option, but it was really the only one; and it is surely preferable to the alternative. If we think we lose a lot by going there, it is because we are 'bot mokke and mul' — dirt and dust — and cannot understand what bliss is really like. It is the *Pearl* poet's distinction to have told us about bliss by showing how far it is from our understanding, and what we must lose to gain it.

References

1 See Ann Chalmers Watts, '*Pearl*, inexpressibility, and poems of human loss', *PMLA*, 99 (1984), pp.26–37.

2 See Colleen McDannell and Bernhard Lang, *Heaven: a history*, New Haven, CT, 1988. A convenient collection of accounts of heaven may be found in Eileen Gardiner, ed., *Visions of heaven and hell before Dante*, New York, 1989.

3 *Paradise Lost*, III 380.

4 E. V. Gordon, ed., *Pearl*, Oxford, 1953. In quotations I have modernized the obsolete letters. I have also used the edition by Malcolm Andrew and Ronald Waldron, *The poems of the Pearl manuscript*, Berkeley/Los Angeles, 1982.

5 A problem for even the most robust believer; *cf.* Luther's words at the death of his 14-year-old daughter, Magdalena: '*Du liebes Lenichen*, you will rise and shine like the stars and the sun. How strange it is to know that she is at peace and all is well, and yet to be so sorrowful.' Roland Bainton, *Here I stand: a life of Martin Luther*, New York/Nashville, TN, 1950, p.304.

6 *Decameron*, VIII 3.

7 R. H. Robbins, ed., *The land of Cockaygne. Historical poems of the xivth and xvth centuries*, New York, 1959, pp.121–7.

8 'Ubi non praevenit rem desiderium/nec desiderio minus est praemium': Peter Abelard, 'O quanta qualia' in F. Brittain, ed., *The Penguin book of Latin verse*, Harmondsworth, 1962, p.195.

9 Alan Lomax, ed., *American folk songs*, Harmondsworth, 1964, p.130.

10 See the Glossa Ordinaria to Apocalypse, xxii 4: *Et videbunt* . . . 'Videre enim faciem dei vivi, hoc est summum bonum, gaudium angelorum, praemium vitae aeternae, gloria spirituum, letitia sempiterna, corona decoris, bravium foelicitatis, requies opulenta, pulchritudo pacis, intimum et aeternum gaudium, paradisus dei, Hierusalem coelestis, vita beata, etc.'

11 Discussed in Thomas Aquinas, *Summa theologiae*, Sup. q.92 and q.95.

12 Aquinas, *Summa*, Sup. q.94 art. 2: 'Et ideo beati qui erunt in gloria, nullam compassionem ad damnatos habebunt'; art. 3: 'Hoc modo sancti de poenis impiorum gaudebunt, considerando in eis ordinem divinae justitiae et suam liberationem de qua gaudebunt.'

13 St Augustine's discussion is contained largely in *The city of God*, XXII; see also the little treatise in BL, Royal MSS. 7 D xxi: 'De futuro judicio etc.' esp. fols 153v–156r, 'De futura mercede justorum'.

14 A brief account of heaven in the works of some female mystics is given in C. McDannell and B. Lang, *Heaven*, pp.98–107.

15 'Now every tree bore twelve harvests each year, and they had various and diverse fruits.' *St Paul's apocalypse* (late 4th century) in E. Gardiner, *Visions of heaven and hell*, p.29.

16 The four rivers appear in St Paul's apocalypse, where they are equated with the four rivers of Paradise in Genesis ii 10–4; ibid., p.31.

17 By Joannes Balbus of Genoa, printed by Gutenberg, Mainz 1460, and photographically reproduced by Gregg International, 1971. See entries under *beatus, defunctus, oratio, sanctus*, and *vita*.

18 Compiled by Gregor Reisch and first published in Freiburg im Breisgau, 1503. There are many editions; I have used the one published in Basel (Johann Schott), 1508.

19 *Margarita philosophica*, XI cap.31, quoting St Augustine and Canon Law.

20 Discussed at length in *Margarita*, XI cap.33.

21 See Aquinas, *Summa,* Supp. q.81: the blessed will be resurrected *in aetate iuvenili*, which begins at 30. They will not, however, all be of the same height, since each individual nature will have its own proper height. The question is also discussed in *Margarita*, XI 37.

22 This is discussed in detail in *Margarita*, XI 39–40; the source is mainly St Augustine, *De civitate dei*, XXII 19. See also Aquinas, *Summa*, Supp. qq.82–82. The seven qualities of the risen bodies of the righteous (*pulchritudo, velocitas, fortitudo, libertas, sanitas, voluptas, diuturnitas*) in Anselm are quoted in J. Balbus, *Catholicon*, s.v. 'sanctus'.

23 'Caro a quocunque comesta resurget in illo in quo primo erat animata': *Margarita*, XI 38; the authority is St Augustine, *Enchiridion*, 8 and *De civitate*, XXII 20.

24 All these questions are discussed in *Margarita*, XI 38.

25 Aquinas, *Summa*, Supp. q.81, art. 3; *Margarita*, XI 37. The answer is no; the authority is St Augustine, *De Civitate*, XXII 17.

26 Abu Bakr Ibn Tufayl (d.1185), *Hayy ibn Yaqdan*. There are many English translations; I used the one by Lenn Evan Goodman, New York, 1972. The 'Beatific Vision' is at pp.149–56 in Goodman's edition.

27 St Augustine, *Confessions*, IX 10 describes his experience of God, which, however, he shared in some sense with his mother Monica.

28 C. McDannell and B. Lang, *Heaven*, p.95.

29 BL Harley MS., 813, fol. 60r.

30 Aquinas, *Summa*, I q.1, art. 9.

31 See the excellent article by Rosalind Field, 'The heavenly Jerusalem in *Pearl*', *MLR*, 81 (1986), pp.7–17.

32 See Warren Ginsberg, 'Place and dialectic in *Pearl* and Dante's *Paradiso*', *English Literary History*, 55 (1988), pp.731–53.

33 *Olympia* is eclogue xiv of Boccaccio's *Bucolicum carmen*. Latin text and English translation are provided by Janet Levarie Smarr, *Giovanni Boccaccio: Eclogues*, New York/London, 1987, pp.154–73. Olympia was Boccaccio's daughter Violante, who, as he says, 'died at an age in which we believe the dying become citizens of heaven'; she was five and a half. Ibid. p.257.

34 David Aers, 'The self mourning: reflections on *Pearl*', *Speculum*, 68 (1993), pp.54–73.

11

The Chester Mystery Plays
and the limits of realism

DAVID MILLS

IN THIS PAPER I want to suggest some ways in which Chester's sixteenth-century Whitsun plays arose from and responded to the political and social realities of the community. I begin by suggesting the possible significance for Cestrians of the newly established genre of Whitsun processional performance when viewed alongside the traditional Corpus Christi procession. I continue by offering some examples of the way in which the content of the plays speaks of and to the concerns of the community. And I conclude with some reflections on 'The shepherds' play'.

A divergence of genres

From at latest 1521 to 1548, at least in certain years, two distinct celebratory genres were enacted in Chester within the space of eight to eleven days.[1] On Corpus Christi day, a Thursday which might fall on any date between 23 May and 24 June, the Blessed Sacrament was conveyed through the streets in procession, escorted by the clergy and by the city's companies dressed in their ceremonial livery and bearing lights. And on the Monday, Tuesday and Wednesday of the previous week, Whit week, the handsomely decorated carriages of the Whitsun plays rolled through the town from station to station. Placed side by side in this way, the two genres must have seemed to contemporary observers distinct and mutually defining.

During the fifteenth century, play and procession had been interconnected; the civic play had been an integral part of the liturgical Corpus Christi celebration from before 1422 to at least 1471–72.[2] But the civic plays seem to have been abstracted subsequently from the Corpus Christi procession. The pre-Reformation Banns to the Whitsun plays, which R. M. Lumiansky and I believed were composed at the time of the separation of the two genres,[3] advertise both plays and procession, and also announce that on Corpus Christi Day the clergy will put on a play in honour of the feast. Although we cannot be sure that the clergy's play remained a regular feature of the Corpus Christi celebration, its introduction into the occasion in place of the civic Corpus Christi play suggests a responding impulse, under clerical control, to the transfer of the civic plays to Whitsun.

What messages did these two processional occasions transmit? Every large town had, and still has, its symbolic geography. The great buildings of church and government, the houses of the wealthy, the concentrations of traders' shops in certain streets, the quays and customs house of the waterfront all made physical statements of different kinds of power, past and present. The mutually defining genres of play and procession were enacted along different routes, and the geography of the two processions assumed a symbolic significance which might continue to change as the years passed.[4]

That Chester had a Corpus Christi procession by 1398 is confirmed by a record of a serious affray that broke out that year in its course.[5] The processional route was thus long established; it linked the older centres of power in the city. The procession began and ended in the south of the town. It started at the church of St Mary on the Hill, near the impressive castle that formed the seat and emblematized the power of the earls of Chester. The monk Lucian, in his celebration of the city written *c.*1195, says that at St Mary's

the earl, the head of the citizens, observes divine
solemnities customarily with his court,[6]

thus confirming that the link was not merely one of geographical proximity. The 1398 record indicates that the procession passed the church of St Peter at the crossing point of the four Roman streets in the centre of the town. It ended at the collegiate church of St John the Baptist, upstream of the town and outside its walls.[7] Lucian says that on feast days there was a procession from St John's to St Mary's, suggesting that the Corpus Christi procession reversed an already established route.[8] Until the fifteenth century this enormous Norman foundation was the most important ecclesiastical centre in Chester. For a short time it had been the seat of the bishop of West Mercia and its relic of the true cross was much revered locally.[9] Physically, it was a large and impressive building. The Corpus Christi procession thus continued to link the old-established seats of civil and ecclesiastical power.

In contrast, the Whitsun plays, first recorded in 1521,[10] began in the north of the town and in all probability moved no further south than the end of Upper Bridge Street.[11]

Their first station was in front of the gate of St Werburgh's abbey in the Northgate, where the clergy watched the plays. The abbot had become a powerful figure in the city and the abbey continued to expand physically through the great building programmes of the fifteenth and sixteenth centuries, which were still not completed at the Dissolution.[12] Physically, it dominated the town from its high site and, as its power grew during the fifteenth century, it overtook St John's in wealth and influence. From 1540 its authority was confirmed when it became the cathedral for the new see of Chester.

The second station was at the cross, at St Peter's, where the mayor, aldermen and common council watched the plays. With the completion of the north side of the civic annex to the church, the pentice, in c.1498–99, the city had a central civic building that signalled its economic confidence and growing administrative autonomy. The so-called Great Charter of 1506 created the city a county palatine and gave it unusual juridical independence. It is perhaps significant that the mayor was granted the right to have a sword borne in front of him, a mark of dignity hitherto possessed only by the earl. The Whitsun processional route thus linked the new centres of power in Tudor Chester, signalling a shift of authority from the southern part to the central and northern sectors of the city.

This physical separation of the two processions is reinforced by the textual claims made for the plays in the pre- and post-Reformation Banns, and in the extant Proclamation of 1531–32 and its subsequent revisions.[13] The claim, made in the pre-Reformation Banns, lines 176–7, that the plays began in the mayoralty of Sir John Arneway, who was supposedly the first mayor of Chester and was therefore thought to have introduced the plays in his mayoralty of *c*.1327, presents them as a civic initiative, in contrast to the ecclesiastical occasion of Corpus Christi which manifested and affirmed the power and authority of the clergy.

The strong emphasis in those Banns upon the companies and the spectacular displays of wealth further reinforces a sense of the plays as a civic and commercial venture.[14] Other documents assign a dual purpose to the plays:

> not only for the augmentation and increase of the holy and catholick faith of our saviour Jesu Christe and to exort the mindes of comon people to good devotion and holsome doctrine thereof, but also for the comon welth and prosperity of this citty[15]

— that is, for both the spiritual edification of the populace and the promotion of the city's economic wellbeing. Such descriptions perhaps suggest the somewhat more relaxed relationships between town and abbey/cathedral which resulted from the resolution of the disputes between the abbot and the city following the transfer of many of the abbot's judicial and financial rights to the city under the Great Charter. The continuation of this link after the establishment of the see, with the alleged division of responsibilities between an abbey-based authorship by Ranulf Higden and a civic-based promotion by Sir John Arneway, provided a convenient Protestant shelter for the plays in times of local and national opposition to such cycles.[16]

The plays were not, however, merely a convenient alliance of the ruling establishments. From the pentice the carriages moved on to stations 'in every street', that is, in each of the three other Roman streets — Watergate Street, Bridge Street and Eastgate Street.[17] Such a dispersal of the plays evenly throughout the town was not possible in the goal-directed Corpus Christi procession. It suggests a wider sense of communal ownership, carrying the plays to the different parishes and to the localized sites of particular trades. This situation looks different from that in York, where stations were purchased in front of inns and the homes of prominent citizens. When in 1575 the plays were not performed along the familiar route, one annal records:

> The whitson playes played in pageantes in this cittye at midsomer to the great dislike of many because the playe was in on part of the Citty,[18]

implying the proprietorial concern that was fostered by processional production. But there was more than mere sentiment engaged here. Ownership had financial implications. The members of each company had paid a compulsory levy for the cost of their production. In return, the plays attracted large crowds to the city, and processional production spread the crowds and the trade across the city over a three-day period.[19]

The plays and the community

It is easy to forget how readily the daily processes of law and order bore upon the scriptural and apocryphal material of a cycle such as Chester's.[20] The doubting midwife, Tebel, who seeks to test the Virgin Mary's virginity after her painless delivery in play six, lines 533–9+SD, is both a figure from the apocryphal gospels and enacting a kind of judicial service in that she is undertaking what a Chester midwife might be asked by the city courts to do in a case of rape or suspected infanticide — 'free from all carnall knowledge', as the midwives Dorothy Rogers and Kate Streete certified of the alleged rape victim Sara Stretch in 1628.[21] Repeated visitations of plague lend an added dimension to the rapid death of Lazarus in play thirteeen (*cf.* lines 357–68). The Pharisees preside over contemporary ecclesiastical courts which can summon the parents of the blind man to testify to his innate blindness (play thirteen, lines 149ff.) or bring an adultress to justice (play twelve, lines 217ff.). The whipping of Christ has familiar echoes of the public flogging of idle vagrants until their backs were bloody (play sixteen, lines 305–22+SD). The dicing for Christ's cloak at the Cross is another example of the illegal games that the parish constables regularly brought before the justices (play sixteen A, lines 67–148). Our reception of the Crucifixion will assuredly be different from that of an age when public execution was itself a kind of theatre, with criminals escorted from the city's Northgate gaol to the gibbet at Boughton with which Octavian threatens his messenger in play six, 'The Nativity', lines 276–80.

The opportunity for commercial display also strengthened communal links. The allocation of certain plays provided an opportunity for craftsmen to show off their skills or employ their wares. The subject might suggest a jocular or actual appropriateness in its allocation — the ironmongers have responsibility for 'The Passion' and show off the articles they sell:

> And here are, by my pon,
> nayles good wonne
> to nayle him upon
> and he were my brother
>
> (16A/lines 156–60)

which, in commercial terms, the actor playing Christ is; while the cooks, responsible for 'The harrowing of hell', build upon the apparently jocular association of kitchens and hell by introducing an ale-wife who has been damned for breaking Chester's licensing laws. The Bakers, with equal appropriateness, undertook 'The Last Supper' and, as instructed in line 137 of the post-Reformation Banns, seem to have distributed samples to the crowd — 'caste Godes loves abroade'. The carriages, which are given particular emphasis in the pre-Reformation Banns and were evidently a major part of the parade, offered

additional opportunities for self-advertisement, as with the
brilliant colours of the fabrics on the mercers' carriage:

> velvit, satten, and damaske fyne,
> taffyta, sersnett of poppyngee grene.
>
> (lines 70–1)

The text sometimes indicates the gratuitous introduction of
properties appropriate to the performing company:

> Have done and fill the wyne in hye;
> I dye but I have drinke!
> Fill fast and lett the cuppes flye,
>
> (8/lines 416–8)

says Herod suddenly at the end of 'The visit of the magi',
performed by the Vintners, asking for their product; was he
played as if in a semi-inebriated state throughout? In the
Goldsmiths' play of 'The slaughter of the innocents', Herod
protests at the death of his son:

> He was right sycker in silke araye,
> In gould and pyrrie that was so gaye,
> They might well knowe by this daye
> he was a kinges sonne,
>
> (10/lines 409–12)

suggesting something of the visual splendour which evidently
accompanied their production.

But 'realism' is to be sought less in these annotatable details
than in the constant emphasis upon the community as a whole.
Two examples must suffice. The waterleaders and drawers in
Dee had responsibility for play three, 'Noah's flood'. God
addresses not just Noah but his whole family at the start of the
play (lines 17–52) and much of the early action consists of the
rhythms of corporate work. Each of the sons has his tool —
axe, hatchet, hammer; the women fetch wood, set up the
workbench, gather clay, make a fire (lines 53–80). The image of
organized labour, each with an appropriate task to perform, is
in contrast to the more individual and comic construction of
the ark in York or Towneley. What detains Mrs Noah is not
waywardness as such but a desire to have her 'gossips', to keep

faith with a wider society which is here presented as reprehensible, drinking and singing and distracting Mrs Noah from her proper sense of values. Their cheerful drinking song gives way to the communal singing of a psalm by Noah's family, reflecting the union of honest communal industry and faith which the play promotes (lines 225–36 and 260+SD).

Even more revealing, because of the connection of its central episode with the independent play in the Book of Brome, is play four, the Abraham play.[22] It is perhaps appropriate that the sacrifice of Isaac, which includes the institution of circumcision, should be performed by Chester's barber-surgeons; again one assumes an opportunity for the display of tools of the trade. Leading the captive to the place of execution, removing the clothes, blindfolding him, are reminiscent of execution rituals. But this play, coming immediately after the Noah play, explores the mutual relationship between individual and community, with Abraham as primary exemplar. In his exchange of gifts with Melchizedeck (lines 17–148) — an episode unique to this cycle — we see the image of the mutual contract of the individual and the Church, the voluntary donation of tithes to the Church and the administration of the sacrament by the Church to the individual. The covenant of God and His people is sealed in the blood of circumcision, and then confirmed in the willingness to sacrifice Isaac — not a test of Abraham's faith as in Brome, but a necessary act to ensure the greater good of the community, prefiguring God's later sacrifice of his own Son.

Chester also reminds the audience of their obligation as a community to those who are dependent upon it, by exhortations to active charity. In play thirteen a boy comes on, leading a blind man and begging for alms for a member of the community:

> If pittie may move your jentyll harte,
> remember, good people, the poore and the blynd,
> with your charitable almes this poore man to comforte.
> Yt is your owne neighbour and of your owne kynd.

(lines 36–9)

This is not a vagrant, but a neighbour deserving of support.
While the recital of the acts of mercy is a recurrent feature of
the judgement plays, Chester reinforces them by the insistence
of the redeemed:

> contrytion yett at my last daye
> and almes-deedes that I dyd aye
> hath holpen me from hell.
> . . . almes deedes, yf any paste,
> and great repentance at the laste
> hath gotten me thy grace.
>
> (24/lines 134-6, 154-6)

While the damned provide the alternative warning:

> Of poore had I never pittie
> Sore ne sycke would I never see.
>
> (24/lines 249-50)

The redeemed and damned have committed the same sins, but
the redeemed are saved by their acts of practical charity
throughout their lives combined with final repentance. A variation
on the theme is given by the aged Joseph, the carpenter of
Nazareth, who is played in Chester by a wright or carpenter
from the company of wrights. Faced with the demand to pay his
penny tribute to the emperor Octavian, he complains at length
of his age, infirmity and poverty in terms recognizably those of
petitions for exemption from parish poor levies (6/lines 389-
406):

> And for greate age and noe powere
> I wan no good this seaven yere.
>
> (6/lines 393-4)

In 1574 George Taylor petitioned the city in comparable
terms:

> Wheras heretofore I haue payd toward the releiff *and*
> sustenance of ye poore a peny a weeke and other of better
> habylyty than I am not so muche as I am credibly Informed
> and now not so able to labour and travayle as I haue done
> because of age . . .[23]

In contrast, the corrupting force of worldly goods and power is seen as a threat to that communal solidarity. The attempted usurpation of God's throne by Lucifer unites the ranks of angels in opposition. The regular parade of offenders against the assize of bread and ale, illegally brewing, adulterating their beer, or serving false measures, is reflected in the recurring condemnations of tapsters, culminating in the appearance of the Chester ale-wife at the end of the 'Harrowing of hell'.[24] The damned at the Judgement include not only the social leaders — emperor, king, queen and pope — but also the petty profiteers of society, the crooked justice who takes bribes and the false merchant who takes usury and cheats in land-deals.

English and Welsh

An important group in Chester's community, often forgotten by modern critics, was the Welsh, and as the city made social space for Welsh incomers in its society, so it also made dramatic space for them in its play-cycle, in play seven, 'The shepherds' play'.

There is no sense in Chester that the shepherds are comic yokels or oppressed peasantry, as in the famous shepherds' plays of the Towneley collection. Chester's is a Tudor cycle and its play can most profitably be set in the context of the amused but sympathetic presentations of the Welsh in English Tudor literature, of which Shakespeare's kindly image of the Welsh captain Fluellen in *Henry V* will probably be the most familiar. Wales is an ethnically distinct country with its own language and culture, and Chester's population included a large number of people of Welsh origin, some trading and others visiting. Chester's rood, and its plays, were readily reached from many districts in north Wales. The bridge across the Dee was known as 'the Welsh bridge'.[25] Chester's religious houses owned lands in Wales, and until the 1840s its diocese included some border parishes, including the large parish of Hawarden.[26] The records of the town abound in names in the Welsh patronymic *ap*, 'son of', across several generations. Welsh was spoken in the streets of the town. This mix of language and race gave Chester a character unique among English towns. In this low-lying dairy area, the sheep were raised on the mountains of Wales and were brought down to the Saltney pastures for shearing by the shearmen's company. Such is the local context for the painters' play of the shepherds.

The play insists from the outset upon the Welshness of its characters; the first shepherd announces that he has pursued his sheep 'from comlye Conwaye unto Clyde' (line 5). Tudd, the second shepherd, has the abbreviated form of Tudor for his name. 'Call him Tudd, Tybbys sonne' (line 65) urges the first shepherd, using the form of Isabel that traditionally connoted a strumpet or woman of low morals; as a metronymic, it jocularly inverts Welsh patronymic styling.[27] And, in the painters' play, the company to which the Chester heralds belonged, one suspects another local joke, on the Tudor concern of Welsh gentry to establish their pedigrees:

> In the absence of any form of political independence, a chain of relationships, carefully defined by the art of genealogy, and the celebration of the loyalties and obligations and qualities of character that went with it, were an essential framework to sustain the sense of nationhood.[28]

The national emblem of Wales is said to be appropriate to their boy Trowle:

> Leekes to his liverye is likinge.
>
> (line 157)

Trowle's own name, incidentally, has always been something of a puzzle, and it may therefore be worth noting that in 1572 ı William Garfield was brought before the city court accused of maintaining an illegal game called 'trowle game', suggesting some game of chance.[29]

This ethnic identification lends a kind of foreign exoticism to the 'English' foodstuffs which the shepherds consume as delicacies —'butter that bought was in Blacon' (line 115), 'ale of Halton' (line 117), 'a jannock of Lancastershyre' (line 120) — which further strengthens our sense of their 'otherness'. And to these specifics may be added a perceived national characteristic. The musical reputation of the Welsh is reflected in the pride that the shepherds take in their own singing and in their appreciation of the angel's 'performance'.

More importantly, the shepherds' play has a remarkable variety of stanza and metrical forms, standing out against the eight-line stanza which dominates the rest of the cycle. The survey by R. M. Lumiansky and myself revealed twenty different stanza-forms in this play, most commonly quatrains of the *abab* type, with considerable variation in the number of syllables in each line.[30] Additionally, there is insistent alliteration in the verse-form which obtrudes to a greater extent than elsewhere in the cycle. An admittedly extreme case is Trowle's taunt to his masters:

> Fye on your loynes and your liverye,
> Your liverastes, livers, and longes,
> Your sose, your sowse, your saverraye,
> Your sittinge withowt any songes!
> One this hill I hold mee here.
> Noe hape to your hot meate have I.
> But flyte with my fellowes in feare,
> And your sheepe full sycerly save I.
>
> (lines 202–9)

At the very least the music of rhyme and alliteration and the changes of verse-pace point to an attempt to give the Welsh shepherds a distinctively different speech-form. That there was antiquarian interest in alliterative verse in sixteenth-century Cheshire is known, and possibly there is a jocular antiquarianism in the use of the device.[31] There may even be a more specific model for these forms. I understand that a characteristic Welsh form is the *cynghanedd* measure, employing a fixed number of syllables (usually seven) in a line, with intricate alliteration and internal rhyme.[32] It is possible that the shepherds' verse forms seek to imitate features of Welsh verse; at the very least, they may reflect an attempt to reflect Welsh intonation patterns. These Welsh shepherds are incomers from a different culture, both ethnic and rural, with a specialist knowledge of sheep salves that accords with the Welsh reputation for magical powers (lines 9–40, 77–84), and a delight in eating and drinking (lines 101–48) and in violent sport (lines 226–99). But, like the shepherds of the Bible, they are outsiders who have been granted a revelation that is denied to the insiders of the town, a sense that is there also in the Towneley plays on the subject. Though comic in their boisterous alterity during the first part of the play, they warrant respect as well as amusement because of that special knowledge. Having brought that knowledge into the city, they leave the community, not as literal pastors but as novitiates in spiritual pastoralism, to become hermit, preacher, missionary and anchorite (lines 651–79). The play moves from a kind of realism to a symbolic conclusion which, in the simple parting of the four, is also strangely moving.

I do not seek to argue that the dominant dramatic mode of Chester's Whitsun plays is 'realistic' — rather, that the plays depended for their effect in large measure upon acknowledgement of the communal concerns of its citizens. Nor do I consider that a matter only of dramatic relevance, of dissolving the gap between past, present and future and making scriptural history accessible to the populace. Both as artefact and as text, the plays were integral to Chester's concept of itself as a social and economic entity.

So it was that, when the mayor of 1574–75, Sir John Savage, was summoned before the Privy Council accused of being personally responsible for the 1575 production, he could claim with justification that the decision to put on the plays enacted by the City Council acting on behalf of the all citizens was:

> don by thassent consente good will and agreamente of the aldermen sheriffes peeres and Comen counsell of the saide Citie and so determyned by seuerall orders agried vpon in open assemblie acordinge to the auncyent and lawdable

custom of the saide Citie whereunto and for the performance whereof the whole Citizens of the Citie are bounde and tyed by othe as they are to other their orders.[33]

The entire community owned the plays and was fully implicated in their production.

References

1 On the development of the plays, see R. M. Lumiansky and David Mills, *The Chester Mystery Cycle: essays and documents, with an essay, 'Music in the Cycle' by Richard Rastall*, Chapel Hill, NC, 1983, ch. 1, 'The texts of the Chester Cycle'; L. M. Clopper, 'The history and development of the Chester Cycle', *Modern Philology*, 75 (1978), pp.219–46. Documents are transcribed in L. M. Clopper, ed., *REED: Chester*, Manchester, 1979, and selected documents appear in edited form in R. M. Lumiansky and D. Mills, *Essays*, ch. 5.

2 *REED*, pp.6–7 and 13–4; R. M. Lumiansky and D. Mills, *Essays*, pp.168–81.

3 Ibid., p.181; for an edition of the pre-Reformation Banns, see pp.278–84.

4 On the medieval development of Chester, see N. J. Alldridge, 'Aspects of the topography of early medieval Chester', *Journal of the Chester Archaeological Society*, 64 (1981), pp.5–31.

5 *REED*, pp.5–6.

6 M. V. Taylor, ed., *Liber Luciani de laude Cestrie, Publications of the Record Society of Lancashire and Cheshire*, 64 (1912), pp.1–78; quotation from p.61.

7 On St John's, see S. C. Scott, *Lectures on the history of St John the Baptist's church and parish in the city of Chester*, Chester, 1892.

8 Ibid., p.63.

9 Sally-Beth MacLean, *Chester art: a subject list of extant and lost art including items relevant to early drama*, Kalamazoo, MI, 1982, p.42.

10 *REED*, pp.24–5; R. M. Lumiansky and D. Mills, *Essays*, pp.182–92.

11 The route is described in *A breviary of Chester history*, first compiled in 1609 by David Rogers from the antiquarian notes of his father, Robert Rogers, archdeacon of Chester and rector of Gawsworth, who died in 1595. The *Breviary* was re-copied on a number of occasions, with variations. The relevant sections from the 1609 *Breviary* are transcribed

in *REED*, pp.238–52, with collation of recurring sections from the later copies; 1618–19 version, pp.324–6; 1636–37 version, pp.435–6. Edited transcriptions appear in R. M. Lumiansky and D. Mills, *Essays*, pp.260–71. The most detailed account of the *Breviary* is Steven E. Hart and Margaret M. Knapp, *'The aunchant and famous cittie': David Rogers and the Chester mystery plays*, New York, 1988.

12 See R. V. H. Burne, *The monks of Chester: the history of St. Werburgh's abbey*, London, 1962, and B. R. Harris, ed., *The Victoria County History of Cheshire*, vol. III, Oxford, 1980, esp. pp.142–4.

13 For an edition of the post-Reformation Banns, see R. M. Lumiansky and D. Mills, *Essays*, pp.285–95; for the proclamation, see *REED*, pp.27–8; R. M. Lumiansky and D. Mills, *Essays*, pp.213–7.

14 See lines 17–20, 45, 55–6, 65–71, 81, 92–5, 98–9, 104, 113, 119, 141–2.

15 Proclamation; R. M. Lumiansky and D. Mills, *Essays*, p.215.

16 Post-Reformation Banns, lines 1–7.

17 *REED*, p.239.

18 BL Harley MS. 2125, f.40, transcribed in *REED*, p.110.

19 *Breviary*, 1636–37: *REED*, p.436: 'all beinge at the Cittizens charge, yet profitable for them, for all bothe farr and neere came to see them.'

20 All references and quotations are from R. M. Lumiansky and David Mills, eds, *The Chester Mystery Cycle*: vol. I, Text (*EETS*, supplementary series, III), London, 1974.

21 CCRO, QSF 73/64.

22 On the relationship between the two plays, see R. M. Lumiansky and D. Mills, *Essays*, pp.90–2.

23 CCRO, QSF 27/88.

24 See, e.g., the case of Janet Endesey, CCRO QSF 4/3 (1533–34) 'for puttyng hoppes in hir hale', or the residents of St Olave's ward in CCRO QSPE 56 (1634) who were fined for mixing their ale with hops and ashes.

25 Glanmor Williams, *The Welsh church from Conquest to Reformation*, revised edn, Cardiff, 1976.

26 C. N. L. Brooke, *The church and the Welsh border in the central Middle Ages*, Woodbridge, 1986, p.12.

27 E. G. Withycombe, *The Oxford dictionary of English Christian names*, 2nd edn, Oxford, 1950, pp.156–7.

28 Emyr Humphreys, *The Taliesin tradition: a quest for the Welsh identity*, London, 1983, pp.50–1.

29 CCRO, MB 20, f.55 (11 January, 1572–73).

30 R. M. Lumiansky and D. Mills, *Essays*, p.313.

31 The last extant poem in the alliterative long line in English is *Scottish Field*, written by a 'gentlemane from Bagguley in Cheshire' *c*.1570; see the edition by John Robson in *Remains historical and literary connected with the palatine counties of Lancaster and Chester* (Publications of the Chetham Society, XXXVII: Chetham Miscellanies, II), Manchester, 1856.

32 See further, E. Humphreys, *Taliesin tradition*. A convenient summary of the diversity of Welsh verse-forms may be found in *The dictionary of the Middle Ages*, vol. XII, New York, 1989, pp.598–9.

33 *REED*, p.114.

12

Marian devotion in post-Reformation Chester: implications of the smiths' 'Purification' play

SALLY-BETH MacLEAN

TEN YEARS AGO pageant wagons rolled again, as the plays of the Chester cycle were recreated on both sides of the Atlantic in Leeds and Toronto. Both productions attempted historical reconstructions rather than modern reinterpretations of the cycle, but with this difference: where the Leeds production committee chose the mid-1550s as their focal point, the Poculi Ludique Societas organizers in Toronto opted for 1572, in order to emphasize the continuation of what is typically seen as a medieval dramatic tradition well into the Elizabethan period.[1] For those of us producing plays in Toronto, this decision posed some challenging questions. With the later date we entered into the complex era of protestant ascendancy under Elizabeth, a period of 'reformation and resistance' which has recently become the subject for fresh investigation on a local level by historians such as Christopher Haigh.[2]

The play texts are late — dating from the late sixteenth to early seventeenth centuries. We know that the wives' 'Assumption' pageant and the clergy's Corpus Christi play were suppressed under Edward VI when efforts began to eradicate papist ceremonial and 'superstition'.[3] After a brief restoration of the old order under Mary, Elizabeth followed Edward's lead in issuing her 1559 Injunctions for church reform. Of particular relevance is injunction XXIII where the clergy are instructed 'that they shall take away, utterly extinct, and destroy all shrines, coverings of shrines, all tables, candlesticks, trindals, and rolls of wax, pictures, paintings, and all other monuments of feigned miracles, pilgrimages, idolatry, and superstition, so that there remain no memory of the same in walls, glass windows, or elsewhere within their churches and houses ... and they shall exhort all their parishioners to do the like within their several houses.'[4]

In tracking the impact of Elizabethan reforms on the drama long associated with the old order of religion, we had to consider the following questions. Were the plays altered to remove liturgical associations and non-biblical content? Was the choice of music in the cycle affected? Both the liturgy and music that may have influenced the cycle in the past were linked with the Sarum rite, abolished in favour of the 1559 English prayer book.[5] How were the plays costumed? Was there an effort to alter costuming which must have paralleled religious iconography now doomed to obliteration in local churches?

Although extensive research has been done by David Mills, Larry Clopper, and others on the Chester cycle and its dramatic records, there is still relatively little detailed information extant to help us with confident reconstruction of the Chester cycle as live theatre — how it looked and sounded. Of the four pageants in the cycle of twenty-five for which accounts survive, the blacksmiths' play is of most provocative interest for post-Reformation study. A representative stretch of pageant expenses for the years 1554, 1561, 1567, 1568, 1572 and 1575 reveals some intriguing, if elliptical, production details which my troupe of parish players used in their 1983 reconstruction of the Chester original.[6]

The smiths' play is titled 'De Purificatione Beatae Virginis' in all five late cyclic texts and the 'Purification of our Lady' in the Harley 2150 listing of companies and plays; the Early Banns, deriving from a pre-1540 original, call the pageant 'Candilmas dey'. Only the protestant-influenced Late Banns change the focus to 'Criste amonge the Doctors'.[7] Do the Late Banns then reflect a reform in the production itself in the last days of the cycle? Both the play texts and performance records would seem to deny radical reform; the section on Christ among the Doctors takes up only 128 of the 334-line play text and the guild expenses, even in 1575, correspond with the play cast list, including among payments to actors, the Virgin, Joseph, Simeon, Anna, angels and singers associated with the Purification.[8]

The play, in fact, falls into three sections — Simeon and the angel, the Purification, and Christ among the Doctors. The opening section features Simeon's attempt to emend the word 'virgin' in Isaiah's prophecy to what he considers the more plausible 'good woman'. Twice he scrapes the word from the manuscript and twice when his back is turned, an angel reinscribes it as 'virgin', the second time in indisputable gold letters. Of some interest to the question of protestant revision is the fact that this episode comes not from the Bible, but from a legend in the fourteenth-century *Stanzaic Life of Christ*.[9] Although these lines serve dramatically to establish Simeon and Anna as characters awaiting the prophesied coming of the Christ child, the sequence also emphasizes — by divine intervention — the purity of the Virgin.

The second episode combines the traditional three elements of Christ's presentation in the temple familiar to medieval art and drama.[10] St Luke's account (Luke ii 22–39) describes Mary's purification forty days after childbirth as coinciding with the presentation of Christ, as first-born son, in the temple thirty days after birth. These two events were further associated with the fulfilment of Isaiah's prophecy in the meeting with Simeon and Anna in the temple. The feast commemorating these combined events was known as the Purification or, as the Early Banns reflect, Candlemas, because of the liturgical procession with lights and blessing of candles for the year which occurred in pre-reformation churches on 2 February.

Candlemas was one of the great Marian feasts of the medieval church and provided the occasion for singing special devotional antiphons and responsories in honour of the Virgin.[11] Although the feast continued to be known as the Purification in the Elizabethan prayer book, the candle ceremony and the liturgical music in honour of the Virgin were proscribed by church reformers.[12] The Early Banns would suggest that the play's association with Candlemas was strong and the inclusion in the cycle of this episode from the life of Christ — which has been described as of 'only marginal dramatic value'[13] — may well be explained by its liturgical significance as a Marian feast, comparable to the play and feast of the Assumption which were suppressed under Edward VI. It is worth noting at this point that the medieval cult of the Virgin appears to have flourished in early Tudor Chester: the 'Assumption' play was singled out for special presentation three times and when John Birchenshawe added the present west front to St Werburgh's during his first abbacy, the Assumption was featured as the subject for the carvings above the main entrance.[14] Furthermore, when the abbey church was saved as a cathedral of new foundation in 1541, its dedication was to Christ and the Blessed Virgin Mary, with the apocryphal appearance of Christ to his mother after the Crucifixion chosen as subject for the dean and chapter's seal.[15]

While the 'Assumption' play produced by the wives of Chester may not have survived to the Elizabethan period, the 'Purification' did under the auspices of the craft guild. As mentioned above, the purity of the Virgin is emphasized in the opening episode with Simeon and the angel. In the second sequence, twenty-four of the eighty-six lines are devoted to aspects of the Purification — Mary's willing obedience to Mosaic law despite her absence from sin, the offering of three birds in the temple as part of the traditional purification rite, and Joseph's gift of the candle, not taken here as signifying Christ, 'the light to lighten the Gentiles', but rather, by its clean wax, Mary's own virginity.[16] Clearly, there are associations with Candlemas surviving in our play-text.

If we consider the music indicated in the play-text and the related performance expenses, there is further corroboration of conservative liturgical associations. The Latin incipit at line 167 directs the actor playing Simeon to sing the 'Nunc dimittis', the antiphon traditionally sung at Mattins on the pre-Reformation feast of the Purification during the distribution of candles. Both the incipit and the English paraphrase following (lines 167–74) suggest that the antiphon continued to be sung in Latin by Simeon into the Elizabethan period; the fact that Simeon receives the highest rate of pay in the smiths' accounts further implies that an experienced singer was required for the part. The accounts imply rather more than this about music in the play, however.

Although the play-text gives us no further direct musical clues, the smiths' accounts consistently record extensive payments to the Chester Cathedral precentor, conducts and choristers, and, in the later 1560s, to one of the great contemporary composers and organists, Robert White.[17] The only likely places for choral music in the play, as Richard Rastall has suggested, are surely during the angels' appearances after Simeon's revisions of the prophecy.[18] It is generally accepted that music was used in biblical plays to represent divine intervention in human affairs and here such intervention would be well illustrated by a celestial chorus singing antiphons in honour of the Virgin and perhaps derived from the Candlemas liturgy itself.[19] The size and liturgical training of the choir hired probably indicates the singing of Latin polyphony, consistent with the elaborate musical effects traditionally associated with other cycle plays in honour of the Virgin.[20]

The Lincoln Cathedral injunctions of 1547–48 are undoubtedly representative of official disapproval of such devotional music in post-Reformation churches: 'they shall from hensforthe synge or say no Anthemes off our lady or other saynts but only of our lorde, And then not in laten but choseyng owte the beste and moste soundyng to cristen religion they shall turne the same into Englishe, settyng therunto a playn and distincte note, for euery sillable one, they shall singe them and none other.'[21] However, outside officially sanctioned liturgy, it would still have been possible for conservatively-inclined musicians and laity to continue to perform such antiphons. The smiths paid for the commissioning of cathedral singers in the 1560s as they had during the Catholic reign of Mary; even in the final year of production, 1575, four singers are hired and Simeon continues to be paid more than any of the other actors.[22]

The role of Robert White, in this context, is worth

highlighting. White first appears in the Chester Cathedral Treasurers' Accounts in March, 1567 as organist and choirmaster; in the same year he is paid 4s. by the smiths, presumably for music in their play, and the following year, when musical expenditures are at their most lavish, he is paid 4s. for singing, while a minor canon, Randall Barnes, receives 3s. 4d., presumably for the cathedral singers to provide angelic music.[23] Because Simeon is not named amongst payments for either 1567 or 1568, it is possible that White's payments are for playing that role, over and above the participation of the cathedral singers.[24] Evidently White was enthusiastic about his involvement with the local drama; we may speculate that some of his own compositions may have been featured during these years. It is now accepted that most of his surviving pieces date from the Elizabethan period and of these the majority are in Latin; included among them are several devotional pieces in honour of the Virgin.[25]

The evidence does seem to point to the survival of liturgical associations with the Marian feast of Candlemas both in textual allusions and elaboration of music. But what of the visual elements in the play? Do the costume and props expenses give us any clues about the post-Reformation look of the 'Purification'? Is there contemporary English iconography to help us reconstruct the theatrical impact of this pageant? The answer to the last question, sadly, is no. Religious art virtually stopped after 1559, when most churches were whitewashed and decorated with the ten commandments.[26] Elizabethan portraits and monumental effigies can provide useful details of contemporary costume, but it is not to them that we can look for depictions of the 'Purification'.

Expenses for costumes in the smiths' records are few. In 1572 there is a payment of 10d. for the loan of a cope, altar-cloth, and tunicle to a clerk, undoubtedly from the cathedral.[27] The cathedral's involvement in the smiths' play has already been indicated and it is quite consistent that supportive cathedral authorities would loan vestments which should not have been available at other parish churches in the city. As a result of the vestiarian controversy in the 1560s, archbishop Parker's advertisements of 1566 had specified that a cope might be worn by principal ministers at Communion in cathedrals and collegiate churches, but parochial clergy were reduced thereafter to the surplice.[28] Copes and tunicles had gone the way of other 'popish gear' in many parts of the south, but in Chester such vestments escaped, both at the cathedral and even at the church of Holy Trinity where 'an ould cope of Redd velvett' was sold by a parishioner in Spain as late as 1573.[29]

Holy Trinity was, in fact, the most recalcitrant of the Chester parishes with records dating from this transitional period; several of its parishioners appear in the play accounts. Intriguingly, two of them, Robert Jones and John Shaw, received some fine vestments and furnishings from the church at the time of the legislated delivery of church goods to the mayor, Henry Hardware, in 1560, but it was another decade and several episcopal visitations later before Holy Trinity made all the changes required to its fabric and furnishings.[30] At any rate, the cathedral loaned the smiths a cope and tunicle, presumably for Simeon who was confused with the high priest in the temple in the Middle Ages and so costumed in medieval art as a bishop in full vestments — cope and mitre, stole, tunicle and dalmatic. Such a costume, of course, reinforces the conservative liturgical associations of the play, as does the altarcloth. Altars had been slated for removal in favour of communion tables as part of the 1559 injunctions, but an altar would appear to have been part of the ecclesiastical stage set for Simeon.[31]

Another medieval element in the expenses is the regular payment, at least until 1572, for gilding Christ's face. The gilding stressed Christ's divinity over his humanity and also served the practical purpose of immediately identifying him in his appearance with the doctors after the twelve-year lapse within this play. Gilding, however, does smack of idolatry and the Late Banns apologist is at some pains to account for this theatrical effect in the cycle as a whole.[32]

By far the single most revealing smiths' costume payment is towards the crown for the Virgin. The crown is only infrequently itemized, in 1561 and 1567, probably because it required periodic repair or repainting.[33] We are all familiar with statues of the Virgin crowned as queen of heaven with the child in her arms, but to see her in narrative sequences from the life of Christ with a crown emphasizing her pre-eminence rather than her maternal humanity is startling to the modern sensibility. In fact, protestant reformers in England tried energetically to eradicate such imagery connected with the cult of the Virgin, but there remain some telling analogues for this post-Reformation Chester stage depiction in late medieval art.

Worship of the Virgin Mary reached a peak in England in the fifteenth and early sixteenth centuries when most of the narrative windows of her life were painted.[34] Among some fine glass surviving from the late fifteenth century in Norfolk are fifteen scenes depicting the joys and sorrows of the Virgin, remarkably preserved in the east window of the church of East Harling (see Figure 1).[35] Throughout the series, the Virgin wears a damask gown — her blue mantle is lined with ermine and edged with a gilded design. Ermine was traditionally associated with royalty; the artist's intention to stress the Virgin's position as queen of heaven is further emphasized in the Annunciation, Visitation and Marriage at Cana panels where she is seen wearing a crown. Although she is bareheaded in the Purification scene, other parallels with our play are manifest in Joseph, who holds a basket with two doves and a candle (see Figure 7).[36]

Also of mid- to late-fifteenth-century English manufacture are the famous and remarkably preserved painted glass windows of Malvern Priory. There are two almost intact Purification panels, both of which have many of the same features.[37] The earlier window includes apocryphal scenes connected with the Nativity of Mary, as well as the Annunciation and Purification (Figure 2). Two lights form what may have been intended as a continuous scene: on the left, the Virgin, in a white ermine-lined mantle over a blue dress, carries the infant who holds a dove. Behind her are two veiled women in wimples — the first holds a candle, the second is scarcely visible. In the right-hand light, Simeon, vested as a bishop, stands to the left of an altar

Figure 1 — East window of East Harling church.

Figure 2 — Painted glass windows of Malvern Priory.

Figure 3 — The Circumcision, depicted on part of an alabaster table obtained from a collector in Pietrain.

Figure 4 — Alabaster table in the Germanic Museum at Nuremberg.

Figure 5 — The Circumcision, depicted in an English woodcut.

Figure 6 — The angel chorus, from the west front of Chester Cathedral.

Figure 7 — The Purification, east window, East Harling church.

holding the child. The focal importance of the altar in this composition and the placing of the child upon it suggests the element of sacrifice in the Presentation and foreshadows the Passion and Crucifixion.[38]

Painted glass is not the only medium to survive from English parish churches to give us iconographic witness of the Purification as ordinary men and women must have visualized it. English alabaster carvings, as Hildburgh has demonstrated, were 'a people's art' like the mystery plays, 'not an art, like that of the goldsmith, of the illuminator of manuscripts, or of the embroiderer, designed rather for appeal to wealthy noble or to richly endowed abbey'.[39]

The crowned virgin appears in a number of fifteenth-century alabaster renderings of incidents in the Nativity narrative; a rare instance of the Circumcision provides but one example (Figure 3).[40] Of greatest interest is another alabaster table where the Purification is stressed above other elements in a traditional rendering of the biblical account (Figure 4).[41] The Virgin, crowned, carries a candle and leads a procession of five, each also carrying a candle in the right hand. Hildburgh comments that 'It would seem probable that the way the incident is shown in alabasters reproduces in some degree the way it was presented on the stage; and we need hardly doubt that the stage version was itself inspired by folk-practices associated with Candlemas Day'.[42] The left hand of the prophetess Anna directly behind the Virgin is raised, thereby distinguishing her; the bearded figure to the left of the Virgin must be Joseph, but he does not carry the birds, nor does the Virgin have the child to present to Simeon, the mitred high priest standing in a pointed arched doorway representing the temple.

Hildburgh suggests that this arch has 'the air of a stage-property, of pasteboard or of painted cloth, such as we might well expect to meet on a small stage'.[43] Of related interest to this possible stage set detail is a contemporary woodcut of the Circumcision (Figure 5).[44] The ornate double-arch frame includes canopied niches with statues and is surely designed to render the Jewish temple in the familiar style of the Gothic cathedral façade. Through the entrance arch we can see the columns of the church interior, leaded windows, and the altar. In 1567 there is a further payment for a steeple, an imposing stage effect, which would seem to confirm that a Gothic church style was used for their temple wagon, even as a bishop's vestments were used to costume Simeon as the high priest.[45]

Chester, which suffered great damage during the Civil War, can offer us little relevant iconography for a study of the Purification. However, the North-West cannot go ignored in this context, and an example of the type of angel chorus which may have embellished the visual and aural splendour of the smiths' 'Purification' may serve as a visual postscript (Figure 6). On the west front of Chester Cathedral, accompanying the Assumption above the main door, a procession of six singers in albs holding music, moves towards the centre; not quite visible (apart from the head to the far right) is the angel playing the positive organ, an instrument related to the regals paid for in the smiths' accounts for 1567.[46]

Patrick Collinson, in *The birthpangs of Protestant England*, has remarked on the cultural watershed which the Reformation represents. In studying the period of transition between what he terms 'the culture of orality and image to one of print culture', we should recognize the valuable witness of a play such as the 'Purification'.[47] The rare combination of production records with play text, together with corresponding iconography, helps us to glimpse this play as theatre not just as literary text. Catherine Dunn has suggested that such vernacular mystery plays are in the tradition of paraliturgical composition, reflecting 'much of the inner life and dynamism of popular devotion'.[48] I would argue that the 'Purification', considered in all its details, maintained some of the key elements of popular Marian devotion into the 1570s. But perhaps this is not so surprising after all. The bishop of Chester under Mary was an arch-conservative and did much to consolidate the Catholic faith in the diocese. His successor, William Downham, was notoriously lax, even indulgent, in administering a diocese described as a 'very sink of popery' in the 1570s.[49]

There is remarkable continuity in key personnel at the cathedral itself through the 1550s and '60s, so that their active support of the 'Purification' production fits well with what would appear to have been conservative inclinations. Seen in this broader historical context, then, we may conclude that the 'Purification' is a striking example of popular resistance to religious change in a transitional period, worthy of particular note not only by theatre historians but also by historians tracking the progress of the Reformation at the local level.[50]

References

1 Lawrence M. Clopper, the editor of *Chester*, (*REED*), Toronto, 1979, has described the final performance of the Chester plays as a scaled down production; see L. M. Clopper, 'The history and development of the Chester cycle', *Modern Philology*, 75 (1978), pp.219–46. The Chester plays ended within a year of the opening of the first professional theatre in London by James Burbage. The famous Coventry plays had the longest run, ending in 1579.

2 See Christopher Haigh, *Reformation and resistance in Tudor Lancashire*, Cambridge, 1975. Other important revisionist studies include *idem*, ed., *The English Reformation revised*, Cambridge, 1987, and J. J. Scarisbrick, *The Reformation and the English people*, Oxford, 1984.

3 See R. M. Lumiansky and David Mills, eds, *The Chester Mystery Cycle: Essays and documents*, Chapel Hill, NC, 1983, pp.190–1. The bakers' 'Last Supper' appears also to have been temporarily suppressed under Edward VI, but re-entered the cycle in the form we now have it in the MSS play texts, possibly under Mary.

4 As quoted by Henry Gee and William John Hardy, eds, *Documents illustrative of English church history*, London, 1896, p.428.

5 Based on the second Edwardian prayer book of 1552. See Hugh Benham, *Latin church music in England* c.1460–1575, London, 1977, pp.162ff, for the effect of liturgical change upon English music after 1549.

6 The two Toronto Anglican parishes of St Thomas and St Mary Magdalene pooled their acting, musical and backstage resources

to present pageant 11, the 'Purification', as part of the Chester cycle production at the University of Toronto. The production was memorable for the torrential downpour which drove all but the hardiest audience members indoors and ran the 'gilding' on God's face into his mouth in an indigestible stream recorded on the PLS archival videotape. For the relevant smiths' records, see L. M. Clopper, ed., *Chester*, pp.53–106. I have followed Clopper's dating of the smiths' records in this discussion, for ease of reference to the *REED* Chester volume. John Marshall has questioned the 1554 date of the earliest performance records in the seventeenth-century transcription made by the Chester antiquarian Randle Holme (BL Harley MS. 2054, ff.14v–15). His arguments in favour of a transcription error for 1545 and a pre-Reformation performance of the cycle in 1546 are set out in his article, 'The Chester Whitsun Plays: dating of post-Reformation performances from the smiths' accounts', *Leeds Studies in English*, new series 9, 1977, pp.51–61.

7 See R. M. Lumiansky and D. Mills, *Chester Mystery Cycle: Essays and Documents*, p.191. For the texts of the Early and Late Banns, see L. M. Clopper, *Chester*, pp.32, 36, and 244.

8 For the play text, see R. M. Lumiansky and David Mills, eds, *The Chester Mystery Cycle*, *EETS*, second series 3, 1974, pp.204–17. Occasional payment omissions occur in the accounts between 1554 and 1575, but there is no evidence for wholesale removal of characters. For example, Mary and Simeon do not appear among the actors' payments in 1567, but Dame Anne, Joseph, and the angel are paid as usual. See L. M. Clopper, *Chester*, p.78.

9 For discussion of the close parallels between *The Stanziac Life*, lines 2741–2804 and the Chester 'Purification' see the introduction to Frances A. Foster, ed., *A Stanzaic Life of Christ* (*EETS*, original series, CLXVI), London, 1926; rpr., New York, 1971, pp.xxxv–xl.

10 For a discussion of the traditions and iconographic representation of the Presentation in continental art, see Dorothy C. Shorr, 'The iconographic development of the Presentation in the Temple', *Art Bulletin*, 28 (1946), pp.17–32.

11 See 'Candlemas', Charles G. Herbermann *et al.*, eds, *The Catholic Encyclopedia*, vol. III, New York, 1908, pp.245–6, and Terence Bailey, *The processions of Sarum and the western Church*, Toronto, 1971, pp.165–6. See also E. Ann Matter, *The voice of my beloved: the Song of Songs in western medieval Christianity*, Philadelphia, 1990, pp.151–2: 'Three events in the Virgin's life became the focus of major devotions: her special nativity, her bodily assumption into heaven (both testified to by extra-canonical Christian writings), and her ritual purification according to Jewish law after the birth of Jesus (testified to by the Gospel of Luke).'

12 The Candlemas ceremony was first abolished by an order of Council in January 1547/48, together with the blessing of palms on Palm Sunday and imposition of ashes on Ash Wednesday; see James Gairdner, *The English church in the sixteenth century from the accession of Henry VIII to the death of Mary*, London, 1902, p.254. Although it was restored under Mary, the Elizabethan reformers were quick to suppress it again in 1559; see 'Elizabeth's Act of Uniformity, AD 1559', in H. Gee and W. J. Hardy, *Documents*, pp.458–9.

13 Patrick J. Collins, 'Narrative Bible cycles in medieval art and drama', *Comparative Drama*, 9 (1975), pp.125–46. Collins proposes that 'it is the traditional selection of biblical episodes in the pictorial art of the Middle Ages which best accounts for the subject matter and chronological pattern of the later English mystery cycles'. Of some relevance is Emile Mâle's general remark: 'The Church would not offer the Christian the whole of the life of Christ any more than she would place the four Gospels in his hands, but she chose out a few events of profound significance as suggestions for the meditation of the faithful. These events are precisely those which the Church celebrates each year in the cycle of her festivals. Sculptors, glass-painters and miniaturists simply illustrate the liturgical calendar.' See E. Mâle, *The Gothic image: religious art in France of the thirteenth century*, transl. Dora Nussey, New York, 1958, p.179.

14 See L. M. Clopper, *Chester*, pp.20–4 for special performances of the wives' 'Assumption' play.

15 See my description of both iconographic subjects in 'Chester art: a subject list of extant and lost art including items relevant to early drama', *Early Drama, Art, and Music*, Reference Series, 3, Kalamazoo, MI, 1982, pp.44–7.

16 See lines 127–50; all play citations are from R. M. Lumiansky and D. Mills, *Chester Mystery Cycle*. Rosemary Woolf [*The English mystery plays*, London, 1972, p.199] also notes the 'neat rendering of the famous paradox in one of the responsories in the office for the Purification: "Though I beare thee nowe, sweete wighte, / thou ruleste me, as it is righte"' (for responsory, see *Sarum Breviary*, iii, p.144).

17 The accounts of the Chester Cathedral dean and chapter treasurers surviving for the years 1561–63, 1567, 1571–72, 1574–79, and beyond reveal that the Cathedral employed a master of choristers, 6 conducts and 8 choristers throughout this period, with the exception of 1567 when only 6 choristers' names are recorded (CRO: EDD 3913/2, esp. pp.58, 67, 74, 109 and 115).

18 For a detailed analysis, see Richard Rastall, 'Music in the Cycle', in R. M. Lumiansky and D. Mills, eds, *Chester Mystery Cycle: Essays and*

Documents, pp.111–64, esp.130–1, 134–7, and 148. Rastall suggests angelic singing would be most appropriate at lines 40 and 71. In the same article (p.129), he also discounts the possibility that the English paraphrase of the Nunc dimittis in the text might have been sung — it is not a metrical version associated with a musical setting. Douglas Cowling, our music director for the Toronto production, came, independently, to the same conclusions about appropriate places in the play for liturgical music by an angelic chorus.

19   Terence Bailey mentions the following antiphons for use in the Candlemas procession: 'Adorna thalamum tuum, Sion', 'Responsum accepit', 'Ave gratia plena', 'Ave Maria'. At the end of the procession, the choir usually sang the responsory 'Gaude Maria Virgo' or another antiphon in honour of the Virgin.

20   See, for example, John Stevens, 'Music in mediaeval drama,' *Proceedings of the Royal Musical Association*, 84 (1957/58), pp.93–5, with reference to the York play of 'The appearance of Our Lady to Thomas' and the Hegge play of 'The Assumption'.

21   Quoted in Stanford E. Lehmberg, *The reformation of cathedrals: cathedrals in English society, 1485–1603*, Princeton, NJ, 1988, p.56. The Acts of Uniformity for 1559 forbade the continued use of old Latin texts; as Lehmberg points out in a related article, 'Clauses providing penalties for those who did not "sing or say" the services according to the form set out in the Prayer Book obviously dictated abandonment of existing musical settings of the Mass and other liturgies . . .' See 'The reformation of choirs: cathedral musical establishments in Tudor England', in Delloyd J. Guth and John W. McKenna, eds, *Tudor rule and revolution: essays for G. R. Elton from his American friends*, Cambridge, 1982, p.45.

22   See L. M. Clopper, *Chester*, pp.53, 66–7, 77–8, 85–6, 91, and 105–6. Nan Cooke Carpenter, in a seminal article, 'Music in the Chester plays', *Papers on English language and literature*, 1 (1965), pp.215–6, sums up the use of music in this and other Chester plays as follows: 'The many parallels that we have seen between the music of the plays and the music of the liturgy are, in fact, effective means of emphasizing the highly devotional function and the strong moralistic purpose of the plays. And the traditional character of the hymns, antiphons, and psalms underlines the traditional character of the plays generally — plays performed well into Elizabethan times virtually unchanged in essentials since their medieval beginnings.'

23   See L. M. Clopper, *Chester*, pp.78, 85–6. The musical expenses that can be confidently calculated for 1568 are 8s. 4d., including a preliminary meeting with White and Barnes. An additional 3d. was spent 'at the hyerynge of the Menstrells & Consell of Simion'. First notice of White's quarterly

wages appears on p.59 of the Dean and Chapter Treasurers' Accounts, CRO: EDD3913/2. The expenses for 1567 appear to be incomplete: the precentor (Sir John Genson) receives a total of 15d. and two clerks of the minster are noted for 8d. There is no reason to think that the hiring of cathedral choristers by the painters for their play in 1568 might have precluded their employment by the smiths in either 1568 or 1567 as Rastall has suggested: see 'Music in the cycle', pp.135–6; the painters' play of the shepherds ran on the day before the smiths' in the three-day cycle.

24 Frederick Hudson first suggested this possibility in 'Robert White and his contemporaries: early Elizabethan music and drama', in Georg Knepler, ed., *Festschrift für Ernst Hermann Meyer Zum 60. Geburtstag*, Leipzig, 1963, p.168.

25 For White's revised dates see David Mateer, 'Further light on Preston and Whyte', *Musical Times*, 115 (1974), pp.1074–7, and Judith Blezzard, 'A note on Robert Whyte', *Musical Times*, 115 (1974), pp.977–9. Blezzard describes the characteristics of White's Latin church music thus: '. . . he favours a predominantly dense texture of usually five or six voices, and his work is often deeply expressive. In style he ranges from very florid writing on the one hand to a much simpler, almost syllabic style on the other, which is reminiscent of older contemporaries during the Reformation period such as Tye and Tallis.' See also F. Hudson, 'Robert White', pp.163–84, for an account of his career and list of compositions. Among the Latin compositions surviving are two votive antiphons, 'Tota pulchra es' and 'Regina coeli', and a setting of the Magnificat, all associated with devotion to the Virgin.

26 See the 'Order concerning rood-lofts, etc.' in Henry Gee, *The Elizabethan prayer-book & ornaments*, London, 1902, pp.273–6. In Chester, churchwardens' accounts record the whitewashing and putting up of the ten commandments in St Mary-on-the-Hill in 1562 and in Holy Trinity in 1566: see J. P. Earwaker, 'The ancient parish books of the church of St. Mary-on-the-Hill, Chester', *Journal of the Chester and North Wales Architectural, Archaeological and Historic Society*, new series 2 (1888), p.144, and J. R. Beresford, 'The churchwarden's accounts of Holy Trinity, Chester, 1532 to 1633', ibid., new series 38 (1951), p.124.

27 See L. M. Clopper, *Chester*, p.91.

28 The Advertisements are quoted by H. Gee and W. J. Hardy, *Documents*, see esp. pp.470–1.

29 See J. R. Beresford, 'Churchwarden's accounts', p.127, and see p.125 for other vestments sold for making players' garments in 1570. The latter record has also been published in L. M. Clopper, *Chester*, p.89.

30 John Shaw received a vestment of white damask and Robert Jones 'the greate candlestick of brass': see J. R. Beresford, 'Churchwarden's accounts', p.123. Jones and Shaw appear in the smiths' accounts for 1560–61 and 1574–75 respectively: see L. M. Clopper, *Chester*, pp.66 and 106. K. R. Wark, *Elizabethan recusancy in Cheshire*, Manchester, 1971, p.155 mentions a 'Robert Johns ... listed as an alderman of Chester who was unfavourable to the religious settlement, 1564'. For the names of Chester citizens later suspected as recusants, including Shaw, see K. R. Wark, *Elizabethan recusancy*, Appendix 1, pp.138–73, especially p.163. Two other individuals named in the smiths' accounts appear in Wark's list: Richard Ledsham, pewterer (p.156), and Richard Smith, cutler (p.164): see L. M. Clopper, *Chester*, pp.65, 77, 85. Wark also notes (pp.16–7) that in 1578, during a visitation authorized by the archbishop of York after bishop Downham's death, Holy Trinity was one of a handful of Cheshire parishes where the majority of absentee parishioners were identified (three of the nine parishes were in the city of Chester). Absence from church was the charge 'most closely allied to recusancy'. The churchwardens' accounts of St Michael's parish indicate a similar reluctance to disperse the furnishings and vestments of the old faith. An inventory of 1564 includes a chalice, cope, altar cloths, sepulchre frame and other remarkable items; many of these were sold in 1565: see J. P. Earwaker, 'Notes on the registers and churchwardens' accounts of St. Michael's Chester, *Journal of the Chester and North Wales Architectural, Archaeological and Historic Society*, new series 3 (1890), pp.36–7.

31 Among the many areas of resistance to reform highlighted in archbishop Grindal's Injunctions for the Province of York in 1571 was the maintaining of altars: '5. ITEM, That the churchwardens shall see that in their churches and chapels all altars be utterly taken down, and clear removed even unto the foundation, and the place where they stood paved ... And that the altar-stones be broken, defaced, and bestowed to some common use:' see William Nicholson, ed., *The remains of Edmund Grindal, D.D.*, (Parker Society Publications, XXIII), Cambridge, 1843, p.134.

32 Gilding is paid for in 1554, 1561, 1567 and 1572, as well as mentioned among midsummer expenses for 1568: see L. M. Clopper, *Chester*, pp.53, 67, 78, 86, and 91. For the relevant passage in the Late Banns, see ibid., p.247.

33 An unspecified amount is spent on 'payntinge & dressynge ... a Crowne for Mary' in 1561 and the crown is mended in 1567, together with a diadem, presumably for Christ. The diadem is mentioned again in 1572. See L. M. Clopper, *Chester*, pp.66–7, 78 and 91.

34 See Brian Coe, *Stained glass in England: 1150–1550*, London, 1981, p.62.

35 I would like to thank Professor Kenneth Hamilton for his generous permission to use photographs of East Harling glass from the estate of his wife, the late Alice B. Hamilton, who shared my interest in the relationship of medieval iconography to English biblical drama.

36 There is a similar panel in St Peter Mancroft, Norwich. For descriptions of both, see Christopher Woodforde, *The Norwich school of glass-painting in the fifteenth century*, London, 1950, pp.26, 47. For a discussion of costumes in the late fifteenth-century play of *Wisdom* associated with royalty (and restricted by sumptuary laws), see Milla Cozart Riggio, ed., *The Wisdom symposium: Papers from the Trinity College medieval festival*, New York, 1986, pp.8–10.

37 The earlier panel described is located in the third window of the north clerestory in the choir. The plate is reproduced from G. McN. Rushforth, *Medieval Christian imagery as illustrated by the painted windows of Great Malvern priory church*, Oxford, 1936, figs 38, 39. The second panel referred to is now in the second nave window (from the east) on the north side of the church. Dating from the late fifteenth century, it shows many of the familiar features — Simeon as officiating bishop, the female attendant with candle, Mary in her ermine-lined robe. In the background on the left is Joseph holding a wicker basket with three birds. Here is another parallel with the play where the same confusion about the original Mosaic requirement of a dove or two young pigeons resulted in three birds being brought to the temple. (The Vulgate, Luke ii 24, reads 'par turturum, aut duos pullos columbarum'.)

38 Another version of the Purification in the early sixteenth-century Magnificat window illustrating the joys of Mary is too fragmentary to provide useful detail for analysis.

39 W. L. Hildburgh, 'English alabaster carvings as records of medieval English drama', *Archaeologia*, 93 (1949), p.52.

40 The Circumcision is depicted on part of a table obtained from a collector in Pietrain in Brabant. Reproduced from W. L. Hildburgh, 'Notes on some English alabaster carvings', *Antiquaries Journal*, 4 (1924), p.379 and plate LIII, fig. 12.

41 W. L. Hildburgh located this table in the Germanic Museum at Nuremberg: see 'Notes on some English alabaster carvings in Germany', *Antiquaries Journal*, 5 (1925), pp.56–7 and plate XI, fig. 2.

42 W. L. Hildburgh, 'Folk-life recorded in medieval English alabaster carvings', *Folk-Lore*, 60 (1949), p.263.

43 W. L. Hildburgh, 'English alabaster carvings as records', p.72.

44 The woodcut is listed as no. 1480, 'The Circumcision', among those used by Richard Pynson, in *Edward Hodnett's English woodcuts, 1480–1535*, revised edn, Oxford, 1973, p.343 and fig. 127. Its earliest recorded use is in 1497 in the *Hore intemerate beatissime virginis Marie*.

45 See L. M. Clopper, *Chester*, p.78.

46 Ibid. For a more detailed description of the carvings on the west front of the cathedral, see S-B. MacLean, *Chester Art*, pp.46–7, 86–9, and plates I–II. There are, in fact, two parallel angel choruses on the west front in procession from left and right above the doorway. The late Brian Harris, editor of the *Victoria County History of Cheshire*, took the photograph of the carving on the west front included here.

47 See P. Collinson, *The birthpangs of Protestant England: religious and cultural change in the sixteenth and seventeenth centuries*, London, 1988, pp.99ff.

48 E. Catherine Dunn, 'Popular devotion in the vernacular drama of medieval England', *Medievalia et Humanistica*, new series 4 (1973), p.67.

49 See especially C. Haigh, *Reformation and resistance* for a detailed analysis of the conservative character of the Chester diocese and an outline of Downham's ineffectual episcopacy. The memorable phrase 'sink of popery' appears in the Privy Council's reply to a report by the earl of Derby in 1574, quoted by Haigh, p.223. R. V. H. Burne first pointed out the relatively smooth transition experienced at Chester during the dissolution. The last abbot of St Werburgh's became the first dean, four of the six prebendaries were St Werburgh's monks, and a fifth was William Wall, ex-warden of the Grey Friars in Chester. Wall continued at the cathedral throughout the next 30 years of religious changes until his death in 1572 or 1573. Similarly durable was one of the St Werburgh monks, the prior Nicholas Bucksey, who stayed on until his death in 1567. See R. V. H. Burne, 'What happened at the Reformation', *Cheshire Historian*, 4 (1954), pp.1–4. Although the Marian bishop, Cuthbert Scott, was deprived under Elizabeth (21 June 1559), members of the cathedral chapter continued. In 1563, when Downham attempted to extract subscriptions to the three articles of the Act of Uniformity, little over half the cathedral staff complied, and even this is no firm assurance that they did so with conviction: see B. E. Harris, ed., *Victoria County History of Cheshire*, vol. III, Oxford, 1980, p.21.

50 Although K. R. Wark, *Elizabethan recusancy*, has explored the topic, his conclusions are somewhat contradictory regarding the transitional years of the 1560s and 1570s, a period for which visitation records are fragmentary or unspecific. See, for example, the following passage (p.20): 'Twenty of the 47 recusants dealt with by the authorities in these

years [late 1570s] were from the city of Chester; no other such concentration emerges. In itself the number is not large, but it is strange that recusancy should apparently be stronger in the city than in the rural areas of the county in the 1570s. It is usually assumed that Chester was strongly Puritan at this time and it is thus possible that it was the very desire of the city council to eradicate the Romanists that makes the city seem to contain almost as many recusants as the whole of the rest of the county.' A fresh study of Chester in this period would be welcome, in light of discoveries relating to popular conservatism in religion at the local level by Reformation historians led by Christopher Haigh.

13

'Selling the Bible to pay for the bear': the value placed on entertainment in Congleton, 1584-1637

ELIZABETH BALDWIN

A SUBSTANTIAL PORTION of the Cheshire volume of *Records of Early English Drama*, which is currently in preparation, will consist of extracts from the Borough Accounts of Congleton, an East Cheshire town which made a surprisingly large number of payments for entertainment in the late sixteenth and early seventeenth centuries. These accounts were discovered in Congleton by Professor Alan Coman, and as Professor Coman has already written elsewhere on the companies of players who visited Congleton,[1] I have chosen to focus mainly on bearwards and bearbaiting, a sport for which Congleton's enthusiasm became a byword: 'Congleton rare, Congleton rare, sold the Bible to pay for the bear.' I shall, however, make references to various items concerning other entertainment from time to time, where I feel this can help to shed light on how the bearbaiting fits into an overall pattern of municipal spending on entertainment.

The allegation that the Mayor and Council of Congleton once 'sold the Bible to pay for the bear' is still generally known in and around Congleton, mostly in the somewhat apologetic version favoured by Robert Head in his book, *Congleton past and present*, who tried to protect the town from the charge of sacrilege by explaining the allegation in the following manner: 'The Wakes being very near, when the greatest bearbait took place, one of the shaggy brutes happening to die, the event plunged the promoters of the display into a sorry strait. The bearward, applying in vain for sufficient money to replace the defunct bruin, at last consulted the authorities, who, having a small surplus contained in the "towne's boxe" intended for the purchase of a new chapel Bible, agreed to help him, and lent the required sum, namely, 16/-.'[2] It is unfortunate that no one assigns even a vague date to this purchase, and that although the price is firmly stated, no source is given. I would also like to know to whom the bearward applied in vain before turning to the town authorities as a last resort. If the bearward was sponsored by the town, the Town Council would be the first body to whom he would apply for money, and if the bearward was not sponsored by the town, they would be exceedingly unlikely to pay sixteen shillings to replace his bear when they could simply hire another one somewhere else. From the evidence of the earliest borough account book, which contains accounts from 1584 to 1637, the Victorian story would have been a far worse insult to Congleton than the original taunt. The suggestion that Congleton should be so unprepared that the success of the wakes depended on one old and decrepit bear would have been a serious affront to the town council of the late sixteenth and early seventeenth centuries.

The accounting year at Congleton was divided into four quarters, beginning at Michaelmas, and it will therefore be necessary for me to refer to years by double dates: 1584–85, and so on. The accounts are generally set out separately for each quarter. Most payments are listed, as far as can be determined, under the quarter in which the expense occurred, although there are a few instances of items being included in a different quarter from that in which the events took place. For example, payments which refer to January dates in the accounting year 1622–23 were included under the previous quarter's accounts.[3] Precise dates within the accounts occur somewhat haphazardly, with the exception of the first two quarters of 1620–21, when an exceptionally tidy-minded clerk set out all the items under month headings, with the actual date beside each one.[4]

Unfortunately he seems to have tired of this practice by the third quarter, but it is very useful in giving precise dates of visits of players and bearwards, and the dates of the play performed by the scholars in February of that year, and that performed by the Townsmen in April.

Entertainment does not seem to have been confined to any one season of the year. Bearwards appear in the accounts in every quarter of the year, as indeed do visiting players. Besides the wakes, which were the occasion especially associated with bearbaits, there are also references to Martinmas, Shrovetide and May fairs, as well as celebrations in Whitsun week. In 1602–03 there is a reference to 'the great beare bayte' occurring in the second quarter.[5] This was probably one of the occasions which are elsewhere described as 'the great Cockfight', in which case it is likely that it took place around Shrovetide. Payments to individual bearwards may be associated with occasions such as Christmas or Candlemas, or they may happen on dates with no particular significance: the 9th of October, the 15th of November (although this is suggestively close to Martinmas) or the 12th of January.[6] Most frequently they occur with no supporting date at all. Of the three dates which I have quoted, the first two occur in 1620–21 and the third in 1622–23, when the scribe is still fairly precise about dates. There are a total of three mentions of bearwards in the first quarter of 1620–21 (the third visit was on the 31st of December), and the scribe gives the names of the bearwards involved. As they are three completely different individuals, it would appear that rather than supporting an official town bearward, Congleton was visited fairly frequently by travelling bearwards. From the accounts and from the judicial files, one gains an impression of Congleton as a reliable place for a bearward to go, the kind of town that every travelling company of players would try to include on their itinerary, because they were certain of payment. When an unnamed company of players performed in Congleton on the 31st of January 1631–32, they were paid 6s. 8d. — a fairly moderate fee for Congleton, but the players evidently considered it worth their while to come back five days later, as the accounts explain, somewhat apologetically that 6s. 8d. was 'geoven more vnto the same company of Players beinge heare agayne the 5th day of ffebruary 1631 towardes there Charges in regard mr deputie wagge & the 2 Justices would not suffer them to play on the Saboth day'.[7] Performing plays, or allowing them to be performed, on a Sunday was strictly illegal, and could involve trouble with both secular and ecclesiastical authorities — yet in 1623–24 the accounts specify that the king's players were paid 10 shillings 'who played heare vpon Sondaie next before Martlemas daie'.[8] The Sunday before Martinmas in 1623 fell on the 16th of November, and the king's players were back in Congleton on the 14th December, this time performing with, or as well as, the earl of Derby's players, at the Swan Inn, which was owned by Randle Rode, an ex-mayor of Congleton.[9] Repeat visits by players within the same year, even within the same quarter, occur on three other occasions. A repeat visit by the same bearward within the same accounting year occurs only once, but bearwards are not always individually named. Travelling companies such as the King's Men, who would have travelled ultimately from London, would no doubt have been anxious to get as many performing opportunities as possible. Bearwards had fewer time constraints, and a more versatile form of entertainment.

Congleton wakes began on the Vigil of the Feast of St Peter ad Vincula, that is, the 31st of July, during the fourth quarter of the accounting year, and bearbaits were a major attraction at the wakes, although bearwards are also paid at other times within the fourth quarter. The earliest payment for bearwards at the wakes recorded in the Congleton accounts, in 1589–90, specifies two bearwards, who received ten shillings between them. The following year, 1590–91, sees the first appearance of Shelmerdyne the bearward, about whom I shall have more to say later. Payments were considerably lower in this year, however, with Shelmerdyne only receiving 2s. 6d., and the earl of Worcester's players, who appeared in the same quarter, receiving 3s. 4d. In these early accounts, prices do not yet seem to be fixed, as both the bearward and Lord Darcy's players in 1591–92 were paid 6s. 8d.[10]

The absence of any payments in connection with the wakes before 1590 may, of course, be accidental. It is not clear whether there were accounts from the period earlier than 1584 — certainly borough orders are preserved from as early as 1538, but this does not mean that regular accounts were also kept. It may also be the case that the town did not make official payments to bearwards at the wakes before about 1590. This would explain some initial fluctuation in the amounts paid. We have, of course, no way of knowing what other income the bearwards got at the wakes. Was the payment made by the town a blanket payment to cover all bearbaits, or did the bearwards receive further payments from the audience? The two payments made to the bearward Edward Hall in 1633–34 are intriguing in this regard. The first payment, of ten shillings, was specifically 'bestowed vpon Edward Hall the bearward by Consentt for makeinge sportt with his beares, the 16th and 17th of Iuly 1634'. Taken in conjunction with a second payment, of 30 shillings, which is specifically associated with the wakes, and is stated to be 'over and besydes that which was Collectted for him by Consentt' it appears that the town bestowed a full two pounds on the bearward. Prices for bearwards at this period seem to have been inflated; the King's Revellors, who appeared in the same quarter, only received 10s. from the town.[11] If the bearward was able to earn further money from betting and gratuities from the crowd, it is not surprising that bearwards favoured Congleton.

There is evidence that the bearward did expect to receive some money from the crowd. The Congleton men, not to mention the Congleton women, were in the thick of a disturbance at a bearbait at Astbury, in 1605. Congleton lay in Astbury parish, and quite a few people, including at least one ex-mayor, had come from Congleton for a bearbait on the 23rd of September. According to one witness, Hugh Whitacres, son of Richard Whitacres of Congleton, the affray began because 'he beinge at

Astbury the mondaie aforesaid & had a dogge of his father to put one the beare, and offered to put the same dogge one the beare, which the bearwarde mislikinge because (as this examinate thinketh) he would haue his beare to fight to more, forbadd this examinate to put one the dogge & therwith offered to drawe his dagger'.[12] A quarrel thereupon broke out, and another witness deposes that 'he sawe the Bearward lift vpp his staffe & laie his hand on his dagger, to whome he heard Robert Wilkenson of Congleton aforesaid saye, take heide what you doe for if you offer anie blowes to anie Congleton man it were better for you, you did not'.[13] The name Robert Wilkenson, incidentally, occurs frequently in the Congleton Borough Accounts and he was responsible, among other things, for the mending of the cockpit. It is not clear whether the suggestion that the bearward 'would haue his beare to fight to more' indicates that he wanted more dogs, to make the baiting more impressive, or more spectators, to make it more profitable. The fact that one of the payments to Edward Hall which I mentioned earlier was 'over and besydes that which was Collectted for him', combined with the evidence from the Astbury riot, strongly suggests that the bearward was receiving money from the crowd as well as the authorities.

To look at a few bearbaiting statistics for Congleton, between the years 1588–89 and 1635–36, there are fifty-three items in the Congleton Borough Accounts relating to bearwards and bearbaiting. Thirty-three of these refer to bearwards who are either named or identified by their patron. Of these, eleven bearwards are individually named and seven more are associated with a patron, ranging from the town of Northwich to the king. There is also one name who may be a bearward, but as the reference is vague I have not included it in the statistics. Most of the named bearwards appear only once in the accounts. Even the generously-paid Edward Hall only appears in the accounts of 1633–34, although he may have been the unnamed bearward paid by the town in the preceding year. Unfortunately these payments come at the end of the period of bearbaiting in Congleton — the only later mention is of the Northwich bearward in 1635–36.[14] The four bearwards whose names do appear more than once in the accounts all appear earlier than 1625. Although only four names are repeated, there may actually have been five bearwards involved. I mentioned Shelmerdyne the bearward at the beginning of my paper. He appears ten times in the accounts, twice as much as the next most frequent name, and he may well have been more than one person. His earliest appearance is in 1590–91; he then appears three more times between 1600 and 1602, and once more in 1608–09.[15] In all of these instances he is referred to only as Shelmerdyne, with variations of spelling. One of the references of 1601–02, refers not to bearbaiting, but to a letter carried to Shelmerdyne. This may, of course, refer to a completely different Shelmerdyne, not the bearward, but it may also have been a letter sent to the bearward to ensure his presence in Congleton for the wakes.

Between 1608–09 and 1620–21 the name Shelmerdyne does not appear in the Congleton accounts. It is worth noting that William Kelsall or Kelshaw, who is the second most frequently named bearward, makes all five of his appearances during this time.[16] In 1620–21 the name Shelmerdyne appears again, twice. The second item, which refers to the wakes specifies Raufe Shelmerdyne, and he is named as Raphe Shelmerdyne when he appears twice in 1621–22, and once in 1623–24.[17] The sudden appearance of a first name may indicate that this is a different Shelmerdyne from the earlier one. Given that the name Shelmerdyne occurs over a stretch of thirty-five years, with a ten-year gap, it is more than likely that two individuals are involved. It would also seem that the Shelmerdynes were a bearwarding family, like the Whytstones of Ormskirk who appear in the Lancashire volume of *Records of Early English Drama*.[18] Bearwarding Shelmerdynes are not confined to the Congleton accounts: a Shermadyne was paid for baiting bears at the High Cross in Chester in 1610–11,[19] and a Ralph Shelmerden was prosecuted in the ecclesiastical court in Lancashire for ape-baiting at Rusholme in April, 1601.[20] This latter individual is described as a native of Withington in Lancashire, and this and the date make it difficult to clearly identify him with either of the Congleton Shelmerdynes. It seems unlikely that one individual would go from baiting bears in Congleton at Candlemas to baiting apes in Lancashire in April. It is quite possible, however, for there to be a family connection between the various Shelmerdynes.

The Town Council of Congleton went to considerable lengths to ensure that they had bears and bearwards for their wakes, although there is no evidence that their transactions involved Bibles. They seem to have been anxious to ensure the presence of enough bears at the wakes in 1613–14. Not only was William Stathome paid to fetch the bearward to the wakes, there are also two payments for fetching bears which are especially interesting: 'Item geeuen to Iohn Pursell for Rydinge to procure Beares in the nyghte for the wakes w*h*ich before were denyed ij s vj d Item geeuen to will*i*am Horderne for goeinge to fetche two beares more at the wakes and w*h*ich came not to Knuttesford xij d.'[21] These items raise all sorts of interesting questions: why were the bears denied, and why was it necessary to fetch them at night? Was there some secrecy necessary because they had been denied earlier? Was the Town Council sanctioning bear-rustling? Although the thought of a Great Congleton Bear Caper is an attractive one, there is probably a much more mundane story behind these items. There are other instances in the accounts of messengers being paid extra when their errands involved travelling after dark, or upon their own horses, in the case of urgency. The mention of fetching two more bears *at* the wakes in the second item quoted suggests that there was some urgency involved in the arrangements, which could have justified the travel by night, and the higher payment to John Pursell. As for the reason for the bears being denied, the most obvious choice is that the price was not high enough. Riding to fetch the bearward occurs fairly regularly about this time. In the second quarter of the same year, 1613–14, William Hordern rode — again in the night — to Northwich to procure a 'belward' and also went to fetch Kelshaw the bearward. The belward in this item was probably a bullward, as a bull ring was set up in Congleton in that year.[22] Of course, bearwards could also be bullwards, as in 1622–23, when 'Boelance the Bearewarde' was paid on the 12th of January 'for spourte he made with his beares and bull'.[23]

It would appear from these and other entries that it was possible for the Town Council to make a good guess at where the bearwards were likely to be. The bears which did not come to Knutsford evidently necessitated a special messenger because they were not where they were expected. Similarly, in the following year, 1614–15, Rafe Hordren was paid 'to fetch brooke the bearward at our wakes', and William Hordren the younger 'for goeyng to fynd broke whome Raffe hordren myst of at our wakes'.[24] The bearwards could, in general, be expected to be at the various wakes and fairs, but Congleton evidently found that it was safer to ensure their presence by going to look for them. Perhaps competition from other towns about this time made it necessary for Congleton to hire bearwards in advance in order to maintain their reputation. Messengers were still being sent for bearwards in the following decade: in 1622–23, Edward Bryon 'wente to seeke for Beares and broughte Wardles beare to the Wakes', and in 1623–24 John Pursell went 'towardes Bvnburie to hyre Beares'.[25]

There is a good deal of fluctuation in prices paid to bearwards throughout the accounts, of course, and probably factors such as the number of bears a bearward possessed — for possession of more than one bear seems to have been common — and what price he could, or claimed he could, get for his skills somewhere else, and possibly how much had been taken from the audience, were all taken into account. The three bearwards named in 1620–21 all received different amounts: five shillings for Boeland in October, 6s. 8d. for Shelmerdyne in November and another ten shillings at the wakes, and only 3s. 4d. for Kelsall in December.[26] But it was the early 1630s which saw the highest prices paid to bearwards: four pounds to the bearward at the wakes in 1631–32, and three pounds in 1632–33, followed by the payment of two pounds to Edward Hall, mentioned earlier, and dying away with a payment of 2s. 6d. to the bearward of

Northwich in 1635–36, the last payment to a bearward by the Congleton Town Council before the Civil War.[27] Players in these years were doing well to get 13s. 4d.[28]

To conclude by going back to the suggestion of selling the Bible, these payments contrast sharply with the 3s. 4d. paid for wine to the two preachers 'who preached heare vpon wednesdaie in the greate Cockfight weeke' in 1623–24. A total of thirty shillings was spent on bearwards in the same year, and 24s. 8d. on players.[29] It would seem that the neighbouring towns and villages who alleged that Congleton sold the Bible to pay for the bear had a fairly clear idea of the value placed on entertainment in Congleton before 1637.

References

1 Alan C. Coman, 'The Congleton accounts: further evidence of Elizabethan and Jacobean drama in Cheshire', *REED: Newsletter*, 14:1 (1989), pp.3–18.

2 Robert Head, *Congleton past and present*, Congleton, 1887, rpr. 1987, p.66.

3 Congleton Borough Account Book, I, 1584–1637, f.216r.

4 Ibid., ff.176r–186r.

5 Ibid., f.70r.

6 Ibid, f.15r (Christmas); ff.62v, 234r (Candlemas); f.176v (9 October); f.178r (15 November); f.216r (12 January).

7 Ibid., f. 274r.

8 Ibid., f.230v.

9 Ibid., f.232r.

10 Ibid., f.12r; 17r.

11 Ibid., ff.306r, 307v, 308r.

12 CRO, Quarter Sessions Files, QJF/34/3/22.

13 Ibid, QJF/34/3/38.

14 Congleton Borough Account Book, I, f.335r.

15 Ibid., ff.17r; 52v, 72r; 62v, 75v; 88v.

16 That is, in 1610–11, 1611–12, 1613–14, 1615–16, and 1620–21; ibid., loose gathering separately numbered, ff.1v; 10v; ibid., ff.99r; 127v; 146r; 179v.

17 Ibid., ff.178v, 192r, 200r; 204v; 210r; 234r.

18 David George, *Lancashire, REED*, Toronto, 1991, pp.l, 31–2, 73–4.

19 Lawrence M. Clopper, *Chester, REED*, Toronto, 1979, p.263.

20 D. George, *Lancashire*, p.90.

21 Congleton Borough Account Book, I, f.115r.

22 Ibid., ff.127v; 105r–107v.

23 Ibid., f.216r.

24 Ibid., f.131r.

25 Ibid., ff.224r; 237v.

26 Ibid., ff.176v; 178r; 179v.

27 Ibid., ff.281r; 294r; 306r; 335r.

28 Ibid., ff.274r; 275r; 287v; 288r; 308r; 316r; 333r; 337r; 345r.

29 Ibid., ff.230v–241r.

Index

The titles of literary works are printed in italics.

Ab Owein Gwynedd, Hywel, 96.
Acton, 6.
Aelred, abbot, 169.
Aelred of Rievaulx, 148, 153 n.16,
    see Ailred of Rievaulx.
Aethelred II, king, 'the Unready',
    (r. 978-1016), 148
Aethestan, king, 78, see Athelstan,
    Æþelstan, Aðalsteinn.
Ailred of Rievaulx, 157, see Aelred of
    Rievaulx.
Aire Gap, 72.
Aldersey, 21, 23, 25, 29, 30, 33 n.4
Aldersey Green, 20, 22, 28-30,
    see Great Aldersey.
Aldersey, John, 22.
    Thomas, 22.
Aldford, 9-11, 17, 18, 21, 25, 33 n.4,
    34 n.16.
Álfgeirr, earl, 112, 113, 117.
Aneirin, 88, 101, 107 n.29.
Angantýr of Saxony, 125, 126.
Anglesey, 42, 72, 135 n.17, 168.
Anglo-Saxon Chronicle, 2, 40, 89, 90,
    119, 136 n.20, 143, 155.
Anlaf, see Guthfrithsson, Guðfriðsson,
    89, 91, 105 n.9.
Annales Cambriae, 42, 72, 135 n.17
Annals of Ulster, 61, 135 n.16.
Annandale, 119.
Anselm, 217.
Antrim, 61.
Ap Llyweelyn, Gruffydd, king of
    Gwynnedd, 165-7.
Aquinas, Thomas, 218 n.21, n.22, n25,
    219 n.30.
Argoet, 99.
    Llwyfein, 100.

Arneway, Sir John, Mayor of Chester,
    224.
Arran, 66.
Arvynyd, 99.
Ashburnham House, 89.
Aspatria, 73.
Astbury, 6, 261, 262.
Aston, 4, 14 n.19, 118.
Athelstan, king, (r. 924-39), 111-13,
    115, 117, 118, 120, 122, 130,
    see also Aethelstan, Æþelstan,
    Aðalsteinn.
Atlantic, 61.
Apisl, see Aðils, 136 n.21.
Aðalsteinn, king, 113-16, 130,
    141 n.87, see also Aethelstan,
    Athelstan, Æþelstan.
Aðils, see Apisl, 112, 117.
Ælfgar, 167.
Ælfgar of Mercia, 166.
Ælfred, 110.
Ælfwine, 102.
Æthelflæd, 5, 8, 41, see also Æþelflæd
    Edelfrida.
Æþelflæd, 11, see also Æthelflæd,
    Edelfrida.
Æþelstan, king, 89, 92, 97, 100, 101,
    see also Aethelstan, Athelstan,
    Aðalsteinn.

Bagguley, 236 n.31.
Balbus, Joannes, 218 n.17, n.22.
Baldwin, archbishop, 160, 163.
Balladoole, 43, 68, 76, 83 n.68.
Ballateare, 75, 76, 83 n. 68.
Ballinderry Crannog, 47.

Bardney, 8.
Barra, 46.
Barthomley, 33 n.10.
Barton, 23, 25, 28–30, 33 n.4.
Battle of Argoet Llwyfein, 99, 101.
Battle of Brunanburh, 87, 88, 92–9,
    100, 107 n.34, 116, 121.
Battle of Gwen Ystrat, 97, 99, 100.
Battle of Maldon, 87–9, 92–7, 100–2,
    132.
Beachin, 31.
Becket, Thomas, 151.
Bede, 107 n.28, 140 n.78.
Berdal, 65, 70.
Bernicia, 88.
Berwickshire, 71.
Bettisfield, 9.
Bickerton, 8.
Bickley, 8.
Bigot, 14 n.31.
Birchenshawe, John, abbot, 240.
Birrens, 120, 121.
Birsay, 64.
Bjarkamál, 106 n.24.
Blackwater, river, 89.
Blacon, 232.
Boccaccio, 206, 214, 219 n.33.
Bodels/Bodles, 118.
Boethius, 180, 201 n.22.
Boleslaw, king, 144.
Bollin, river, 2, 5.
Book of Kells, 43.
Book of Taliesin, 96.
Boughton, 25.
Bovium, 10.
Bowdon, 5, 6.
Braddan, 49, 50.
Bradshaw, Henry, 175 n.66.
Brihtwulf, 110.
Brinsworth, 121–3.
Bristol Channel, 42.
Britain, 38, 59, 61–3, 85, 97, 111.
British Isles, 38–40, 44, 46, 48, 54, 67,
    87.
Bromborough, 89, 112, 119, 121–4,
    136 n.20.
Bromswald, 122.
Broxton, 7, 9, 10.

Bruen Stapleford, 25, 33 n.4.
Bruera, 25.
Brunanburh, 89, 112, 118, 119, 121,
    123, 136 n.20.
  battle of, 78, 112, 121, 122, 124,
    131.
Brunburh, *see* Brunanburh, 136 n.20.
Brunefeld, 122.
Bruneswald, 122.
Bruneswerce, 119.
Brut, 131.
Brut Tysilio, 131.
Brut y Tywysogyon, 135 n.17.
Bucklow, 2, 3, 6, 10.
Bucolicum Carmen, 219 n.33.
Budworth, 14 n.19.
Buerton, 25, 33 n.4.
Bulkeley, 8.
Bunbury, 6, 11.
Burnley, 89.
Burnswark, 89, 119–21, 137 n.37.
Burton, 22, 23, 25, 28, 29.
  near Tarvin, 33 n.4.
Bute, Isle of, 46.
Byrhtnoth, 132, *see also* Byrhtnoþ.
Byrhtnoþ, 89, 94, 95, 100, 102,
    see also Byrhtnoth.
Byzantium, 145, 147.

Caedwalla, 11.
Calveley, 22, 34 n.12.
Capture of the five boroughs, 90.
Caradog, 103.
Carden, 22, 25, 33 n.4.
Carlisle, 96, 120.
  cathedral, 53.
Carmen de Hastingae Proelio, 144.
Carrick, 71.
Castlefield, 56 n.27.
Castleford on the Aire, 118.
Catholicon, 208, 218 n.22.
Catraeth, 97, 101, *see also* Catterick.
Catterick, 88, 101, *see also* Catraeth.
Chapmonswiche, 3.
Chaucer, 181, 182, 200 n.12.
Cheshire, 1–4, 6–8, 10–12, 15, 17–19,
    23, 27, 28, 30–2, 45, 72, 89,

109, 112, 119, 124, 135 n.17,
136 n.20, 165, 167, 232,
236 n.31, 252 n.30, 257.
Ridge, 9.
Chester, 6, 9, 12, 13, 13 n.9, 17, 40,
48, 72, 111, 149, 150, 155-7,
160-9, 173 n.40, 174 n.52,
175 n.71, 221-6, 228-31, 233,
234 n.4, 240, 243, 244, 246,
247 n.1, 251 n.26, 252 n.30,
254 n.49, 255 n.50, 263.
cathedral, 241-3, 246, 249 n.17,
254 n.46.
cycle, 237, 238, 240, 243, 247 n.3,
248 n.6.
Cheswardine, 157.
Chowley, 21, 23, 25, 33 n.4, 34 n.16.
Christleton, 21, 25, 27, 31, 33 n.4.
Chronicle of Laôn, 149.
Church Shocklach, 17.
Churton Heath, 27, 31, 33 n.4.
Cirencester, 131.
City of God, 217 n.13.
Claughton Hall, 73.
Cleanness, 183, 184.
Clibberswick, 65.
Clontarf, 117, 136 n.26.
Clotton, 28, 34 n.16, 35 n.21.
Hoofield, 23, 25, 28, 31, 33 n.4.
Cluny, 166.
Clutton, 25, 30, 33 n.4.
Cnut *see* Knut.
Coddington, 9, 27, 31, 32, 33 n.4,
35 n.26.
Coel Hen, 100.
Colonsay, 43, 68, 69, 76.
Confessions, 218 n.27.
Congleton, 257.
Connaught, 61.
Constantine II, king (r. 900-43), 112,
123, *see also* Constantinus.
Constantinus, 89, 91, 92, 98.
Cork, 42.
Cornovii, 12.
Cotton Abbots, 27, 31, 33 n.4.
Edmunds, 25, 33.
Cronk Mooar, 83 n.68.
Cross Canonby, 48.

Cuddington, 8.
Cuerdale, 41, 43, 73.
Cumberland, 28, 45, 49, 73, 109, 167.
Cumbria, 40, 44, 64, 72, 97, 110.

Darebury, 5.
De Arithmetica, 180, 201 n.22.
De Civitate Dei, 218 n.22, n.23, n.25.
De Inventione Sanctae Crucis, 159,
161, 169, 172 n.36, 176 n.90.
De Laude Cestriae, 165.
De Nugis Curialium, 166.
De Pisan, Christine, 125.
De Venables, Gilbert, 3.
De Vernon, Richard, 14 n.19.
De Vick, Henri, 178.
Dearham, 45.
Decameron, 206.
Dee, river, 7. 9, 17, 21, 34 n.12, 157,
167, 230.
Deira, 88.
Denmark, 39, 44, 70.
Depenbech, 7, 11.
Descriptio Kambriae, 164.
Domesday Book, 2, 3, 11, 30, 35 n.26,
106 n.26.
Doncaster, 118.
Donegal, 61.
Donnán of Eigg, 61.
Douglas, 50.
Dover, 144, 149, 156, 161.
Downhan,William, bishop of Chester,
246, 252 n.30, 254 n.49.
Dublin, 41-4, 47-9, 51-3, 59, 64,
66-72, 76, 81 n.43, 92, 105.
Duddon, 22, 25, 28-30, 33 n.4,
35 n.21.
Dudestan, 7, 9, 10.
Dumfries, 40, 45.
Dumfriesshire, 89, 110, 119.
Duncan, 176 n.83.
Dunham, 6.
Dunnere, 94.
Dunragit, 96.
Durham cathedral, 54.
Dutton, 14 n.20.
Dyfed, 52.

Eadmund, prince, 92, 100,
see also Edmund, prince.
Eadred, king, (r. 946–55), 77.
Eadric the Wild, 168.
Eadweard, 100.
Eadwine, 167.
earl, 167.
Ealdgyth, 166–8.
Eanred I, king (r. 808–41), 68.
East Anglia, 2, 88.
Eaton-by-Tarporley, 33 n.10.
Ecclefechan, 119.
Eddisbury, 13 n.19.
Edelfrida, 111, see also Æthelflæd,
Æþelflæd.
Eden, river, 97, 98, see also Idon.
Edgar, king (r. 957–75), 10.
Edinburgh, 88.
Edmund Ironside, 167.
king (r. 939–46), 77.
prince, 89, 112, see also Eadmund,
prince.
Edward I, king (r. 1272–1307), 4.
VI, king, (r. 1547–53), 237, 240,
247 n.3.
the Confessor, king (r. 1042–66),
147, 148, 150, 151, 172 n.36.
the Elder, king (r. 899–924), 10.
thegn, 4, 14 n.20.
Edwin, earl, 6, 7, 9, 14 n.31.
Egerton, Sir Philip, 23.
Egils saga Skallagrímssonar, 111, 112,
117–25, 127, 128, 130–3,
136 n.27.
Eigg, 61.
Elizabeth I, queen (r.1558–1603), 23,
237, 254 n.49.
Enchiridion, 218 n.23.
England, 2, 8, 12, 15, 38–43, 47–9,
51–4, 72–6, 78, 88, 92, 96, 99,
105 n.9, 109, 110, 112, 113,
143, 145, 148, 149, 155–7, 203,
244.
Essex, 89, 94, 149, 156.
Ethelred, ealdorman of Mercia, 8.
Eudeyrn, Welsh prince, 107 n.29.
Eugenius, see Owen, 112.

Farndon, 9, 10, 13 n.13, 17.
Faroe islands, 63.
Fitz Nigel, William, 14 n.19.
Fitz Tezzo, Osbern, 4, 14 n.20.
Flamdwyn, 99, 100.
Flateyjarbók, 146.
Flatholm, 42.
Florence of Worcester, 105 n.9, 121.
Fluskew Pike, 44.
Fordun, 119.
Fóstbrœðra Saga, 117.
Foulk Stapleford, 25, 33 n.4.
Frank, Roberta, 106 n.24.
Frickley, 118, 136 n.29.
Fridleif the Swift, 131.
Frodsham, 6.
Fulk of Orby, 161.

Gaimar, 119.
Galloway, 40, 45.
Gautr, 46.
Gawain and the Green Knight, 177, 183,
185, 187, 191, 192, 199,
201 n.22.
Gawain-poet, see Pearl-poet, 177, 183,
190, 199, 201 n.21, 203.
Geir, 126.
Genson, Sir John, 251.
Germania, 106 n.24.
Gervase of Tilbury, 149.
Gesta Danorum, 127.
Giraldus Cambrensis, 131, 149, 160,
161, 163–6, 169.
Glastonbury, 151.
Gloucester, 8.
God and All Saints, church of, 5.
Godeu, 99.
Gododdin, 88, 97, 101–3.
Goðrekr, earl of, 112, 117.
Godwinson, Harold II, king (r. 1066),
143–5, 148–51, 155–69,
170 n.8, 171 n.10, 172 n.29,
n.30, n.36, 174 n.52, 176 n.90.
Gokstad, 39.
Golborne Bellow, 27, 31, 33 n.4.
David, 27, 31, 33 n.4.
Gordon, 71.

Gormund the Dane, 131.
Gosforth, 45, 47, 74.
Gotland, 44.
Gowy, river, 6, 9, 17, 21, 34 n.12.
Gramsson, Hadding, king, 131.
Grappenhall, 14 n.20.
Great Aldersey, 22, 30,
    see also Aldersey Green.
Great Boughton, 33 n.4.
    Budworth, 3–5, 14 n.19.
Grey Friars, Chester, 254 n.49.
Grosseteste, 179.
Guðfriðsson, Óláfr, 112, 118, 123,
    see also Anlaf Guthfrithsson.
Guthfrithsson, Olaf, 89, 118, 120, 132,
    see also Anlaf Guðfriðsson.
Gwen Ystrat, 97.
Gwen-y-ddavid, 17.
Gyrth, 155, 157, 162, 171 n.20.
Gytha, 144.

Halfdan, 125.
Hallsson, Þorsteinn, 117.
Halton, 4, 6, 14 n.19, 45, 232.
Handley, 25, 27, 31, 32, 33 n.4.
Harald, king of Denmark, 165.
Haraldsson, Óláfr II, 143.
Hardware, Henry, mayor of Chester,
    243.
Hargrave, 25.
Haroldson, Edmund or Edwin, 168.
    Godwin, 168.
    Harold, 168.
    Magnus, 168.
    Ulf, 176 n.83.
Hastings, battle of, 143, 144, 145,
    148, 149, 155, 156, 160–2, 167,
    169, 171 n.20.
Hatteberg, 44.
Hatton, 21, 25, 33 n.4.
    Hall, 25.
Hawarden, 230.
Hayy ibn Yaqdan, 218 n.26.
Healfdan, 110.
Hebrides, 47, 67.
Heiðrekr, 127, 139 n.64.
Heimskringla, 146.

Hemings þáttr, 150.
Henry II, king (r. 1154–89), 42, 149,
    150, 156, 157, 159–62, 164,
    169, 170 n.8, 171 n.12,
    175 n.71, 176 n.90.
    III, king (r. 1216–72), 165.
    IV, emperor (r. 1056–1106), 166,
    175 n.70.
    V, emperor, (r. 1106–25), 166,
    175 n.71.
    of Ghent, 180.
Hereford, 167.
Hervarar sage ok Heiðreks, 127.
Hesket-in-the-Forest, 44, 45, 48, 73.
Higden, Ranulf, 164, 166, 224.
High Legh, 3.
Higher Huxley Halls, 25.
Hingamund, 111, 135 n.17, see also
    Igmund, Igmunt, Jgmwnd.
Historia Brittonum, 88, 96.
Historia de Antiquitate Regum
    Norwagiensium, 146.
Historia de Sancto Cuthberto, 110.
Hjorungavágr, 117.
Holmgarðr, 126.
Holy Cross, church of, 144, 149, 150,
    153 n.21.
    Trinity, church of, 243, 251 n.26,
    252 n.30.
Hordaland, 44.
Horton, 22, 23, 25, 33 n.4, 34 n.16.
House of Fame, 182.
Hringr, 112, 117.
Hronesness, 132.
Hugh II, earl of Chester, 164, 165,
    174 n.62.
Hugh of Avranches, 168.
Humber, river, 105 n.9, 121.
Huntingdonshire, 122.
Hussa, 107 n.28.
Huxley, 21, 25, 33 n.4.

Iceland, 131, 144, 145, 148.
Ida, 107 n.28, n.29.
Idon, river, 98, see also Eden.
Igmund, 135 n.17, see also Hingamund.
Igmunt, 135 n.18, see also Hingamund.

Inchbrock, 46.
Ingemund, 41.
Ingimund, 72.
Inisbofin, 61.
Inismurray, 61.
Iona, 45, 47, 61, 62.
Ireland, 40–5, 47–9, 51–4, 59, 61–4,
    68, 69, 72, 74, 78, 80 n.22, 92,
    111, 167, 168.
Irish Sea, 37–40, 43, 45, 48, 50, 54,
    59, 66–9, 71, 74, 75, 77, 78,
    80 n.22.
Irton, 44.
Islandbridge, 41, 68–70, 76, 81 n.49.
Itinerarium Kambriae, 149, 160.
Izkorostén, 131.

Játvarðar saga, 150.
Jelling, 39.
Jerusalem, 145, 147, 148, 151.
Jgmwnd, 135 n.17, n.18,
    see also Hingamund.
Jutland, 39.

Kells, 62.
Kilbar, 46.
Kilmainham, 68–70, 76, 81 n.49.
Kiloran Bay, 43, 68.
Kirk Braddan, 49.
    Michael, 46, 47, 51.
Kirkmaiden, 43.
Knight's Tale, 182.
Knock y Doonee, 83 n.68.
Knut, 41, 51, 53, 167.
Knutsford, 33 n.10, 264, 265.
Kolbrúnarskáld, Þormóðr Bersason,
    117.
Kuli, 46.

Lai de Havelock, 127.
Lakeland, 111.
Lamlash Bay, 66.
Lancashire, 1, 40, 43, 45, 72, 73, 89,
    109, 232, 263.
Lancaster, 73.
Langland, 181.

Largs, battle of, 42.
Laxton, 18.
Layamon, 131.
Lea Newbold, 27, 31, 33 n.4.
Leche, John, 22.
Leo VI of Byzantium, 124.
Leofric, earl, 167.
Leofwine, brother of King Harold II,
    155.
    ealdorman, 166, 167.
Lewis, 43.
Life of Christ, 239, 248 n.9.
Liffey, river, 69.
Limerick, 42.
Lincoln cathedral, 241.
Littleton, 25, 33 n.4.
Livre des faites d'armes et de chevalerie,
    125.
Llanfaes, 135 n.17.
Llech Wen, 99.
Llywelyn, Welsh prince, 165.
London, 49.
Longest saga of Óláfr Tryggvason, 146–8.
Lough Ennell, 71.
Lucian, 163, 165, 174 n.53, 222.
Lundy, 42.
Lymm, 3, 14 n.20.
Lyvennet, river, 97.

Macefen, 8.
Maelor Saesneg, 7, 9.
Maes Rhosmeilon, 135 n.17.
Maiden Castle, 10.
Malcolm of Scotland, 165.
Maldon, 89.
Mâle, Emile, 249 n.13.
Malew, 48.
Malory, 192, 195.
Malpas, 7, 9, 11.
Man, Isle of, 39, 40, 42, 43, 45–51,
    53, 63, 64, 68, 74–8, 109, 110,
    167.
Manaw Gododdin, 101.
Manchester, 56 n.27.
Map, Walter, 166.
Margarita Philosophica, 208, 218 n.19,
    n.20, n.21, n.22, n.23, n.24, n.25.

Mary, queen (r. 1553–58), 237, 241, 246, 247 n.3, 249 n.12.
Matilda, 166, 175 n.70.
Mein Water, 121.
Mercia, 6, 7, 111, 166, 167, 223.
Mersey, river, 5, 6, 75, 112.
Middlebie, 120, 121.
Middlewich, 6, 10.
Midlands, 32.
Millington, 4.
Milton Green, 25, 27, 31.
Montacute, 156.
Morcar, earl, 6.
Morecambe Bay, 75.
Morkere, earl, 167.
Morte D'Arthur, 192.
Mynydawc Mwynvawr, 101.
Mynyddog, 107 n.37.

Nantwich, 6, 10,
  see also Waermundestou.
Njáls saga, 117.
Norfolk, 244.
Normandy, 165.
North Uist, 66.
Northamptonshire, 122.
Northern Isles, 62–4.
Northumbria, 110, 112.
Northwich, 10, 264.
Norton, 4.
Norway, 39, 44, 59, 61, 63, 66, 145, 147, 148.

Odard, 14 n.19.
Odd's cross, 49.
Ogier le Danois, 127.
Óláfr the red, 112–17, 120, 121, 123, 130.
Óláfs saga Tryggvasonar, 117, 150.
Olafsson, Magnus, 168.
Olgar, queen, 131.
Olympia, 214, 218 n.33.
Orkney, 50, 62, 64–6, 67.
Orm, thegn, 4.
Orme's Head, 42.
Ormside, 73, 82 n.61.

Ormskirk, 263.
Orton Scar, 71.
Osmeilon, *see* Maes Rhosmeilon, 135 n.17.
Otia Imperialia, 149.
Otley, 54.
Óttarsson, Hallfreðr, 144, 146, 147.
Over, 6.
Owein, 99, 100.
Owen, *see* Eugenius, 112.
Oxfordshire, 156.

Pagen, thegn, 4.
Pant, river, 132.
Paris, 178, 179.
Paschal I, pope, 165.
  II, pope, 166.
Patience 183–5, 197.
Pearl, 177, 178, 183, 185–7, 191, 197, 198, 201 n.16, 204–7, 211, 214, 215.
Pearl-poet, *see* Gawain-poet, 203, 204, 212, 214–6.
Peel, 42, 56 n.30.
  Castle, 77, 78.
Pennines, 44, 49, 75, 110.
Peovers, 3.
Philomena, 127.
Piers Plowman, 181.
Pitney, 51.
Poulton Lancelyn, 34 n.16.
Preston, 72, 73.
Preston-on-the-Hill, 5.
Priestholm, 42.
Pulford, 23.

Rabani, Geoffrey, 159.
Racedham, 106 n.26.
Ralph, abbot of Coggeshall, 149, 161.
Rampside, 73.
Ramsey, 51.
Ranulf II, earl of Chester, 160, 164.
  III, earl of Chester, 164, 165, 174 n.63.
Rathlin, 61.
Reget, 99.

Reisch, Gregor, 218 n.18.
Rheged, 96.
Rhuddlan, 167.
Ribble, river, 72, 73.
Ribe, 70.
Richard of Wallasey, 173 n.40.
Riknild Street, 118.
Rochdale, 96.
Rode, Randle, mayor of Congleton, 260.
Rogers, Robert, archdeacon of Chester, rector of Gawsworth, 234 n.11.
Roman de Brut, 131.
Rome, 11, 129.
Roncesvalles, 132.
Rostherne, 2, 3.
Rotherham, 121.
Rousay, 65.
Rowton, 25, 33 n.4.
Ruloe, 6, 10, 11.
Runcorn, 4–6, 13 n.9.
Rusholme, 263.
Rushton, 6.
Russian Primary Chronicle, 131.

Saebeorht, 156.
Saighton, 25, 33 n.4.
St Alexius, 158.
    Augustine of Hippo, 207, 208, 211, 217 n.13, 218 n.19, n.23, n.25, n.27.
    Bertelin, church of, 4.
    Chad, church of, 9.
    James, chapel of, 157, 160.
    John, church of, 150, 156, 157, 160–4, 167.
    John the Baptist, church of, 223, 234 n.7.
    Mary-on-the-Hill, church of, 222, 223, 251 n.26.
    Michael, parish of, 252 n.30.
    Oswald, 7, 8.
        church of, 7.
    Patrick's Isle, 42, 56 n.30, 77, *see also* Peel Castle.

Peter, church of, 160, 163, 176n.40, 223.
    Werburgh, abbey of, 163, 164, 167, 173 n.40, 223, 240.
        monastery of, 163, 165, 254 n.49.
Saltney, 231.
Sanday, 66.
Sandbach, 6, 11.
Santon, 43.
Savage, Sir John, mayor of Chester, 233.
Saxo Grammaticus, 127, 131.
Scandinavia, 37–9, 45, 46, 48, 51, 63, 68, 70, 145, 168.
Scar, 66.
Schott, Johann, 217 n.19.
Scotland, 40, 41, 43, 45–7, 51, 53, 59, 63–5, 67, 68, 78, 96, 109, 115, 116.
Scottish Field, 236 n.31.
Scottish Isles, 61.
Shetland, 65, 67.
Shocklach, 9, 18.
    Oviatt, 17.
Shropshire, 157, 169.
    Union Canal, 7.
Sicily, 131.
Sigurðsson, Haraldr Harðráði, 131.
Simeon of Durham, 122.
Simon, abbot of Whitchurch, 163.
Sink Moss, 2.
Skaill, 50.
Skallagrímsson, Egill, 112, 113, 116, 120, 124.
Skomer, Island of, 52.
Skye, Isle of, 61.
Smalls reef, 52.
Snaefell, 40.
Snorrason, Oddr, 146, 147, 150, 153.
Sodor and Man, diocese of, 53, 77.
Soiscél Molaise, 47.
Solway Firth, 47, 109, 119.
Somerset, 51, 156.
Stanton Harcourt, 156.
Stiklastaðir, 117.
Stockton, 8.
Stranraer, 96.
Strathclyde, 88, 112.

Stretton, 27, 31, 33 n.4.
Sturluson, Snorri, 117, 131, 146,
    152 n.6, n.9, 153 n.12.
Summa Theologiae, 217 n.11, 218 n.21,
    n.22, n.25, 219 n.30.
Sutton, 4.
Svolder, battle of, 143, 148.
Swan-Neck, Edith, 157, 160, 162, 166,
    168.
Sweden, 44.
Swold,132.

Tabley, 3.
Taliesin, 88, 96, 97, 99, 100, 107 n.29.
Tarporley, 6.
Tarvin, 6, 9.
Tattenhall, 21, 22, 25, 27, 33 n.4,
    34 n.17.
Tatton, 2.
    Park, 1.
Thames, 49.
Thelwall, 13 n.9.
Theodoric, Norwegian monk, 146.
Theodric, 107 n.28.
Thorleif's cross, 49.
Thornton-le-Moors, 6.
Three Fragments, 72, 111, 135 n.16,
    n.17, n.18.
Throndheim, 143.
Tilston, 9, 10, 18, 20–2, 25, 28–32,
    33 n.4, 34 n.16, 35 n.26.
Topographia Hibernica, 131.
Tory Island, 61.
Towneley, 227.
Troilus and Criseyde, 182.
Tryggvason, Óláfr, 143–8, 150, 151.
Tufayl, Abu Bakr Ibn, 218.
Tunendune, 2, 4, 6, 10.
Tushingham-cum-Grindlay, 33 n.10.
Tyne, river, 110.
Þórðarson, Flosi, 136 n.26.
Þórólfr, 113.

Udal, 66.
Uhtred of Northumbria, earl, 167.

Uig, 43.
Unst, 65.
Urien, 88, 96–101, 107 n.28.

Valtos, 43.
Vébjörn, 126.
Vígaglúmsson, Vígfúss, 117.
Villifers saga froekkna, 125.
Vínheiðr, 111, 113, 117–19, 121–4,
    127, 128, 130, 140 n.79.
Vínuskógar, 113, 122.
Vita Haroldi Regis, 145, 149, 150,
    156–62, 164, 165, 168, 169,
    170 n.9, 174 n.52.
Vita Sancti Edwardi Regis, 148.

Wace, 131.
Waermundestou 6, *see also*, Nantwich.
Wales, 8, 39–42, 45, 47, 49, 53,
    55 n.14, 109, 149, 156, 161,
    164, 169, 230, 231.
Walter, abbot of Waltham, 157, 170.
Waltham, 144, 149, 150, 153 n.21,
    156, 162, 170, 171 n.21.
    abbey, 155–62, 170 n.9, 171 n.12,
    172 n.30.
Waterford, 42.
Watling Street, 10, 11, 13 n.10.
Waverton, 21, 25, 33 n.4, 34 n.16.
Weaver, river, 5.
Weaverham, 6.
Wendland, 143.
Wensleydale, 97.
Weondun, 122.
Werburg, 165.
West Riding, 121.
Western Isles, 46, 53, 63, 64, 66.
Westmeath, 71.
Westmorland, 45, 71, 73, 109.
Westness, 65.
Weston, 4.
Wettenhall, 22, 34 n.12.
Whithorn, 78.
Whitley, 14 n.19.
Wight, Isle of, 11.

Wigmund, archbishop of York, 68.
William I, king (r. 1066-87), 143,
   144, 149, 150, 155, 160, 161,
   170 n.8, 176 n.83.
   II, king (r. 1087-1100), 176 n.83.
   of Jumièges, 143.
   of Malmesbury, 122, 144, 155,
   157.
   of Mandeville, 173 n.47.
   of Poitiers, 144.
Willmoor, 27, 35 n.18.
Winchester, 156.
Wirral, 3, 6, 10, 41, 72, 112, 119, 122.

Withington, 263.
Woodstock, 162.
Workington, 49.
Wrocen saete, 12.
Wybunbury, 6, 11.
Wych Brook, 7.
Wychough, 8.

York, 38, 44, 48, 49, 72, 73, 75, 77,
   225, 227.
Yorkshire, 27, 30, 54, 88, 101, 118,
   121, 122.